QUEER RACE

gender culture sexuality

William J. Spurlin
General Editor

Vol. 3

PETER LANG
New York • Washington, D.C./Baltimore • Bern
Frankfurt am Main • Berlin • Brussels • Vienna • Oxford

Ian Barnard

QUEER RACE

Cultural Interventions in the
Racial Politics of Queer Theory

PETER LANG
New York • Washington, D.C./Baltimore • Bern
Frankfurt am Main • Berlin • Brussels • Vienna • Oxford

Library of Congress Cataloging-in-Publication Data

Barnard, Ian.
Queer race: cultural interventions in the racial politics of queer theory / Ian Barnard.
p. cm. — (Gender, sexuality, and culture; vol. 3)
Includes bibliographical references.
1. Homosexuality. 2. Race awareness. 3. Gays—Identity. I. Title.
HQ76.25.B375   306.76'6—dc22   2003022438
ISBN 0-8204-7088-0
ISSN 1528-6525

Bibliographic information published by **Die Deutsche Bibliothek**.
Die Deutsche Bibliothek lists this publication in the "Deutsche Nationalbibliografie"; detailed bibliographic data is available on the Internet at http://dnb.ddb.de/.

Cover design by Lisa Barfield
Cover art by Marc Geller © 2003 www.marcgeller.com
Author photo by Aneil Rallin

© 2004 Peter Lang Publishing, Inc., New York
275 Seventh Avenue, 28th Floor, New York, NY 10001
www.peterlangusa.com

All rights reserved.
Reprint or reproduction, even partially, in all forms such as microfilm, xerography, microfiche, microcard, and offset strictly prohibited.

For Aneil

Contents

Series Editor's Foreword ix

Acknowledgments xi

Chapter 1 Introducing a Queer Theory for a Queer Race 1

Chapter 2 Whiteness as Gayness: *The Men of South Africa* 19

Chapter 3 Representing Race in the Discourse of Desire 35

Chapter 4 Gloria Anzaldúa's Queer Mestisaje 63

Chapter 5 Jeff Dahmer 80

Chapter 6 Your Picture Here 101

Notes 115

Works Cited 135

Series Editor's Foreword

In the contemporary world, we have come to understand gender and sexuality as shifting sites of signification. Unlike their traditional constructions tied to the expression of an inner self or essence under a humanist paradigm, postmodern theory, feminism, and academic queer theory have enabled radical rethinking of gender and sexuality as multiple, fluid, variable, contingent, and contextual as they operate under a variety of cultural, historical, rhetorical, and ideological conditions. These fields of inquiry have also helped to denaturalize any causal, normative relation proffered *between* gender and sexuality, exposing these relations as political and deeply imbricated within a heteronormative social order. In particular, academic queer theory, as a mode of analysis and critique, and with its emphasis on the proliferation of social differences, has helped to challenge identic fixity and has enabled more complex theorizations of gender and sexual identity in relation to other sites of subjective identification, including, but not limited to, race, class, geopolitical spatialization, and national affiliation.

This Series is a forum for the critical investigation and analysis of the contested terrain between culture, gender, and sexuality. The books collected in the Series are productive of new directions in queer studies and gender studies as they critically examine the relation(s) between culture and gender and/or sexuality in a range of historical periods, past as well as contemporary. Some projects retheorize gender in relation to, or its constitution through, sexuality, race, class, or culture. Other books are studies of sexuality and sexual identity that produce new understandings of gender, or are broad inquiries into culture that raise compelling implications for the ways in which we think about gender and sexuality as we begin a new century.

While the Series has been influenced by a previous decade productive of queer theorizing, the lines of inquiry undertaken in its aftermath by the authors collected here are both numerous and exciting. For instance, more comparative work and further analyses of gender and sexuality in postcolonial contexts will enable critique of the Euroamerican biases of gender and queer inquiry, while calling attention to their undertheorization in postcolonial studies to the extent that gender and sexuality remain contained within heteronormative frames of reference. The breaking down of national borders, made possible by heightened diasporic migration, the impact of economic globalization, the rapid dissemination of texts and culture worldwide, and the explosion of information technology, further impinge on our traditional understandings of gender and sexuality while continuing to radically transform them. The books in this Series represent highly theoretical engagements with gender and sexuality through a broad range of interdisciplinary inquiry, including anthropology, literary studies, history, psychology, and other areas of the humanities and social sciences. Each volume, as well as the Series as a whole, will make a unique contribution not only to furthering our understandings of gender and sexuality as categories of analysis, but their complex and multiple configurations in the vast, historically specific network(s) of codes, symbols, and signifying practices we have come to understand as culture.

William J. Spurlin
Cardiff University

Acknowledgments

My thanks to the following for assisting me with this book over the many years of its evolution: R. M. Dapper, Sheryl Gobble, Mónica Szurmuk, Cari Svich, Holly Bauer, Donald E. Hall, John Hawley, Bruce M. Abrams, Juan Corona, Robert Prager, Molly Rhodes, Aneil Rallin, Jenifer Fennell, William A. Nericcio, Adriana Novoa, Barney Barnard, Iona Barnard, Louie Crew, Laurence Roberts, Debra Moddelmog, Javier Morillo-Alicea, Anne Shea, Margarita Barceló, Craig Barnard, Maggie Sale, David Botha, Martin Nel, Judith Halberstam, Iñigo Sánchez-Llama, and Cindy Gray and Media Applications Development at The Ohio State University. I am especially grateful to Susi Mitchell for her insightful and helpful suggestions for Chapter 6. I am also grateful to Phyllis Korper, Sophie Appel, Lisa Dillon, and Ace Blair at Peter Lang Publishing for their commitment and conscientiousness, and to William Spurlin, the Gender, Sexuality and Culture series editor, for his enthusiastic support of this project. My special thanks to Marc Geller (the photographer) and Terence Smith (Joan Jett-Blakk) for generously allowing me to use their brilliant poster on the cover of the book.

Earlier versions of excerpts from this book appeared as chapters or articles in the following books and journals. I thank the publishers of those volumes for permission to reprint this material.

Chapter 1: *Social Semiotics*, Volume 9, Number 2, pp. 199–212. © 1999. Reprinted by permission of the publisher. All rights reserved.

Chapter 2: John C. Hawley, ed., *Postcolonial and Queer Theories: Intersections and Essays*, pp. 129–38. Greenwood Press, © 2001. Reprinted by permission of the publisher. All rights reserved.

Chapter 3: *Literary Studies East and West* Volume 16 ("Re-placing America: Conversations and Contestations"), ed. Ruth Hsu, Cynthia Franklin, and Suzanne

Kosanke, pp. 227–40. © 2000. Reprinted by permission of the publisher. All rights reserved.

Chapter 4: *MELUS*, Volume 22, Number 1, pp. 35–53. © 1997. Reprinted by permission of the publisher. All rights reserved.

Chapter 4: Renée R. Curry and Terry L. Allison, eds., *States of Rage: Emotional Eruption, Violence, and Social Change*, pp. 74–88. New York University Press, © 1996. Reprinted by permission of the publisher. All rights reserved.

Chapter 5: *Thamyris: Mythmaking From Past to Present*, Volume 7, Numbers 1–2, pp. 67–97. © 2000. Reprinted by permission of the publisher. All rights reserved.

I also thank the authors and publishers for permission to reprint material from the following texts:

Chapter 2: from Michael Grumley, *Life Drawing*, Foreword by Edmund White, Afterword by George Stambolion, © 1991 by The Estate of Michael Grumley. Used by permission of Grove/Atlantic, Inc.

Chapter 4: from *Borderlands/La Frontera: The New Mestiza*. Copyright © 1987, 1999 by Gloria Anzaldúa. Reprinted by permission of Aunt Lute Books.

Cover poster © 2003, Marc Geller www.marcgeller.com.

Chapter 1

Introducing a Queer Theory for a Queer Race

I

The title of this book, *Queer Race*, juxtaposes two nonanalogous demarcations of identity, sexuality and race (assuming for the moment that "queer" refers to sexuality and that the word "race" is self-explanatory) in order to inaugurate a third term that conjures up a cacophony of new epistemological questions, identificatory possibilities, and theoretical problematics I want to variously pursue, articulate, and contest precisely as each problematic is suggested, enabled, abjured, and reinvented by the others.

Queer race could suggest that there might be a queer race in a similar way that humanistic, racist, and/or homogenizing nationalistic discourse constructs a human race, a black race, and so on. I have no sympathy for such a project, and am equally unsympathetic to the humanistic or racial versions of this formula. In the latter case this is not because I don't consider race to be an important politico-analytic category or because I want to multiply the constituents of whiteness in order to dilute a radical postulation of systemic racism, but because of the unitary and monolithic subjectivities and identifications that all these formulas assume and demand. To postulate queers as a race is not only to fix sexuality by a logic antithetical to what I want to suggest is the productive potential of the meaning of queer, but also to analogize sexuality and race in a manner that seeks to compare and equate noncongruent orders of identity and oppression. This analysis of homophobia and racism usually results in the occlusion of white gay racism and the erasure of the identities of queers of color, two political and cultural sites where sexuality and race do not work along parallel but separate logics.[1] I hope that my readings of the other possible explications of queer race will show why my antipathy is so strong here.

A second interpretation of queer race purports to talk about race that is queer (unlike the first understanding of my title that takes queer race in toto as a term in itself, here queer is merely modifying race) or to ask what is queer or can be queer about race as a political, cultural, or biological designation (i.e., not a particular race but racial constructions in general), or, conversely, to ask what the race is of queer, or how queer is raced. My interest in this book lies in the last questions, that is, in delineating and theorizing the racial inscription (both as it is already constructed and as it may be productively deployed) of the "queer" in queer theory, queer politics, and queer identity. Sexuality is always racially marked, as every racial marking is always imbued with a specific sexuality (gender, class, and other classificatory inscriptions are equally determined and determining). In other words, I do not see sexuality and race as disparate constituents of subjectivity or axes of power. Thus I do not want to write race and sexuality as two separate trajectories of identity that cross and overlay in particular subject positions, but instead as systems of meaning and understanding that formatively and inherently define each other. Race does not exist independently of sexuality (and vice versa) to become variously sexualized when particular sexual identities are considered in conjunction with specific racial attributes. Rather, race is always already sexualized as sexuality is always-already raced.[2]

Up to now there has been little work on the racialized construction of sexual identity and the sexualized marking of race to match the growing body of feminist explorations of the ways in which gender is always racially specific, and racial categorizations are inevitably gendered. The construction of sexuality is usually treated separately from the construction of race, as if each figuration of subjectivity could develop independently of the other.[3] We see this aporia tellingly in queer theory: with few exceptions all the already canonized white queer theorists have failed to theorize queer race or to adumbrate the always racialized nature of every queerness in the context of academic institutions and epistemological imperialisms from which queer theory makes its Western postcolonial advance.[4]

Teresa de Lauretis, writing of the cumulative oppressions distinguishing lesbians from women and from each other, adds, "What cannot be elided in a politically responsible theory of sexuality, of gender, or of culture is the critical value of that 'also,' which is neither simply additive nor exclusive but signals the nexus, the mode of operation of *interlocking* systems of gender, sexual orientation, racial, class, and other, more local categories of sexual stratification."[5] De Lauretis cites Audre Lorde's *Zami*, and continues, "Neither race nor gender nor homosexual difference alone can constitute individual identity or the basis for a theory and a politics of social change. What Lorde suggests is a more complex image of the psycho-social-sexual subject . . . which does not deny gender or sex but transcends them."[6] Here de Lauretis articulates the theory that I will be fleshing out in the arena of race/sexuality. De Lauretis's tracing of representations of lesbian difference focuses largely on particular narrative strategies in lesbian literature and film to show how the specificity of lesbian desire is rendered through the transcendence of normative gender binaries. My own readings of culture, while sharing de Lauretis's commitment to charting the interlocking of multiple categories of identity, are more deconstructive: the transcendence I trace is less a utopian escape from predetermining parameters than an exegesis of the impossibility of ever inhabiting the categories without *interlock*, without contamination.

In the United States, from where I argue this transcendence, many contemporary political and theoretical formulations of communitarian subjectivity assume that every identity is merely the accretion of so many other base identities (thus, in popular liberal parlance, a Chicana lesbian is said to be triply oppressed as a woman, a Chicana, and a lesbian), a paradigm that denies the specificity of identity and the inseparability of the supposed constituents of a particular identity (Chicana lesbian might be an identity in itself, rather than a conglomeration of other identities). Consequently, this paradigm normalizes the modes of subjectivity privileged by material power relations in a particular cultural-historical moment (to compute Chicana lesbian as the sum of Chicana, woman, and lesbian, is to establish heterosexual male Chicanoness, white heterosexual femaleness, and white male gayness as the central identities from which the Chicana lesbian draws her constituent parts) and thus erases the experience of those who occupy more than one of the canonized subject positions: discourses that speak of oppression directed against one's gender, race, or sexual orientation make no space for the Chicana lesbian. In these types of sortings one is a person of color *or* one is a woman *or* one is gay.

There is by now a well-documented history of racism in the lesbian and gay movement in the United States,[7] a racism that has inevitably accompanied these problematic liberal conceptions of subjectivity and the single-issue homogenizations implied in such terms as "the gay community" that these conceptions have generated. This fantasized gay community is ritually invoked by the institutions of the state as they attempt to enforce the regimen of compulsory heterosexuality, and by right-wing religious organizations and political interests who construct the state as kowtowing to the homosexual lobby.[8] But those assimilationist lesbians and gay men who seek access to these institutions invoke this fantasy gay community as insistently. Thus when wealthy lesbians and gay men are featured on the cover of *Newsweek* or in television interviews, or when polls "prove" that lesbians and gay men are more prosperous than their heterosexual counterparts, the media is praised for the positive depiction of "our community" by the elite group of lesbians and gay men who are criminally ignorant of (or systematically ignoring) homeless queers, poor queers, and jobless queers.[9]

Those who think of their own identity as singular, those who are unable to imagine multiple subjectivities in others, and those who experience only one site of oppression against themselves tend to universalize their limited understanding by colonizing other subjects. Since most institutionalized lesbian and gay organizations in this country are controlled and dominated by middle-class gay white men, these organizations inevitably have infused the category "gay" with a middle-class white male content. This isn't news. However, even nonassimilationist groups that organize around singular categories reproduce dominant structures. For instance, in the late 1980s and early 1990s, conflicts within the political organizations ACT UP and Queer Nation regularly centered around the opposing interests of white men, on the one hand, and people of color and white women, on the other. It was a struggle over whose experiences and agendas would define the group's identity and politics. Most of the white men usually wanted the group to devote itself exclusively to contesting homophobia and/or to AIDS activism, while many of the white women, white transgendered participants, and people of color often felt that racism and sexism demanded as urgent attention. The white men found these issues irrelevant and divisive. The white women, transgendered participants, and people of color were unwilling to condone sexism and racism for the sake of an oxymoronically impossible queer unity, and unable to divide up their identities in order to decide why a particular act of discrimination was being committed against them. Group identity was constructed so that one's concerns were only pertinent to the group if they were a result of one's gayness as gayness was usually understood by white gay men, and sometimes by white lesbians. If you were being attacked on the street because of your sexual orientation, your outrage and pain were relevant. However, if you had been attacked because of your gender or color rather than your gayness your concerns belonged elsewhere. Those who had been assaulted for all three reasons or who didn't know exactly why they had been assaulted often confused the group's very raison d'être.

The conflicts in these queer organizations stem from specific ways of constituting and designating group formation. Any US politics, no matter how coalitional its compass, that identifies itself in terms of gender and/or sexual orientation only (lesbian separatism, Queer Nation, Lesbian and Gay Studies) will be a white-centered and white-dominated politics, since only white people in this society can afford to see their race as unmarked, as an irrelevant or subordinate category of analysis. Women means white women; lesbian and gay means white lesbians and gay men.[10] When any marginalized subjectivity (i.e., gayness) becomes the basis for community, it will, in turn, create and enforce marginalizing prioritizations and exclusions. The idea of a/the gay community is conjured up to celebrate deviance in the face of a massive structure of compulsory heterosexuality, but also in order to re-inscribe other relations of domination and to silence diverse queer voices.

This policing of identity was vividly illustrated in a 1993 issue of the San Diego, California, "gay" newspaper *Update*,[11] in "Tribal Writes,"[12] the regular column written by the late Connie Norman, a white male-to-female transsexual HIV-positive queer AIDS activist.[13] Norman's article is representative of prevailing attitudes not only within the lesbian and gay establishment but also among many participants in more militant, nonassimilationist groups like ACT UP and the now defunct Queer Nation. In this particular article, Norman, quite appropriately, is raging against homophobic violence. But she begins her column as follows:

> All right folks, don't you think it is just about time that we started circling the wagons? And I don't really give a shit if "indigenous peoples" object to my use of the phrase "circle the wagons" or not. I don't give one whit if that phrase comes from the dominating white imperialist culture and therefore is racist in connotation and is the tool of language that western culture has used to dominate and oppress people of color and on and on and politically correct this and multiculturalism that, I'm just sick of it!
>
> When in the hell are we going to come together as a community and start fighting our real enemy, *homohatred*![14]

The community Norman invokes is a racist one; only queers who do not think that racism is as pernicious as homophobia are welcome in it. Her "we" assumes that all queers are white, since it is primarily white queers who can enjoy the luxury of constituting "homohatred" as the only real enemy. Her "we" also erases the alignments and experiences of those white queers who are irrevocably committed to antiracist work. In Chapter 2, I will examine the consequences of these kinds of separation by showing how gayness can actually be used to signify whiteness and to shore up white supremacist power structures. Chapter 4, on the other hand, will suggest an alternative conception of queer identity through an analysis of Gloria Anzaldúa's book *Borderlands/La Frontera*. Here a fragmented, conflictive, and even anti-identitarian conception of queerness not only evokes multiple queer subjects, but also confronts the racist assumptions of the gay establishment.

As I have already suggested, in intellectual discourse, queer theory and characterizations of queer theory have often (re)produced the kinds of racial normalizations and exclusions demarcated by queer community and political organizations. For instance, in an article for the 1994 queer theory issue of *Sociological Theory*, Steven Seidman cites several lesbian and gay writers of color in making the point that in the 1980s the "concept of lesbian and gay identity that served as the foundation for building a community and organizing politically was criticized as reflecting a white, middle-class experience or standpoint."[15] But in the very next page of his article Seidman cites only white writers in his characterization of queer theory's affirmation of a "radical politics of difference."[16] He continues,

> Drawing from the critique of unitary identity politics by people of color and by sex rebels, and from the poststructural critique of "representational" models of language, queer theorists argue that identities are always multiple or at best composites, with an infinite number of ways in which "identity-components" (e.g., sexual orientation, race, class, nationality, gender, age, ableness) can intersect or combine.[17]

Here people of color are explicitly opposed to queer theorists. While the work of people of color is drawn from by queer theorists, it does not itself qualify as queer theory. Queer theory and queer theorists are thus constructed as white, while queer intellectuals of color are situated at an earlier—less sophisticated, more primitive?—moment that enabled but does not participate in queer theory. Another review article in this issue of *Sociological Theory* follows suit in constructing queer theory as white by citing only white writers in a list of "many works . . . emblematic of the 'queer turn.'"[18]

I situate my own work in the context of various analyses of constructions of race, and as participating in, interjecting into, articulating, and interrogating queer theory, insofar as it seeks to specify the race of queer theory, and queer theory's marking of or failure to mark race. Rather than showing that racial difference is not a significant variable of queer articulation and performance, however, this absence points to the continued normalization of whiteness by these queer theorists, and suggests that in at least one important respect some queer theory might not be as different from the epistemologies and methodologies that it so frequently claims, whether explicitly or implicitly, to contest. In this sense, under a trendy new name and poststructuralist vocabulary, this queer theory merely reproduces the racism of the lesbian and gay organizations, structures, struggles, campaigns, studies, and curricula that normalized and continues to normalize whiteness by failing to acknowledge the racial constitution of lesbian and gay identities and their own racial inscriptions.

The expositions of queer theory that I have mentioned raise a number of troubling questions. Is queer theory white, and are these merely accurate descriptions of it? If so, antiracist work might contest queer theory (the theorists I have mentioned who characterize queer theory as white do not, of course, do so explicitly, and they do not lament their queer theory's monoracial nature). And is this whiteness intrinsic to the epistemological work of queer theory or merely a reflection of some practitioners of queer theory? Might the queer theory of the future not be a white theory? If these dispensers of queer theory are wrong, is this because they have misdefined queer theory, defined queer theory in such a way that it only encompasses white theorists or theorists who do not explicitly work on race? Or have they simply failed to recognize other queer theorists?

My strategic response to these questions is to resist conceding queer theory to whiteness, both in order not to remarginalize queer critics who do work on race, and because I see my own project as very much enabled by and part of the project of queer theory. The subtitle of my book, then, "Cultural Interventions in the Racial Politics of Queer Theory," affirms not only that queer theory already has a racial politics, even if only by default, but also indicates my desire both to intervene into this politics and to point to what I see as cultural texts that already make such interventions. So the "in" of my title points to my own situation within queer theory as much as it indicates an entrance from elsewhere. I want to constitute these interventions as part of queer theory's project, rather than merely as a critique of or addendum or supplement to queer theory. Instead of conceding queer theory to whiteness I want to think through the theoretical possibilities of queer theory that can put it at odds with formations that resist racialization in order to theorize a queer theory for a queer race.

I am interested, then, in the theoretical articulation of queer, rather than in an empirical elaboration of different queer crystallizations. My concerns are cross cultural not in the sense of the coverage model of Western academic and pedagogical multiculturalism that seeks to articulate a comprehensive (and imperialistic) universalism, but in my attempts to bring into strategic juxtaposition certain historical moments of cultural visibility, intervention, and transcendence of raced sexual subjectivity precisely in order to trace the shape of such imperialisms as they generate and are themselves transformed by discourses of deviant sexuality. Much commendable work by social scientists has already been undertaken in the empirical elaboration of geographically diverse queernesses, as has a greater quantity of less careful work in which, typically, a white Westerner uses the trope and privilege of travel and the sanctioned promise of investigating difference to recapitulate a putatively universal and ahistorically transcendent gay identity, and to interpolate the metropolitan traveler as the arbiter and omniscient cataloger of the queer world (commonly in the form of the scientist, historian, storyteller). The production of otherworldly gayness becomes an opportunity only to enrich and expand the reach of hegemonic positionalities, much as the discourse of multiculturalism has avoided confronting racist power relations and institutions by emphasizing the enrichment potential of cultural diversity for a still centralized white subject.[19]

Similarly, literary and historical projects that attempt to locate and claim a lesbian or gay past, or lesbian and gay foremothers and forefathers in order to inscribe them into a linear and unified gay tradition, necessarily impose a specifically Western and modern teleology of identity, sexuality, and liberation onto historically and culturally diverse (and often alien) subjects, and thus re-enforce the imperialist relations that are already inherent in such a project's almost inevitable origin in the white Western academy. Knowledge is never benign, and, certainly, apparatuses and institutions of knowledge production will always contextualize any knowledge thus produced, as will the situation of the investigator of knowledge as someone with the privilege, resources and historically enabling legacy of economic and military imperialism to travel, write, and acquire.

The elite institutions from which queer theory advances complement the paternalistic activist wisdom of lesbian and gay organizers in the United States who judge the level of progress another country is making in the arena of lesbian and gay rights by the uniquely US trajectories of Stonewall, coming out, and identity-based civil rights. Of course, it is always the US standard that these other countries must live up to and, naturally, the United States is always the leader in this race for gay utopia. The far reach of US gay imperialism is evident even in the recently published book *Defiant Desire: Gay and Lesbian Lives in South Africa*, where the white South African editors make an unprecedented effort to treat the diversity of South Africa's queer cultures, but still fall into the trap of internalizing US models of gay progress and thus reproducing US imperialism, too. Mark Gevisser, one of the book's editors, comes to the following conclusion about South Africa: "Only in the 1980s did black men and women begin to play an active role in gay politics."[20] He is apparently oblivious to the ways in which his uncritical deployment of the category gay and his assumptions of what constitutes gay politics, a priori exclude uniquely black and uniquely South African queer identities and formations from his purview.[21]

This, however, is not to say that queerness or theory or queer theory should be contained in their supposed birthplaces. Besides the collusion with postcolonial homophobias that such a reticence would enact, besides the arrogance it would assume in always returning to the West as source, it would postulate a geographic and intellectual purity that belies the bastardized after-effects of imperialism, multinational capitalism, and international telecommunications. As Chris Berry says of the spate of homoerotic representations of East Asians in recent films, "All these instances are further evidence of how the deviationist position constitutes not a Western incursion into a pure Asian frame, but rather a selective borrowing from outside that further hybridizes an already hybridized space."[22] As a consequence, an un-national queer theory "has everything to do with an emergent globalized debate on lesbian and gay rights that affects everyone who engages in same-sex sexual activity, for the effect of this globalization is to put everything back on the negotiating table, so to speak."[23]

Given the global reach of some US queers and the increasingly problematized assumptions of nationalized discourses (especially where categories like race and sexuality necessarily privilege experiences specific to but not congruent with national identity, and recognizing the multiplying diasporic communities around various permutations—and intrications—of both categories), and my own transcontinental social, intellectual, and political formation (in South Africa and the United States), I have not strictly focused my investigation on one national culture—the United States—but have instead also used a sporadic transnationalism to interrogate and exemplify my understandings of both US and other political, cultural, and intellectual formations, and to properly contextualize queerness and theory in the arenas of transnational corporate capital and US imperialism. Although emerging firmly from a training in literary criticism, this study is also a genre-fuck and discipline-fuck in its equal treatment of pornography, Literature, personal advertisements, etc., as literary study per se is imploding in upon itself with its voracious de(re)constructions of categories and normative notions of critical evaluation. Thus in Chapter 2 I treat the constitution of contemporary racial and sexual subjects reciprocally between the United States and South Africa in a pair of pornographic videos, while Chapter 4 notes the written work of Gloria Anzaldúa confounding national and disciplinary purisms, and my conclusion, "Your Picture Here," points to the enduring reach of (post)coloniality in queer theory.

II

The exclusionary rhetoric of gay community has its counterpart in racial nationalism and race essentialism. As peoples of a particular race are routinely homogenized (both by those inside and outside of that race), so queers of color are imagined by some members of the race as a threat to this (fictitious) unity, or are merely claimed not to exist (by some members of the race, by some outside the race). Concomitantly, while the marks of queerness are often mistakenly assumed to be invisible or choosable (not all lesbians pass for straight; not all lesbians can pass for straight), a platitude whose popularity marks the eclipse of common knowledge (gaydar) by an unusual congruency in the effects of liberal civil rights discourse (we're just like everyone else) and constructionist academic theory, popular wisdom has it that race is self-evident: one can look around a room and tell how many people of color are in the room; one can look at a roster of names to determine who on that roster is Latina; a white person knows that she is white; either one is (born) a certain race or one isn't. But the idea of race as it is understood today is a fairly recent concept, and science now tells us that races do not exist.[24] (Science didn't always tell us this.) History tells us: about legal rules in the United States that assigned a race to someone according to the proportion of black blood in her, and that this proportion was quite arbitrary; about South Africans born into one racial classification only to be reclassified as a different race later on in their lives by the apartheid government; about the politically expedient designation of Japanese people as honorary whites by the apartheid government; about slippages between races and nationalities; about someone who changes races when she crosses national boundaries (Mexicans are considered people of color in the United States, but were classified as white in apartheid South Africa. An Argentinean might be white in her home country, but Hispanic in the United States.); of historical changes in the content of particular racial categories; of different and contradictory criteria for determining one's race; and of the different uses of racial categories in different places (the political use of black in South Africa, the inclusion of all peoples of color under the rubric black in the United Kingdom, and the designation of only those of African descent as black in the United States). Personal anecdotes show us people who identify as one race but are mistaken for another: light-skinned black people who have to insist on their blackness, Native Americans who are often made invisible by that non-Native observer looking for tell-tale signs of coloredness in a room. And people of mixed race who get tired of having to check the box marked "Other" on application forms. Race is as much constructed and unstable as sexuality is, and sexuality is certainly one of the factors that determine racial appellations and identifications.

But to understand that biological races are phantoms and that race is a political tool cannot rectify the reality that there was once a science of race and that this (discredited) science is still believed in many quarters. And this understanding cannot eradicate the reality of the material and psychological effects of these constructions on people's lives and identifications, and on they ways in which people are racialized by themselves and others, both historically and today. That is, race may no longer be scientific, but it still holds meaning: it is still social, cultural, and political. My own racial investigations, then, are intricated in this double bind by paradoxically using race to point to its constructedness, by showing how race shifts and shape-shifts under the pressures of sexuality—that is, by showing how queer race is.

My understanding of the queer part in queer race—to return to my beginning disavowal of a queer/race analogy—partly explains why I want to work queer race as an asymmetrical rather than as an explanatory counter-balanced phrase. The debates in the 1990s among lesbians and gay men about the efficacy of the word queer are, of course, more than merely terminological contentions: they encapsulate polarized assumptions and agendas springing from theoretical and experiential premises that are very different yet bewilderingly prone to conflation and co-optation. To begin, then, I should say that, to use the words of an editorial in a 1994 issue of the 'zine *Rant and Rave*, "queer is not a substitute for gay."[25] This is not to deny that at certain times queer may mean (merely) gay and/or lesbian, but rather to insist that the totality of the meaning of queer will always be more or less than or different from its synonymity with lesbian/gay, and that its force, in fact, resides in the way it can be both conflated with lesbian and/or gay and used to disrupt that conflation or deconstruct lesbianness and/or gayness. This is not to deny that terms and categories like lesbian, gay, and even lesbian and gay can serve useful and specific functions, but rather to emphasize the productive potentialities of those places where two different systems of naming might collide, and to adumbrate the reverberations of queer that collide and overlap with its conflation with lesbian and/or gay to produce this asynchronicity.[26]

First, queer understands sexuality as fluid, open ended, constructed; thus those organizers (of conferences, organizations, marches) who take queer to be the (provocative or convenient) shorthand for "lesbian, gay, bisexual, and transgender," or some other such inclusive formulation of minority sexualities, are as misguided as are their less thoughtful counterparts who use queer as a modish synonym for lesbian and gay. These usually tokenistic additions to the descriptor gay (often the name of a group/event is changed to include lesbians and/or bisexuals and/or transgendered people, with no corresponding change in the agendas or understandings of the group/event, which remains as relentlessly gay as ever) only highlight the ways in which all such litanies attempt to catalog and circumscribe identities; not only does the list necessarily exclude a plethora of as yet unarticulated, unimagined, uncategorizable, and unacceptable nonheterosexual identifications, as well as many discursively thriving queer subjectivities, but it also does not explain those identifications that contest this system of classification per se. Identities should not be thought of as fixed; hence minoritizing rhetorics that make well-meaning cases for lesbians and gay men as constituting ten percent of the population, or argue for academic departments of Lesbian and Gay Studies, might miss the opportunity offered by queer to imagine deviance infiltrating or find deviance in an entire population/curriculum.

Second, it follows that queer is not the Other of straight; in fact, its deconstructive position outside of the hetero/homosexual binary makes its relationship to concepts like straight and gay oblique, and its definitional slipperiness means that some straight people might be thought of as queer, whereas some gay people might be thought of as not queer, though to even overlap these categorizations in this way is to confuse different planes of subjectivity: since queer contests the heterosexual/homosexual binary, to speak of queerness in the same sentence as that binary is already to juxtapose conflicting epistemologies and to concede queer to the gays and straights that it counterposes. Queer doesn't seem to have a clearly definable polar opposite, except, perhaps non-queer, a category whose content is as difficult to specify as queer itself is a slippery identity.

Third, queer also has an uneasy relationship with male/female gender binaries: in that queer is nominally ungendered (unlike, usually, the terms lesbian, and, increasingly, gay) it can be said not only not to assume gender as the primary axis of difference among lesbians and gay men but also to leave unspecified the number and scope of possible gender categories and identifications insofar as it risks erasing queer female (including lesbian) specificity as many generic terminologies come to universalize male experience in patriarchal societies. Queer is as ambiguously feminist as is feminism's own deconstructive suspicion of the categories of sex.[27]

Fourth, if in certain circumstances queer includes all gay people, it might also be useful to argue at times that not all gay people are queer (this is not only a strategy of exclusion, but also a concession to people's self-identifications, since many gay people emphatically disassociate themselves from the term queer[28]), and we might come closer to a definition of queer by asking what distinguishes non-queer gay people from queer gays (and non-gays). In a 1994 *Radical Teacher* forum on queer studies/pedagogy versus lesbian/gay studies/pedagogy, Andrew Parker jokingly postulated the telling distinction as one of political alignment: "There are no queer Republicans."[29] One could, however, take Parker's quip seriously in order to posit a politicized and politically particular queerness. Certainly, this kind of criterion speaks to a specific historical moment in a circumscribed geographic, intellectual, and social space. In previous decades in the United States, the identifications gay and lesbian did carry much of the political charge that is associated with queer at the beginning of a new millennium, not only in terms of a sense of otherness and the commitment to activism often assumed by those who identified as lesbian and gay, but also insofar as gay organizing was often undertaken in a context of leftist politics, and, insofar as in and after the 1960s lesbianism became crucially intricated with radical feminism. While gay male politics pluralized and dispersed quickly, lesbianism has retained its politicization much longer. Today it is quite common for both lesbians and gay men to think of sexual orientation as a lifestyle or as happenstance or as irrelevant to anything rather than as a political position and to be politicized neither about sexual orientation nor about anything else. One can no longer fairly or safely assume that a lesbian is also a feminist. Those lesbians and gay men who identity as queer, however, are bound to invest their homosexuality with a political (usually oppositional) component, often also implying—perversely—the desirability of queerness rather than merely submitting to its genetic inevitability or objective immutability.[30] This militant embrace of queerness also means that the queer asks less to be recognized as just-like-everyone-else, than insists on celebrating queer difference (that is, difference from non-queers as well as difference among queers). Hence the reclamation of the derogatory word "queer," one of whose meanings is just odd.

The politicization of queer thus removes it from the logic of liberal pluralism. I have resisted the considerable temptation to say that queer is more inclusive than lesbian and gay, since although it is true that the category-phrase lesbian and gay does not explicitly include, for instance, bisexuals and transgendered people, I do not want to set queer up as an always all-inclusive category. I intend, rather, to emphasize the political agenda behind queer, and, as I have implied above, this agenda might well exclude as many members of sexual minorities from its compass as lesbian and gay does. San Francisco's Queer Nation, for example, was at one time consumed by heated debates over whether lesbian and gay police officers should be permitted to attend the group's meetings. In San Diego during the Gulf War of 1991, Queer Nation was bitterly divided between prowar and antiwar activists, and over the question of whether the group should define itself in opposition to the war, or as welcoming queers of other persuasions, as well (much to my own regret, the latter course was decided upon). Queer, then, has involved as much monitoring, proscribing, and prescribing of actions and affiliations as has any other term of identity.

However, there is a tension between the progressive potential of queer to signify diversity and multiplicity, and the tendency of this multiplicity to become a depoliticized anything goes tolerance—for queer to stand as a purely individual politic. In an address entitled "Queer Theory: Unstating Desire" at one of the plenary sessions of the Sixth North American Lesbian, Gay, and Bisexual Studies Conference in Iowa City, Lee Edelman quite rightly refused the imperative to construct a master narrative of intellectual community, remarking that to "inquire into the state of queer studies—as if it *had* a state and all of us happened to live in that state *together*—is to presuppose a fantasy."[31] But the conclusion that Edelman drew from this caveat sounded suspiciously like a return to the kind of pluralism that queer theory claimed to contest:

> And as we come to Iowa from different states so we come from different disciplines as well, and from differing ideological and political perspectives within those different disciplines. Whatever queer studies may become, then, we have reason to hope that for now, at least, it defies any effort to reduce it to the singularity of a "state" that would be subject to any conceptual or methodological totalization.[32]

Acknowledging various political positions should not mean that one must not promote a particular ideology. Furthermore, experience is not analogizable with political affiliation: there is no causal relationship between the recognition of diverse experiential formations and a liberal tolerance of political diversity.

Fifth, the recognition of experiential difference proceeds from and to an antiessentialist understanding of sexuality that realizes the historical and cultural specificity of and multiplicity within contemporary lesbian, gay, and other identities.

This definition-as-difference makes queer especially amenable to an understanding of sexual identity as formatively shaped by race as opposed to an identity politics model that must premise its generation of subjects on the assumption of commonalities among queers (as it also constructs monolithic communities marked by race, gender, and so on). Because a queer commitment emphasizes the differences among and within queers, rather than positing a transhistorical queer universality, it is less likely to prescribe a single model of sexual identity or sexual liberation and to assume white male normativity in its constructions of lesbian and gay communities. Concomitantly, as the linking commonality between queers become less identifiable, and a plethora of queer identities is articulated, so race can be seen as a marker of queer identity and a determinant of the meaning of any queer identity as much as sexual orientation or any other identification is. Phillip Brian Harper has intimated that queer's destabilization of singular and unitary paradigms of sexuality could usher in a truly multicultural lesbian and gay epistemology:

> we could see multiculturalism as a challenge whereby the lesbian and gay community has to face up to the already multiple nature of lesbian and gay culture itself. This would mean recognizing the diversity of what we already consider to be lesbian and gay culture—recognizing its own diversity in terms of race, class, gender identification, ethnicity, and so on. For me as a Black man, this would have to entail, in particular, more direct treatments of racial difference in what most of us think of as lesbian and gay literature . . . Frankly, as far as I can tell, the phenomenon of racial difference, discussion of racial difference, are all but absent in most of what is currently promoted as gay (male, in particular) literature. This latter way of thinking about multiculturalism would enable a fundamental change in how most of us think about gay identity. That's something I find particularly useful, potentially: that gay identity itself would begin to encompass a whole range of cultural differences within it. It might be precisely this change that constitutes a difference between what we have thought of as lesbian and gay culture, on the one hand, and queer culture, to use the *au courant* term.[33]

Similarly, Gloria Anzaldúa has argued that the word "lesbian" implies white lesbian, while the disaffection, outcast status, and vague compass of queer make it, paradoxically, more generalizable.[34] Anzaldúa has affiliated the queer with "the troublesome, the mongrel, the mulatto, the half-breed, the half dead."[35] Of course, this multi-vocal access is queer's potential rather than its inevitability. There is always the potential for appropriation, too. As Helen (Charles) points out, queer is a working-class word that has been taken up by the middle-classes.[36] Further, there is no guarantee that queer will not be defined or redefined by hegemonic lesbian and gay institutions so that it comes to carry the same force of privileged whiteness that lesbian and gay often do currently.

Some of the progressive potential of queer identity—as well as the frequent failure of this potential to materialize—was enacted in the brief life of Queer Nation. (Despite Teresa de Lauretis's protests to the contrary in her introduction to the Queer Theory issue of *differences*, I think that there are commonalities and continuities between Queer Theory and Queer Nation. I believe that each constituted and qualified the other.[37]) Queer Nation produced guerilla actions that promoted the visibility of lesbian, gay, and other queer identities. The first Queer Nation chapters were formed in 1989, and Queer Nation subsequently prospered and self-destructed to various degrees. In their commitment to a multiplicity of queer identities, not only as these identities define sexual practices, but also as they are constructed by racial, gender, and other identifications, many Queer Nation groupings internalized the lessons learnt by feminism regarding the bankruptcy of the notion of a universal Womanhood. Thus Queer Nation celebrated queerness, rather than attempted to delineate a uniform, correct, or totalizing lesbian and/or gay identity. (As I suggested earlier, this is not to say that Queer Nation multiplicity was a pluralistic—and apolitical—free for all. Queer identities a priori radicalize the assimilationist lesbian and gay identities that work against the visibility that Queer Nation promoted when these assimilationist identities assure the dominant heterosexual order that they are just-like-everyone-else.) Queer Nation enacted a poststructuralist conception of subjectivity as shifting and multiplicitous, but nevertheless aspired to an agenda of political activism that is presumably premised on some notion of commonality. The name Queer Nation itself, juxtaposing irrecuperable difference with the parochialism of nationalism,[38] connoted a paradoxical eccentricity within a coherent political program, thus recognizing the arbitrariness of constituting a community around sexual identity given the heterogeneous ways in which sexual identity is experienced across different races, genders, classes, and so on.

Queer Nation actions encompassed a puzzling and always polysignifying and slippery mix of complicity with, and parody, appropriation, and inversion of dominant institutions and discourses. This polymorphousness was illustrated at 1991 protests of the United States war against Iraq, where some Queer Nationalists were heard chanting "shopping bags, not body bags!" More traditional leftists accused Queer Nation of colluding in the promotion of consumer capitalism. These Queer Nation detractors were unable to see that the consumer capitalism in the slogan was irretrievably inflected (and infected) by its campy context. Since in the United States (and most anywhere else) one cannot *not* make commerce with consumer capitalism, it is precisely in the shopping malls that the battles for queer visibility should be waged—such battles would not only contest homophobia but would also be the pre-eminent way to shape those shopping malls. Furthermore, to demand slogans that would be correct in the terms of more traditional leftist politics would be profoundly homophobic since it would be to require that Queer Nation conform to pre-existing models of oppositional political discourse—it would, in effect, require that Queer Nation not be queer. The slogan "We're not here to educate, we're here to ruin your day," shouted by Queer Nationalists during protests against Hollywood homophobia at the 1992 Academy Awards ceremony encapsulated not only Queer Nation's enactment of *style* as politics but also Queer Nation's refusal to participate in the lip service that hegemonic models of politics pay to the etiquette of polite give and take.

But any unitary definition of Queer Nation necessarily insists on exactly what the movement of Queer Nation seemed to resist: Queer Nation attitudes and actions varied from city to city, and even within individual Queer Nation chapters there seemed to be a delight in contradiction and elusiveness. I do not want to idealize Queer Nation. In fact, the November 1991 decision by San Francisco's Queer Nation to disband because of the group's ongoing failures to contest racism and sexism, both within and outside the group, is symptomatic of the ways in which, in many activist circles, the queer merely has became a trendy recapitulation of the gay white male of the 1970s and 1980s. But for me the moment when Queer Nation San Francisco voted itself out of existence was also a characteristic Queer Nation moment: it illustrated the radical discontinuity and multiplicity within Queer Nation itself, as well as Queer Nation's anti-nationalistic commitment to fragmentation and dissolution—in a way, activists' prescient answer to Donald Hall's call for greater self-reflexivity within queer theory.[39]

Many of the complaints against Queer Nation in the wake of its demise in the mid-1990s certainly suggest that despite its other queer enactments, Queer Nation was from its inception, or rapidly became, very much a white nation (and some would further argue, a male nation). Thus while it is true that the appellation "queer" might invoke a multiple, shifting, and anti-identical logic of interested association that contests reifying and monolithic expositions of sexual identity, its actual political trajectory is unpredictable, and it can easily slip into the habits that I have charted some queer theory falling into when, in particular, white queer theorists reproduce histories and archaeologies that centralize white experiences of gayness and lesbianness: as Anzaldúa says, "Their theories limit the ways we think about being queer."[40]

Contrarily, as queer continues to take up the challenge of describing multiply inscribed subjects, it faces the possibility of diluting its antihomophobic critique. Despite the denotative potential of queer to apply to anything that strays from the norm, its historical legacy and current usage sutures it to lesbian and gay sexualities, and, to a lesser extent, to bisexual and transgender subjectivities. As queer is currently used by queer theorists, it almost without fail refers to sexuality;[41] this very privileging of sex, sexuality, and sexual identity as axis of analysis means also that its model subjects are assumed to be white, since, as I have suggested, in a society structured around race and racism at every level it is only white queers (and white people in general) who can have the luxury of not naming race, of not naming their own race. On the other hand, if queer is made to signify, race, as much as sexuality, is its potential as a tool for antihomophobic analysis not marginalized and erased in its subsumption under or alternation with other analytic categories? Homophobic leftists in the 1960s who didn't openly ridicule lesbians, bisexuals, gay men, and transgendered people trivialized queer concerns by relegating them to the realm of the personal or to the temporal space of later, and most multiculturalists of today will usually refuse to include queer concerns in their monolithic multicultural paradigms, doing so only when pressed to and usually by tokenizing and ghettoizing these concerns by incorporating them under the much more important cultural classifications of race, ethnicity, nationality, and even gender.

In order to define a manageable scope for this project, in order to write something that readers will not find completely arbitrary, and because of my own particular interests and investments in queer theory—not least of which are its antihomophobic impetus, its immersion in homoerotic cultures and practices, in addition to, in spite of, and exponentially invigorated by its playfulness, outrageousness, and negativity (its boredom with the necessity of positive images of previously marginalized subjects)—I have in the remainder of this book taken queer and queer theory to be centrally concerned with representations of sexuality, and of homosexuality in particular. But I have also continually interrogated this focus (both my own and that of queer) in my assumptions throughout that queer is not enough, that queer gestures to something more, that these representations are always also racial representations. I do want queer and queer theory to be about sex—I am not willing to give up queer theory's antihomophobic commitment—while also wanting it equally to not be only about sex, to be about how sex can never be "only." In terms of the sexual meaning of queer, Ellis Hanson has articulated this tension in his description of queer demarcating "a domain virtually synonymous with homosexuality and yet wonderfully suggestive of a whole range of sexual possibilities."[42] My goal is to retain queer synonymity with homosexuality and queer suggestivity of other sexual possibilities, while also showing how queer denotes a whole range of racial possibilities, and, beyond the pages of this book, of other possibilities as well.

III

The following chapters address the problematics I have delineated through readings of specific cultural texts; these readings attempt to show how political narratives of community are assembled. I address the erasure of queers of color from intellectual and popular civil rights discourse throughout the book, but especially as evidenced in a perhaps unexpected overlay of US nostalgia on South African newness that I narrativize in Chapter 2. This chapter brings together several sites of conflict by treating current competing and politically charged depictions of male homosexuality in South Africa. South Africa is both a Third and First World nation. The particular historical juncture in which culture in South Africa is now being produced makes South Africa an especially fertile ground for revealing the interstices and intersections of multiple positions and identifications, and the processes by which new national and communal planes are formed and figured. Because of the long enforcement of formal apartheid, South Africa is only now seeing a tangible fruition to its own equivalent of the Civil Rights movement that is commonly mythologized to have procured similar results in the United States four decades ago. Concomitantly, as questions of lesbian and gay civil rights only entered the realm of sustained public debate in the United States in the 1990s, South Africa in 1996 became the first and only country in the world to constitutionally prohibit discrimination based on sexual orientation.[43] Through exploring the image of South Africa as it is produced by and for gay consumers in the United States (for instance, in all white pornographic videos that define South African gay maleness within the parameters of a landscape conjured up in the terms of an exoticizing colonial rhetoric) in contradistinction to lesbian and gay South Africans' self-representations, I show how homoerotic imaginaries collude with, create, and confront various imperialist regimes.

I conclude Chapter 2 by hypothesizing that racialized representations of desire might be productively used in the service of an antiracist politics. Chapter 3 takes up Robert Reid-Pharr's challenge to queer theorists, and white lesbians and gay men, especially, to theorize "cross-racial desire."[44] I examine the kinds of political interstices of gender, race, and sexuality that can be invested in representations of interracial gay male relationships, in particular, in order to show how the existing discourses about these representations and relationships simplify and thus impoverish the potential trajectories of racialized desire in the arenas of social theory and politics.

Chapter 4 suggests how an antiracist queer politics might be formulated, by treating the work of Gloria Anzaldúa. Anzaldúa's politicized use of the idea of the queer contests the pluralist impetuses that I have described while it also conjures up the specter of queer losing its antihomophobic force. I argue that Anzaldúa's writings, as they disrupt canonical genre designations, and cross the borders between and within countries, cultures, languages, genders, and the self, embody a queerness that retrieves the radical agendas of much pre-Stonewall US lesbian and gay activism, yet at the same time transform that queerness with social signs and practices from some Native American cultures. Anzaldúa's work embodies a fragmentary queerness that selectively produces the past to offer a vision for the future of queer theory; in addition, it refigures accepted notions of reading and teaching as it refuses mastery to any one reader, and moves in and out of the academy, and across national boundaries. I read Anzaldúa's work not only as archetypically queer but also as archetypically American to the extent that it revolutionizes restrictive parameters of Americanness and undercuts the very discourses of nation and nationalism. In this sense her work invites consideration of the disjunctions and overlaps between the queer nation and the nation state in general, and is radically skeptical of the spectrum of institutional academic specializations.

Chapter 5 offers an alternative reading of queer from that implied by Anzaldúa, but in order to show how a distopic queer epistemology is as important a tool for understanding the constitution of racialized sexuality as is Anzaldúa's progressive queerness. I read media and subcultural representations of Jeffrey Dahmer to show the extent to which the degree of Dahmer's homosexualization in a particular representation determines Dahmer's thinking and actions in the sphere of race, and to suggest how spiraling efforts to separate race from sexuality in the Dahmer case only further intricate the two analytic axes.

I see the elaboration of the category queer in relation to race as crucially dependent on a paradigm of identity as self-conceptualization (and self-fashioning), and on a scrupulously diverse delineation of the contextual specificities of queer-as-self-differentiation and queer-as-differentiation-from-itself, rather than on a pre-existing imposition of static phantasmatics of identity onto fractured, incompatible, and elusive subjects. While a number of recent studies have described queer manifestations in various geographic spaces and historical moments, my project differs from these in that its emphasis is theoretical rather than empirical. I am more concerned with charting a theoretical framework for understanding the race of queer theory than in producing a cross-cultural survey of queer practices.

This book tests the limits of queer theory. It will, I hope, intervene from and into queer theory as a theoretical investigation of queer theory's racial inscription, as well as a speculation as to its possible future directions and potential alliances with, interpenetrations with, and subsumptions of and by antiracist studies. "Queer Race" means the ways in which particular racializations are and can be queer, the ways in which queerness is variously racialized and can be racialized differently, a queer race theory, and the enigmatic intersections of these possibilities where race itself becomes/is queer.

Chapter 2

Whiteness as Gayness: The Men of South Africa

I

In this chapter, I narrativize a particular construction of whiteness. Since the means of this narrativization is a series of white South African gay pornographic videos produced for US consumption, my particularity turns on nationalist identifications and relations between the United States and South Africa, various trajectories of US imperialism, and the production of gay identity, and, ultimately, a gay US imperialism.[1] My aim is not merely to point to examples of racism in white gay cultural productions but rather to trace the ways in which sexual and racial identities can define each other in such productions. This story tells us as much about the meaning of gayness as the meaning of whiteness. This is not to suggest that the meaning of gayness or whiteness is fixed or that the relationship between these two categories is stable; in fact, I illustrate that here (and always, I suspect) gayness is as slippery as whiteness: neither identity has meaning in and of itself. I do not make claims, then, for all sites of gay culture and identity or for all sites of white (gay) culture and identity; rather, by delineating one way in which white racism and gayness produce each other I hope to unsettle the conventional wisdom that assumes that racist institutions are also reactionary in the arena of gay rights. Concomitantly, I want to show that by identifying the racist potential of gayness as a category, queer interventions not only make race queer but also constitute integral components of antiracist work.

II

I take it for granted that the specification of whiteness is essential to antiracist work, and that such a specification is not coterminous with a white supremacist celebration of whiteness, or a liberal white insistence on the many ethnicities of whiteness in order to diminish and dilute the naming and analysis of white racism.[2] There has recently been an outpouring of whiteness studies in antiracist articles on whiteness, conferences, anthologies, books, and special issues of journals. I do not here rehearse arguments that have already been made by these numerous cultural critics for the urgency of the project of analyzing whiteness, though this work has, of course, enabled my own.[3] I also take it for granted that the primary responsibility for interrogating whiteness belongs to white people. Too often the burden of identifying and contesting racism has fallen solely to people of color; hence people of color have been forced to teach and caretake white people, and a center-periphery relation between white people and people of color has been re-inscribed, reproducing racist and sexist stereotypes that reduce people of color to self-effacing nannies/mammies.

Many of the existing attempts to analyze whiteness have noted that the terms of whiteness appear elusive (the specifics of the content of whiteness elude white people, in particular), especially when whiteness is not treated in opposition to nonwhiteness; it seems easier to say what whiteness is not than what it is. I suggest that we can create a new perspective on whiteness by looking at the ways in which gendered race and sexuality construct each other, and at what the resulting substitutions, displacements, and conflations suggest about racial definitions and constructions, about the workings of whiteness, and about the disparate uses, denials, and specifications of whiteness.

III

A mail order company based in San Francisco sells gay porn videos to, as its catalog puts it, "men of selective tastes everywhere."[4] However the October 1993 catalog's editorial column entitled "A word from our president" delineates the company's specialties more specifically: "With this brochure, we are beginning a new format to provide you with a monthly brochure alternating between Latino and Asian products each moth [sic]."[5] But the parade of racist exoticizations of men of color that pervades so many arenas of middle-class white gay male culture in the US is interrupted by the company president's next sentence: "Periodically, we will include material which focuses on youth oriented Caucasians as well." These "Caucasians," who, it turns out, are not particularly youth oriented, given the prime career age of most gay male porn video stars in the United States, are usually collected together on one page of the catalog; in keeping with the company's internationalist agenda they represent, for example, Australia, a nationally unspecified Eastern Europe, and The Men of South Africa.

I want to illustrate a specific instance of the conjunction of race and sexuality via a discussion of the tapes featuring these Men of South Africa, the South African gay porn video, *The Men of South Africa*, and its sequel, *Men of South Africa II*. Both tapes seem to feature all white casts, were made in the early 1990s in a South Africa still under formal apartheid, and are distributed by the aforementioned San Francisco mail order company specializing in "exotic" gay pornography. I see these videos as constitutive articulations of a complex relationship not only between race and sexuality but also between the United States and South Africa, and as telling indices of particular cultural conjunctures at this historical moment in the United States and in South Africa as South Africa itself encapsulates the collision and collapse of First and Third Worlds. The videos, then, are emblematic of disparate hierarchies and sequences in the attainment of different kinds of civil rights, and of the multilayered imbrications of queer discourses with other structures of power and formations of identity, particularly as the videos trace the racialized construction of white gay male identities. This construction is a product of its particular South African and US manufacturers as well as the demands of its target US consumers, inasmuch as manufacturer and consumer continually construct and reconstruct each other and their product.

Theorists of film and video pornography have noted the genre's drive for realness: as Linda Williams puts it, "The genre of pornography . . . works hard to convince us of its realism."[6] In viewers' demands for proof that the sexual activity and sexual satisfaction depicted is actual, porn films and videos embody a particular mix of documentary, narrative, and sexual set pieces. This realness variously serves to authenticate viewers' experiences, to give "real" meaning to viewers' orgasms, to titillate viewers with the knowledge that the actors are not acting but are really having sex and really enjoying it (hence the complaint against slicker porn that the actors merely seem to be going through the motions), and to address real life sexual problems, questions, invisibilities, and fantasies. I will be arguing that *The Men of South Africa* tapes inflect this porn convention by bringing it to bear on a parallel tradition of anthropological documentation: pornographic realness (as well as some specific conventions of gay porn) is here appropriated in the service of national and racial logics at the same time that these logics are sexualized.

The Men of South Africa begins with panoramic shots of Hillbrow, Johannesburg. These shots establish both the video's documentary authenticity (the shaky hand held camera and the street noises on the soundtrack seem to confirm it is in fact on location) and its exotic otherness. Authenticity and otherness here mark the intersection of panoplies of problematic and elusive epistemological and political terrains. The opening sequence (and similar ones interspersed between the interior scenes of masturbating men) cannot guarantee that the sex sequences themselves are filmed in South Africa. For all we know, those might have been taped in the United States and then spliced onto the establishing shots of South Africa. The video thus continually attempts to prove its authenticity with real people, real sex, real South Africa, documentary realness. Extended takes and the unusually few number of cuts in the ejaculation scenes assure viewers that they are watching real people coming in real time. The apparently synchronous sound, unusual in a genre where sound is usually postdubbed and where music is often the most consistent feature of the soundtrack, gives viewers privy only to a variety of groaning, gasping, and squelching noises, as well as the performers' few spoken lines, the movements of the videographer, and the traffic and other surrounding sounds.[7] The moderate amount of ejaculate in the money shots (indeed, in the sequel video one of the performers doesn't ejaculate at all, and another does so only after much effort and an off-screen voice generously announces to "give it a couple of minutes"[8] when the performer becomes anxious about his inability to produce an erection) acts as a corrective to the manipulated images of unbelievably extended orgasms common in commercial pornography.[9] In addition, all the performers speak with a variety of convincing South African accents, and several explicitly locate themselves in South Africa ("Hi, I'm John, I'm 27, and I live in Johannesburg. I'll show you what I do in my spare time,"[10] etc.). Each of these characteristics of the video has the effect of making it appear less contrived and thus less like most US gay porn videos; it seems more a "slice of life" to which the viewer is privy than a fictional narrative. These codes of realism also underlie the contradictory way in which the otherness of these men of South Africa is figured. On the one hand, the performers have foreign accents and all except one is uncircumcised (a trait emphasized in the sequel video by close-up shots of some of the performers' foreskins): these are marks of exotic otherness for most middle-class white gay men and some African-American gay men in the United States. On the other hand, the city within which the performances take place is, to some extent, recognizably Western and all the performers are white in terms of South African law at the time and contemporary common popular understandings of whiteness in the United States and South Africa. One even has bleached hair, a costuming effect that has the paradoxical result of inscribing and heightening his whiteness but also ironically emphasizing his otherness—he has to make himself blond. The clearly visible dark roots point to a phantasmatic schizophrenia that I will return to throughout this discussion.

The sequel video to *The Men of South Africa* is advertised in the distributor's catalog with the blurb, "Seven handsome guys with lots of meat in 'original' condition show us the advantages of having a loose and ample foreskin. Interspersed with panoramic images of vast plains, elephants, zebras, etc. to bring you home."[11] The primitivist discourse is more explicit in this blurb, and in case the video's opening cityscapes don't completely satisfy viewer demands for the vaunted wild Africa, later in the video the promised plains, elephants, and zebras are delivered as well. But these images of the wild obviously come from a different locale than the human performers, and human and animal scenes are poorly edited together (it's like watching an old *Tarzan* movie: fake background scenery, naked men, and neo-colonial fantasies). When the two spheres meet, the porn performers traipse around in a bushveld that is clearly closer to the city than the jungle: cars roar past on a nearby road and the scrub is not dense or lush or

Whiteness as Gayness: The Men of South Africa | 23

particularly menacing; in fact, someone might have picnicked there recently. These disjunctive unrealities enable the viewer to have the fantasy both ways: the city and the wild, the city as wild, the wilderness tamed. On the one hand, these shots of the city and the deforested countryside undermine Western stereotypes of wild Africa. On the other hand, given the increasing familiarity of US gay porn viewers with large Third World cities (Rio de Janeiro, for instance[12]), the city in *The Men of South Africa* is still Other enough to make even its urbanity exotic.

Jarring juxtapositions pattern both videos. Almost every sex scene is imbued with the reminder of proximate danger: one performer jerks off on the patio of a high rise building, another in a suburban garden just a low wooden fence away from passers by and the car traffic that is ever present on its soundtrack. In the middle of the latter scene, an overhead shot revealing the suburb just beyond the fence reminds viewers of the proximate potential of discovery and punishment for this illicit public display. The fear or promise of discovery and the titillation of the dangerous and the illegitimate are familiar motifs in all Western pornography, and especially in gay pornography which nearly always contains the eroticizing trace of illegal public sex and the proscription of homosexuality itself. Here, however, this convention also ambiguously intricates gay sex with a mythology of colonialist historiographies.

The most revealing moment in *Men of South Africa II* breaks the pattern of the video by interpolating images of what most South Africans and US Americans would think of as black people with the wild animals as exoticizing frame for the white sex performers. The video encloses the black crowd within the white narrative: we see a young white man masturbating in a bedroom; then, suddenly, we are treated to a series of exterior shots of elephants and ostriches; these are followed by a lengthier scene in which a naked white man masturbates outdoors; we then move to the (old) South African flag, the (apartheid) State President's office (apparently as much to be celebrated as the wild animals and the roaming black people), the crowd of black people walking, and a few springbok and zebra. Finally we return to a masturbating white man. Black South Africans here are treated as props, on the same level as the animals and the landscape (an incorporation confirmed by the "etc." in the catalog blurb about "vast plains, elephants, zebras, etc."), and accorded no individuality, agency, subjectivity, or humanity. Black people serve to enrich the locale with extra Otherness and at the same time by counterpoint to emphasize the normalcy of the "exotically" white characters. The black people in *Men of South Africa II* clearly are scenery, not potential voters (as the conventions of gay porn seldom position anyone as a potential voter), viewers, sex partners, or sexual subjects.[13] As in the first video, all the characters in *Men of South Africa II* seem to be white (a fact that is perhaps anxiously dramatized by the bleached blond I mentioned earlier), but the video's ambiguous discernment of these white characters' relationship to First and Third Worlds, to other South Africans, and to their US viewers, marks a cynical process of neo-colonial appropriation: inasmuch as viewers are supposed to desire the exotic but only insofar as it is containable, white people, here, are much better black people than black people could be themselves. Dominant subjects are more willing and able to know and play out their own fantasies of the Other than the Other is; in so doing they can also hope to annihilate the presence of the Other altogether by incorporating this phantasmatic Other into their own performances. This point has been succinctly enacted in the realm of gender relations in cultural texts like David Henry Hwang's play M. Butterfly (the character of Song), or the cult film hit The Crying Game (Dill, the character played by Jaye Davidson).

IV

The representation of race (and the lack of racial representativeness) in the South African videos has several consequences impacting the racialized construction of both South African and gay identities, and the cultures and organizations for whose benefit these constructions are deployed. In constructing South African subjecthood as all white, the videos are complicit with similar delusory and destructive characterizations of the country by the pre-Mandela South African government, and the institutions and industries it created and nurtured in the heyday of apartheid. Under apartheid South Africans who were designated black by the government were both psychically and literally bracketed out of the white South African imaginary of full South African nationality and citizenship: this psychological work revolved around the fiction that South Africa was a European nation, and a democratic country (all South Africans designated white enjoyed the franchise); the material embodiment of this fantasy encompassed government legislation that created homelands for black South Africans in order to justify denying them citizenship and thus civil rights in South Africa proper. The idyllic all white beach scenes in the typical South African tourist postcard of the 1980s (not that today's postcards are much different) gave no indication that 85.2% of the population of this country was black, and that this black majority was forcibly excluded from the postcard beach (only that much has changed today). Official South African tourist propaganda was in the same vein: white South Africans assumed (usually correctly) that white visitors from other countries would want to visit an all white pseudo-European enclave in darkest Africa; while many white South Africans actually believed that they lived in an all white country (this much has changed today), most overseas white people suspected better. In fact, the attraction of South Africa as a white tourist destination was precisely the promise of danger lurking just outside the comfort zone—fantasies of animal sexuality to spice up the familiar reality of all white action; wild animals, and black people safely cordoned off from luxurious tourist hotels (no wonder tourism dropped off after the publicity generated by the Soweto uprising of 1985!). The videos are especially significant because they attempt to conjure up this picture of South Africa in the early 1990s, with Nelson Mandela released from prison and the African National Congress and South African Communist Party unbanned, with white South Africans being forced to confront the reality of their multiracial nation as never before.

The videos' anachronistically myopic vision of South Africa can be explained partly by the persistence of white South African denial, diminution, and degradation of the black majority in South Africa. Part of the explanation is also a gay porn convention: just as the gay porn convention that excludes all women and usually all representations of femininity from the videos' world circumscribes citizenship as a male prerogative in this world, so the very narrow racial range of characters depicted in the South African videos is in keeping with a porn tradition in which individual products cater to highly specialized and exclusive tastes in terms of race, age, size, and so on. In these videos, then, we see marks of gay culture interdependently appropriating and appropriated by other regimes of identity and domination, and, I would argue, evidence that sexual fantasies in general are integral to narratives of race, and vice versa. But I also think that we need specifically to consider the relation of the videos to the United States in order to fully explain the particular construction of South Africa that they evoke. The fantasized South Africa in these videos (and in other popular homoerotic videos set in South Africa like *Trance*, *Kalahari*, and *Sirocco*) is created for US consumers, and is thus as much a commentary on those consumers as a reflection of the realities and fantasies of a fractured South Africa lurching toward change.

V

On the one hand, the videos inscribe themselves into a long white South African legacy of erasing the black South African majority from citizenry status. Yet, on the other hand, they can also be seen as a fantasy of colonial nostalgia for their US viewers (who might identify along national lines as well as or against racial identifications: thus this assertion could apply to US viewers of color as well as to white viewers). It's unclear to me exactly what role South Africans and US Americans played in the production of the videos, but the tapes were clearly made for US (and perhaps other) overseas audiences. First, they would have been banned in the puritanical apartheid South Africa. Second, the performers' articulation of their South African location is for the benefit of foreign viewers. Third, the performers' use of United States expressions (e.g., "hi") marks an attempt to communicate—that is, establish familiarity and common ground—with an imagined US viewer. Fourth, the exoticizing use of landscape is plainly for the benefit of US Americans who are often embarrassingly ignorant about other countries and ensconced in ethnocentric stereotypes. Fifth, the videos, as I have already indicated, are marketed out of San Francisco (the only place I've found them). Sixth, and last, the first video ends with two of the performers looking directly into the camera and urging viewers to visit South Africa. The videos invite white US Americans to project their own racism onto a utopic bygone South Africa under classical apartheid.

The trope of travel and the travelogue as a literary and cinematic genre (together with its closely related cohort, the adventure film and novel) have for the West been the popular correlatives of the imperialist disciplines of anthropology and ethnography. In her *Imperial Eyes*, Mary Louise Pratt has written of the ways in which travel writing produced "the rest of the world" for European readers. Analogously, in these videos South Africa is constructed for the white United States: onto them these viewers are able to project their nostalgia for a past of pure apartheid in South Africa and the United States. They don't want to let it go. South Africa had always been and continues to be a convenient demon for liberal white people in other countries to point to in order to avoid confronting racism in their own backyards. (I say this not to deny the appalling magnitude of apartheid in South Africa, but in order to stress the ways in which South Africa became a convenience for the rest of the racist West.[14]) While South Africa changes, constructions of it can preserve its sameness to its old self, and to the United States. This sameness gives the lie to international liberal concern about apartheid. While the West focused obsessively on apartheid in the 1970s and 1980s, it often reproduced the spatial imaginary of apartheid by keeping white South Africa at the center of its cultural attention. Trendy big budget international films focused on white South African opponents of apartheid, and white South Africans were awarded (and continue to be awarded) Nobel literature prizes, and otherwise celebrated world wide. Even today, liberal US Americans can easily identify Alan Paton, Athol Fugard, Nadine Gordimer, J. M. Coetzee, and other white South African writers who have been rewarded for their opposition to apartheid, but are almost always hard pressed to name even one black South African writer, despite the fact that people like Paton and Fugard have been vigorously criticized by black South Africans for their liberal appropriations of the anti-apartheid struggle.[15]

In his 1991 article "A Grand Tour: South Africa and American Tourists Between the Wars," James B. Wolf describes the South African travel industry in the early decades of the twentieth century marking a nexus of collaboration between transcontinental tourism and ideologies of white separatism and white supremacy:

> The problem was getting the tourists to come. In South Africa, government officials had a product to sell, the country's unique beauty and its unusually diverse, and alien to western eyes, population. While in the west, and in the United States particularly, a burgeoning wealthy middle class was developing a desire to see new places, to observe different cultures, and to participate in overseas adventure. The seller of tourism and the consumer, the tourist, coming together constituted a part of the imperial process, of linking white South Africa to white Americans, often by specifically setting them apart from the black South African population.[16]

Wolf relates how impressed E. W. Howe, a Kansas businessman, was with his 1910 trip to South Africa:

From the window of the train to Victoria Falls he saw a land in which he could be content, if, "God forbid," he were ever dissatisfied with the United States. Furthermore, the canny Mr. Howe noted that there was a plentiful source of cheap labor. South Africa, he concluded, was a most appealing place for Americans; and Howe found a surprising number of his countrymen already living and working there. In his travel journal Howe left no doubt that Americans felt right at home in South Africa and that South Africans like Americans and America.[17]

Of course, it is the *unstated*, but crucial, qualifier "white" before both US Americans and South Africans that makes possible this camaraderie and this entrepreneurial cooperation, as it was the peculiar conjunction of First and Third Worlds in South Africa that made the country especially amenable and potentially profitable as a tourist destination for white US Americans: "Perhaps the most seductive lure of westerners to South Africa was the appeal of a non-western society in easy proximity to modern conveniences."[18] A 1929 advertisement on the back of *Nomad*, a popular US travel magazine rhapsodized, "In South Africa you find picturesque, quaint, colorful, native Kraal life side by side with modern civilization."[19] The exoticizing racist discourse is perhaps more blatant here, but we see its equivalent sixty odd years later in the *Men of South Africa* videos, with a gay inflection. Hence I read the phrase "to bring you home" in the catalog blurb for the sequel video, "Seven handsome guys with lots of meat in 'original' condition show us the advantages of having a loose and ample foreskin. Interspersed with panoramic images of vast plains, elephants, zebras, etc. to bring you home," not only in terms of its porn meaning, and not only as a signifier of the ways in which the video domesticates the exotic for the comfort of its viewers, but also as indicative of the larger at-homeness of US consumers of the video with its racist landscape, their familiarity and complicity with its intrication of gayness with racist whiteness. The sequence in the sequel video featuring black South Africans reminds viewers who and where they are (or should be).

VI

Now my account of the videos' creation of South Africa for white US viewers needs further qualification, for it is specifically gay South Africa that is presented for the consumption of gay US viewers[20] in the videos. The videos present as whitewashed a face of gay South Africa, and I would suggest, of gayness in general, as they do of South Africa in general. At the same time that South Africanness is whitewashed in the videos, then, gayness is racialized as white. (The men of South Africa are the *white* men of South Africa, and the white men of South Africa are the *gay* white men of South Africa.) This depiction of an all white gay South Africa in stark contrast to the history of queer organizing in South Africa adds force to the argument that the South Africa of the videos is based on their viewers' (and perhaps producers') fantasy of South Africa, which runs directly counter to the evidence of the explicit multiculturalism of South Africa's public lesbian and gay communities, and of their involvement in apartheid and anti-apartheid politics, which multiplied in the 1990s: in Johannesburg's 1993 lesbian and gay pride parade one very visible male marcher brandished a placard reading "Viva! Democratic Erections," a punning reference to the imminent end of formal apartheid;[21] the multiracial South African contingent in the Stonewall anniversary march in New York City in 1994 carried banners reading "Gays and Lesbians for the New South Africa" and "Viva Gay Rights in the New South Africa";[22] the August 1994 issue of the South African lesbian and gay magazine *Outright* sported a full color cover picture of two otherwise naked embracing men—one black and one white—draped in the new South African flag.[23] Recent gay South Africans' self-representations are diametrically opposed to the trajectory of the videos, not only in terms of racial diversity but also of political affiliation.

Given the usual hostility of right-wing regimes to lesbians and gay men, surely the greatest irony of the videos' interpellation into and of the apartheid state lies in their irretrievable gayness: besides the fact that the videos are marked and marketed as gay pornography, almost all the characters in them are coded as gay,[24] a most unusual coding in gay porn videos until very recently. But this congruency represents more than just another instance of gay white male racism, or evidence that an all white cast can be as racist a porn convention as the one that exoticizes people of color as super sexual objects of the white gaze or perfect sex partners for the white subject. The specific permutations of the race/sexuality conjunction are embodied in the final scene from the first *Men of South Africa* video, where the video's two blondest performers urge the viewer, "Come to our country, there are lots of us around, come and see us, we never run out of time."[25] They stand naked looking directly into the camera and repeat variations of the invitation to South Africa several times. The scene—and the video—ends with the two performers embracing. Significantly, when the one performer euphemistically refers to "our country," the other assertively interjects "South Africa," as if to emphasize the specificity of their nationalistic appeal, as if to counteract the white South African shame that characterized the export of South African heterosexuality in the waning days of apartheid—even Jamie Uys's blockbuster film *The Gods Must Be Crazy* was screened in the 1980s in the United States as an African or Namibian film, presumably to avoid producers and distributors the embarrassment and financial loss concomitant upon promoting a white South African film in the face of boycotts and sanctions against South Africa.

This final scene of the video also points to the complex racial and national potentialities for gay porn conventions ("we never tire," "we're waiting for you," "this is your utopia") and particularly for the conventions of amateur or "real-life" porn that has been regaining popularity since the 1990s. The South African tapes are in some ways a throwback to what Linda Williams terms the primitive heterosexual stag film, the precursor to the feature length porn film or video, in their disjointed editing and overt addresses to viewers;[26] this latter tactic is also a characteristic of solo porn.[27] In the South African videos, the primitivism is no doubt partly inevitable, given the technical and financial resources of their creators, and the constraints of illegally taping the pieces in South Africa. But it also works as an added source of arousal for viewers jaded by the slicker productions that characterize commercial porn videos in the United States today. However, there is another type of primitivism at work here. The "we never run out of time" line plays into anthropological reductions of the Other to eternal savagery as analyzed by Johannes Fabian, Chandra Mohanty, and Edward Said.[28] The embrace, unusual in gay porn "solo" videos (that is, videos that otherwise depict only solo masturbation scenes), underscores the illusion that this is a utopic homoerotic space—the earlier hints of danger merely enrich this homoerotic experience. A gay agenda, then, becomes paradoxically congruent with the policies of the pre-1994 South African government that not only enforced apartheid, but that also prohibited public displays of homosexuality, criminalized private consensual homosexual sodomy, and banned pornography. Naturally, no mention is made of witch hunts against gay men or bannings of gay publications taking place in South Africa at the time that the videos were made.[29] The coding of almost all the performers in the video as gay re-enforces the sense of a safe haven for white gay US Americans in South Africa.

This delusory construction of gay South Africa is indicative of ways in which benign narratives of gayness can collude with homophobic repression and even produce increased danger for queers by occluding the evidence of antigay state persecution. This construction also emphasizes the extent to which my own narrative is not so much about real gayness or whiteness as it is about the discourses (including discourses of whiteness and gayness) that produce whiteness and gayness, which is not to say that the textual and the material are easily separable: identity itself is an effect of discourse, and narrative often relates a particular reality or gets taken up by the objects it seeks to narrativize. Further, this narrow construction of gay South Africa is absolutely synchronous with the apartheid South African government's constructions of an all white South Africa and tourist propaganda in the 1980s that denied the realities of apartheid and of racial conflict in South Africa. Given the desperate importance that the apartheid South African government attached to the task of attracting white tourists to the country in the face of sanctions and boycotts and when apartheid was being most strenuously challenged, the scene at the end of *The Men of South Africa* can almost be seen as a commercial commissioned by the apartheid government itself.[30] The opening vistas of the tape, the intermittent shots of the skyline at night, and the lengthy shots of animals in the sequel video nicely underpin the trite characterization of South Africa as "a world in one country" by tourist outreach programs established by the apartheid government.

Such collaboration is not as unlikely as it might sound. While the apartheid South African government does have a history of homophobic legislation and persecution, the history of apartheid in South Africa also fundamentally contests received liberal wisdom in the United States that homosexuality is the final taboo in the hierarchy of persecuted identities and that homophobia should be expected to override racism among bigoted US Americans. In the early 1980s, candidates running for office for the ruling South African National Party had no compunction in appealing specifically to racist white gay voters—vote for us, we'll support gay rights and keep South Africa white.[31] Furthermore, the invitation to visit South Africa at the conclusion to *The Men of South Africa* even suggests that South Africa and the United States might be able to continue their collaborations in white supremacism by tapping into a lucrative gay male US tourist market, one that is already familiar with a host of upscale gay cruises and tours (some specifically to Third World countries to pursue racist sexual fetishes), and that will accept the racist recreation of a disappearing South Africa under the aegis of the erotic conventions of US middle-class white gay male culture.[32] This kind of collusion might also partly explain the current modish popularity of "white" queer theory. In each case, gayness—that is always and only white—sustains whiteness and white supremacy.

VII

We can draw many conclusions about gay representation in general from these videos. But my point is not merely the obvious one that the videos reproduce racist and imperialist ideologies (a truism of most US porn videos); rather, the conclusion that I want to focus on involves a process of substitution. In their work on literary and cinematic representations of race and sexuality Christopher Lane has explained how racial Others can serve as deflected or displaced representations of white gay male sensibilities/relationships/desires and Richard Dyer has traced racial whiteness's enunciation in terms of order and rationality, and, specifically, its colonization of normative (patriarchal) heterosexuality.[33] In the *Men of South Africa* videos, however, substitution has the opposite trajectory from what we might expect, one that is perhaps not as compatible with political formulations of gay sexuality as only oppressed or as automatically subversive of hegemonic institutions. In Lane's argument there is a correlation between gayness and coloredness, suggesting an undisciplined or transgressive or taboo quality to both, and for Dyer heterosexuality and whiteness describe and circumscribe each other, again situating homosexuality in the realm of nonwhiteness or marginality. However, in the South African videos gay maleness comes to stand for white maleness, and vice versa.[34] This congruency and conflation is partly due to the difficulty, on the part of white people, of specifying the content of whiteness per se (thus whiteness is delineated in terms of something else—gayness—or against something else—blackness), but surely is also a response to the increasing social unacceptability of a discourse of

Whiteness as Gayness: The Men of South Africa | 31

white separatism and a concomitant fashionable legitimacy in depicting gay identity, which is putatively white, and all male. Gay is the code for white.

This coding is more than an instance of a metonymic fetishization that caters to the specialized tastes of a particular subculture, because it not only demonstrates the centrality of gayness to other forms of identification and to Western culture in general,[35] but also the ways in which historically dominant configurations of power and privileged individuals and institutions can re-invent themselves as they continually constitute, incorporate, and transform new social subjects and cultural formations in these dominant configurations'/individuals'/institutions' resilience and resistance to real change or loss of power. Dyer points out that whiteness needs to demonstrate its virtues to justify continued domination.[36] We can say that in the videos whiteness seeks to justify itself via gayness. One of the few ways to construct a white South Africa without immediately provoking antiracist outrage is to use the codes of gay maleness: a gay discourse (both in the United States and in South Africa) can appear to be progressive while in fact entrenching racist domination and recruiting new converts to this racist agenda.

There are several resonant implications of this substitution of gayness for whiteness. First, it suggests one possible understanding of the absence of—indeed, the impossibility of—an official discourse of colored queerness in the United States. Together with the trendy litany of minoritized identities that divides people into discrete categories of race, gender, and sexuality, and that thus cannot conceptualize queers of color, or white female queers, this conflation of gayness with whiteness erases the existence of queers of color in the United States, and in South Africa, where an imperialist US gay teleology is already imposing its own models of identity, queerness, and queer progress onto the South African scene. In this context, South Africa is subject to the coercive dictates of US economic, cultural, intellectual, and military imperialism (as are most countries of the world); this relationship complicates the subject positions of white South Africans vis-à-vis the United States. Such a complexity is evident in the *Men of South Africa* videos. I have already described how the videos' paradoxical representational strategies both exoticize and familiarize their white gay South African subjects/objects. All except one of the men are uncircumcised, a trait viewers will associate with other exoticizing videos that use foreskins to signal barbarity. The farewell invitation to visit South Africa, with the promise of insatiability and plentiful availability, is reminiscent of what the natives are supposed to say (and what white women say in misogynistic heterosexual pornography) rather than what the white masters say of themselves. The videos also complicate the relationship of their characters to white dominance by representing them in positions conventionally thought of as subordinate to viewers in terms of class, age, and passive/active and top/bottom sexual roles. Further, hardly any of the men are aggressively masculine, an absence that, by convention, aligns them with racist gay stereotypes of gay Asian men and Latinos. That the second video ends with an exhortation to viewers to look for *Wavelength*'s Asian and Latin products indicates a presumed continuity between these "Asian and Latin products" and the white men of South Africa. An array of international dynamics are as significant and independent a determinant of the power relation in any representation of desire as race is.[37]

The tapes' ambivalent identificatory agendas are embodied formally in the paradoxes of their conventional quest for pornographic realness. The contradictory nature of the first video's attempts to authenticate itself most clearly surfaces in the way in which the performers keep "botching" their lines in their farewell invitation to viewers to visit South Africa. Each time the line is flubbed it is re-taped, but the flubbed versions are not edited out. The fact that the performers stumble over their lines and that the botched scene is (most "unprofessionally") left in the final copy only adds to the tapes' efforts to authenticate themselves and to the sense that the performers in it are not performers at all. When called upon to perform (to say their lines), their failure emphasizes the supposed spontaneity and realness of their earlier (unscripted) masturbation scenes, a distinction that is emphasized when they discuss the flubbed line with each other in Afrikaans, apparently their first language, and a language most of the videos' viewers will not understand. But the irruption of Afrikaans here also points to the inauthenticity of the earlier scenes when the performers address the camera in English, and thus the tapes' complicated and contradictory relationship to their anthropological objects and to the genre in which they attempt to inscribe these objects.

In "Looking for My Penis: The Eroticized Asian in Gay Video Porn," Richard Fung revises Thomas Waugh's elaboration of the fluidity of the position of the gay male spectator of gay porn videos to argue that this fluidity exists only when all the parties in question (spectators and performers) are white. While several writers on gay porn have asserted that, unlike the implied viewer of heterosexual male porn, the gay porn viewer might identify both with the desiring gaze and with the object of desire, as well as with the scene of desire in general (this argument has been followed by Earl Jackson Jr. in his discussion of the simultaneous processes of desire and identification that structure the spectator's relation to gay male porn), Fung notes that representations of Asians in gay porn videos in the United States count on singular viewer identification with the white "tops" in the sexual encounters.[38] However, the all white "Men of South Africa" suggest that porn theory needs to be honed even more. In the light of the new spate of international gay porn, we can further qualify Fung's caveat by limiting Waugh's and Jackson's celebrations of gay porn's disruptions of the heteropatriarchal gaze to all white tapes depicting United States characters only (and no doubt other limitations can also be argued, for instance, around the possibilities of class cross-identifications): *The Men of South Africa* tapes demonstrate how identification can be restricted when the iconography of internationalism, the apparatuses of production and distribution of such internationalism, and the tropes of travel and tourism on which such productions are premised, presume to override more open-ended possibilities for identification and consumption.

The second point I want to make about the process of displacement in the tapes revolves around the irony that the white supremacist substitution of whiteness for gayness colludes with the arguments of some black nationalist organizations and individuals, both in the United States and in South Africa, that homosexuality is foreign to black people, and that black queers have been contaminated and co-opted by imperialist white cultures.[39] Contrarily, this unholy alliance between homophobic black nationalism and homophilic white supremacy could provide one of the best counter-attacks against this black nationalist position, showing how it undergirds homosocial white domination.

Finally, this interdependency of whiteness and gayness undercuts primitivist stereotypes of the pre-colonial Third World as blissfully nonhomophobic that are now popular among many liberal gay scholars in the West.

By arguing that gayness here enables racism, I am also insisting that we have to once and for all abandon not only the notion that gayness can be apolitical, but also the idealistic and complacent hope that gayness inevitably represents some kind of oppositional political position. The collusion of gayness with racist whiteness alerts us to yet another problem with identity politics to add to those already elaborated by feminist, race, and queer theorists wary of the essentialist and homogenizing potentialities in the identity politics traditions in the United States. My skepticism of the assumption of the necessarily revolutionary potential of gayness returns me to the meanings of queer I teased out in the first chapter of this book by suggesting that political affiliation should be as essential a component of queer identity and queer theory as is sexual orientation. What would this kind of queer delineation look like in the arena, of, say, white gay male pornography? First, it would disassociate whiteness from gayness by constructing and depicting gay people of color and envisioning a subject position for viewers of color. Second, it would sexualize politics and repoliticize desire. Since desire and romance in the West are popularly construed by the parameters of bourgeois individualism in cultural and social realms, and the right to privacy in legal and political spheres, the strategic eruption of desire in the public domain would be a truly queer revolution of dominant political epistemologies. This work has already begun among black gay writers, film and video makers like Darieck Scott and the late Marlon Riggs in the United States, and Isaac Julien in the United Kingdom, and feminist theorists and artists responding to campaigns against pornography. But popular white gay male cultural formations in the United States have yet to articulate the political affiliations embedded in, or occluded from, their representations of desire. Pornography is notoriously reluctant to openly engage politics and gay porn is not exceptional: only recently has a small number of gay porn videos dared to present explicitly gay characters, and only a handful of these videos depict a gay pride parade or antihomophobia demonstration. Antiracist politics are even harder to find. Gay pornography that exoticizes people of color is common, but nothing has been done to harness the potential of gay white desire in the service of contesting racism. While white gay politicians adopt the sanitized language of multiculturalism, white gay pornographers continue to decontextualize sex. As part of the latest fad in travel, gay US tourists can embark on expensive gay tours to South Africa, where travel agents arrange for them to meet with desexualized local gay black activists or enjoy oblivious all white sex. Bringing politics and desire together without either refetishizing black sexuality or authorizing white politicality would entail explicitly eroticizing politics and restructuring the conventions of desire. This would be not only to recognize the racial inscriptions of sexuality but also to make the contestation of racism that much more accessible by suturing it to the pornographic imagination.

A political queerness is an especially urgent imperative now, given the increasing visibility of right-wing gays in the United States in recent years.[40] I will explore one possible trajectory of such a politicized queerness in further detail in Chapter 4. In Chapter 3 I examine the sites of gay identity strategically evacuated in the *Men of South Africa* videos and in the possibilities of subjectivity implied by those sites: representations of queers of color, interracial gay desire, and desire among queer men of color. In the preceding pages I have referred to an exoticizing tradition in pornographic gay representations of men of color; in the following chapter we see how this tradition also interacts with queer representations by artists of color, and that the mere representation of colored queerness cannot unproblematically forestall the equation of gayness with whiteness.

VIII

In this chapter I have identified a centrifugal instance of the interdependent interworkings of whiteness and gayness, not to single out white gay men and white gay male cultural productions as preeminently responsible for or illustrative of the machineries of racism, but rather as a beginning strategy to disrupt both undialectical theorizations of race and sexuality, and uncritical celebrations of a reified gay identity that are gaining popularity in glossy lifestyle magazines and yuppie gay publications as debates around lesbian and gay civil rights enter mainstream discourses in the United States. Equally important work remains to be done around the intrication of the multitude of heterosexual and other sexual cultures and institutions with racial markings and racialized fantasies, and the inextricable relationship of this intrication to formations of class and gender, and to gay desires, knowledge, and powers. All of this, too, should be part of the project of queer theory.[41]

Chapter 3

Representing Race in the Discourse of Desire

I

In Chapter 2 I argued that, in the arenas of international cultural consumption and public desire, racist and imperialist epistemological economies can develop and be developed from a gay aesthetic. Here I want to pursue some of the questions and challenges with which I concluded the previous chapter by examining the production and problematization of these racialized transactions of desire and identity in the cultural and intellectual discourses (i.e., popular culture, literary representations, academic and political debate) that have become the intermittently accurate political transcription and instigating conscience of the personal relationships that mark these nodes of gayness. The translation between the personal and the public, as this demarcation itself is constitutive of a range of repressive and dislocative categorizations, documents and monitors the ways in which (in bourgeois societies particularly) the signs, the unfolding, and the effects of this translation are occluded precisely to deny the overwhelming force of nationalized constructions of subjectivity and the interconnectedness of public institutions and local desire. This is a denial that in turn hopes to preserve the delusion of democratic individuality in political life. In this context, tracking the "personal" reinserts it into a continuum of politicized cultural constructions of society, the self, and the Other.

I suggested in Chapter 2 that all-white representations of gayness are problematic to the extent that they can define whiteness in terms of gayness and erase the subjectivities of queers of color. This leaves, then, the possibilities of representations of gay people of color only, of omniracial depictions of gayness, and of the vexed and over determined field of interracial desire, a metonymic site of the discursive conjunction of and struggle between the erotic and the political, as it has come to be reduced to desire between white people and people of color. Other reductions have also ensued and I will discuss these shortly.[1]

II

In the United States, the apocryphally higher frequency of gay and lesbian relationships between people of color and white people compared to heterosexual relationships between white people and people of color is colloquially attributed to the relative ease of breaking a second taboo (miscegenation) once one taboo has already been broken (homosexuality), but this explanation neither accounts for the nature of the causality of progression between the two types of transgression nor for the particular permutations of desire that figure race in a specifically queer context.

B. Ruby Rich has argued that in same-sex desire, "[r]ace occupies the place vacated by gender"[2] in order to sustain an erotics of difference in desire, but, as I will suggest, her unproblematized assumptions about the coherence of gender and the binary division of gender (as Kate Bornstein puts it, "The opposite sex is neither"[3]), are disrupted by the varied interventions of heterogeneously gendered discourses into representations of interracial desire. This is a disruption that must qualify Rich's substitution of race for gender, and suggests that the particularity of lesbian and gay intrications with race may not be of the direct explanatory order (i.e., if race replaces gender, queers have a different and potentially exemplary relation to race, and something new to tell us about the constitution of difference itself) that Rich implies (without actually specifying what the nature of this explanation is).[4] This is not to say that queer race is no different from other racial formations, but rather that race cannot stand on its own in the house of difference, whether as symptomatic syntagma or diagnostic catachresis.

Rich and Jackie Goldsby have pointed out that the race-desire nexus has not been overtly sexualized by lesbians to the extent that it has among gay men. Thus gay male representations of racialized desire, and representations of racialized gay male desire, are uniquely situated to read queer race at the same time that they often figure what is an undercurrent in other economies of race and sex, too. The highly charged but often unexplicated sexual logic around the symbols and practices of interracial gay male desire, together with the relative undertheorization of race among gay men (and gay white men, in particular) compared to lesbians,[5] make representations of interracial gay male relationships rich texts for the interpretation and specification of the discursive interstices of race, gender, and sexuality in general. These texts might suggest what the culturally constructed possibilities are for negotiating the politics of race in a gay relationship between a man of color and a white man, or, contrarily, the feasibility of a black gay nationalist discourse (or any other nationalist discourse of color) as a counter to the delineation of gayness as whiteness in narratives like *The Men of South Africa*.

In the remainder of this chapter I chart a variety of orders of representation of relationships between white men and men of color: from the uncritical racist fetishizations of popular pornography, to the more self-conscious fetishizations of high art; from the humanistic belief in individual exceptionality that recognizes racism but finds comfort in the conviction that a particular relationship or individual is free from racist contamination, to the related loyalty to an ideal of romantic love as transcending all socialization and so the conviction that race is not a determining factor in these relationships; from the positioning of these relationships as contestations of racism, to the insistence that they are necessarily and specifically racist. I argue that many of these accounts are reductive to the extent that they do not account for the complex imbrications of politics in desire and indicate how they might productively be revised and supplanted.

III

White homoerotic representations of black men in the United States date back at least to antislavery writings at the end of the eighteenth century.[6] Twentieth century literary representations of interracial gay desire range from the high art of James Baldwin to pornographic pulp novels of the 1970s and 1980s. My own analysis focuses on more recent texts, not only because I cannot possibly cover centuries of representation in one chapter, but also because my interest here is theoretical rather than historical. Queer Theory as an academic field only came into existence in the 1990s. I want to cross queer theory with contemporaneous cultural discourses of interracial desire in order to shake up both and to intervene into present-day political debate about race and desire as it is shaped by culture and theory.

A wide panoply of racist strategies is deployed in contemporary representations of white people, people of color, and interracial relationships by individuals, organizations, groups of people, cultural producers, and cultural critics interested in manufacturing, selling, participating in, and critiquing forms of desire and stories of desire that are racially overdetermined. These discourses are often contiguous with other orders and arenas of racist representation, but they also take on particular codes, covers, denials, absences, and justifications when they are explicitly conjoined with desire, whether this desire is inscribed romantically or pornographically. Not surprisingly, the authors of racist representations of people of color are usually white.

While the racism of the gay white man who will not consider a relationship with a person of color (as in the familiar personal ad from a G/W/M seeking same, or, more overtly, the one that says "no blacks") is self-evident to many, there is also a tradition to which I alluded in the previous chapter of racist representations by white men who desire people of color in particular. The most blatantly racist of these representations take the form of ritualized fetishizations of stereotypical people of color in many formulations of desire: personal advertisements, private fantasy and sexual encounters, commercial pornography, etc.

For gay men in the metropolitan United States, these racist articulations are readily available in pornographic magazines and videos where whiteness (or, to be more precise, a limited range of very specific whiteness) is normalized either through an exclusive attention to white men or by the reduction of men of color to fetishized stereotypes (black men always have huge penises, Asian men are either big and mean or passive and small in stature and penis size, etc.).[7] The specific fantasies of "rice queens," "taco queens," "dinge queens," and so on, are catered to and intensified by operations like the San Francisco mail-order video company which oversees the distribution of the *Men of South Africa* videos. *International Wavelength*'s catalogs and products are usually divided into homogenizing national, racial, and even continental categories for the benefit of their exotically inclined customers. To my knowledge, there is no such publicly marketed line of products in the United States catering to "snow queens," "matzo queens," or other race-specific categorizations in which the agent of desire might be a man of color.[8] This silence is probably due to the racist and sexist inscription of the desiring gaze in the conventions of mainstream cinema,[9] pornographic film, and in social interactions at large, as well as the distribution companies' perception that the market for such products would be too small compared to the market for the products aimed at white men to be financially worthwhile.

Another video distributor, *HIS*, markets all white, all black, and interracial tapes (the interracial tapes feature sex between white men and men of color, as well as between differently raced men of color) with promotional recourse to (and no doubt instigated by) racist fetishizations in the case of the all black and interracial tapes (the all white tapes are seldom described with racial markers in so many words). In fact, one of the company's flyers goes so far as to explicitly fetishize people of color in announcing a "sex fetish sale" featuring "blacks, latins, shaved sex, orgies and more for a mere pittance." My point is not that fetishism itself is racist or objectionable generally, but that in the context of racist social structures, and for the specific permutations of all-white desire, the objectification of men of color is racist, especially when whiteness is normalized here by remaining the unmarked category, while white desire for black or "latin" men is paralleled with "orgies" and "shaved sex" in a seemingly infinite shopping list (the "and more" of the blurb) of white sexual tastes and practices. The *TLA* video company likewise renders men of color as objects to be selected for white pleasure by including the categories "dark chocolate" and "luscious Latinos" in its cataloging of tapes by director, star, themes (athletics, uniforms, etc.), and type of sex (leather, bondage, orgies, etc.).

Supposedly progressive political programs and identities are appropriated by these videos in the service of a reactionary politics of desire. The boom in multicultural gay pornography might provide an unexpected caveat about multiculturalism. What better argument against the trendy but toothless invocation of multiculturalism could one find than the *HIS* flyer announcing a "XXX MULTI-CULTURAL SALE!" in rainbow lettering, and "MELTING POT SALE PRICES" further down the page? In yet another *HIS* flyer, we see an example of the ways in which culture can attempt to contain political dissidence, an attempted containment here enacted in the sexualization and trivialization of a specific iconography of blackness that might otherwise be threatening to white people in particular: a hook for a scene captioned "Rump Rasta!" from a video entitled *Black Studs* announces that "Superstar (and super hunk) Ryan Block gives a fuck-crazed black stud with spiked hair a good going over! Rasta, mon!" The Rasta and spiked hair are transmuted from the realm of cultural-political identity into a white sexual fetish, while black antiracist militancy and anger are combined with white fears of black power and white demonizations of black political subjectivity as savage and insane, to become the signs of sexual promiscuity and availability: translated here as fuck-crazed.

Men of color are not offered any point of identification with these videos. One flyer makes clear that the "you" it is addressing can only be white by asking seductively, "Wanna be the middle in an Oreo Sandwich?"[10] Because all potential viewers for these videos are assumed to be and positioned as white, even what might appear to be gestures toward recognizing the subjectivity and agency of men of color and acknowledging a politically reconciliatory role for pornography are finally just more grist for the wheel of white racist fantasy. Thus a tape in which "Large, surly black men with even larger blue-black love pistons share cock, asses, mouths and cum, bringing new harmony to the hood" is here not so much an illustration of community problem solving for black viewers as it is a paternalistic display of noble savagery for white viewers. Similarly, while mention of a "Black stud" and his "White Boytoy" in a blurb for another video might suggest some degree of control for a man of color, the invitation that follows that mention emphasizes the centrality of white fantasy and agency: "Do you fantasize about mean, meaty, huge-cocked black studs cramming their giant black cocks up your ass?" The white man might be the black man's boytoy, but this is still the white man's fantasy. What happens when stereotypical race-roles are reversed and black men are addressed without disclaimer? "The white waiter shows up at your room with champagne and pants around his ankles. Being a big, black stud, what do you do? Fuck him 'til he can't sit down!" While the white man's race is mentioned, his actions or appearance are not described as a product of his race. In fact, he is not described in terms of his race at all, a clear signal that this is for and about those who see themselves as the norm (i.e., white people) and who can thus afford to imagine that they think of themselves in unracialized terms. This aporia in the elaboration of whiteness is characteristic of almost all these pornographic (and other explicit) representations of race as a function of sexuality.

In this market context, even the least offensive gestures acknowledging global racial diversity must be understood only as part of the ever expanding marketplace of white pleasure. The advertisement for *What Guys Do Best*, a video in which "New Kids cum from all walks . . . whites, blacks, Latins . . . but all understand the Universal Language: A Cock in the Ass! Their Second Language: A Cock in the Mouth!" is not so much a celebration of homoerotic multiculturalism as it is a tribute to the linguistic imperialism of English, and the universalizing ethic of white US gayness for whose pleasure this diversity is displayed.

The videos that do not feature white men at all are hence no less beholden to the vagaries of a racist semiotics than those expressly depicting white sexual fulfillment with men of color. The blurbs for the all black videos commonly emphasize the videos' exclusion or marginalization of white characters: "Not a white boy in the bunch," "There's a token white boy on the team," etc. But given the framing of the videos' viewers as white, this exclusion can only with great effort be taken as a sign of black separatism or even of independent black desire. Ultimately, the videos featuring sex between white men and black men and the all black videos achieve the same effect, albeit through different arguments. Each scenario presents a different type of fantasy for its putative white viewer/consumer: the all black tapes offer the voyeuristic white viewer an objectified touchstone of unspoiled primitive lust, or an indulgent spectacle of his desire (his disdain for white men—his self-hatred—is, of course, part of the scene of racist exoticization), while the tapes depicting only men of color in interracial sexual activity heighten the array of exotic performances, and those using scenes between white men and men of color give white viewers an explicit point of identification as they imagine participating in their own interracial sexual encounters.[11]

The texts I have discussed in the preceding pages, though they may seem unusually blatant or extreme in their racism, are not only typical of the products and discourses of the companies who create and market them, but also of many other similar companies and publications offering products featuring men of color, and even of companies and publications for which such videos form only a small percentage of overall product stock. For instance, the *Adam Gay Video Directory*, which is a far more mainstream gay publication in the United States and elsewhere compared to the flyers and brochures from HIS and *International Wavelength*, also classifies the videos it reviews by themes that include different types of sexual activities and categories like Asians and Latins. The videos are described with no less sensitivity to the politics of race than is the case in the more "specialized" texts: a caption for an illustration from *Bi-Bi Banjee Boys* featuring two Latino performers asks "How's it hangin' hombre?," while one for *Ricans in the Raw* explains, "Cholos explore each other's hole-o's." "Foreign" languages and cultures become the occasion for ignorant and demeaning jokes and puns that play on ethnocentric and racist stereotypes, while, as usual, the race of the performers in the all white videos (by far the majority in this catalog) are presented without remark.[12]

More importantly, these pornographies of race are symptomatic of a host of other gay Western cultural productions, ranging from magazines like *Passport* that bring together for Western readers erotic photographs of and personal advertisements for/from

Asian men, to gay travel guides to Third World countries, coffee table photograph books set in remote locales, and even nonsexual gay books about other countries, and gay books about people of color within the metropolis. These texts comprise a continuum of primitivist stereotypes and wishful/fearful representations of third world exotic availability at the whim of the white fantasizer. Of course, these texts also influence and recount people's ideas of others, their relationship expectations, and their sexual fantasies and expectations.

IV

Representations of men of color and interracial relationships that draw on the above discourses, but that might appear to be less uncomplicatedly racist, can be found in literary and other artistic works where the relationship of author to representation is sometimes unclear, frequently conflicted, and occasionally critical. White Western homoerotic writing in the tradition of Paul Bowles, Andre Gide, Jean Genet, William Burroughs, and Joe Orton often describes autobiographical encounters with men of color in white tourist sexual destinations (Tangiers, Bangkok, etc.) with a mixture of unflinching racism and self-castigation on the part of the authors and narrators.[13] More recently, work by the South African writer Stephen Gray, the United States writer Tom Spanbauer, and British author Alan Hollinghurst have used narrative personae that allow one to read a critical distance between authors and narrators or characters who elaborate racist fetishes in the service of homoerotic desire. While the narrators themselves (and, in the case of Spanbauer's *The Man Who Fell in Love with the Moon*, also the heroic white character whom the narrator loves) are unreflective about their own or other characters' racism, one can argue that the authors, by dwelling on unpleasant aspects of the narrators' and characters' personalities or the destructive results of their actions, or by emphasizing aspects of their character and ideology of which the narrators and characters themselves seem unaware, in fact invite such reflection on the part of readers, and encourage readers to be critical of the narrators' and characters' racism. Nevertheless, these texts represent a very different kind of engagement with the politics of interracial gay relationships than that seen in much of the explicitly and complexly political work of contemporary black gay writers and filmmakers, as perhaps apotheosized in Darieck Scott's deeply self-conscious novel, *Traitor to the Race*, to which I will return in the final sections of this chapter.

The difficulty of distinguishing social commentary from the reproduction of social norms in the highly charged arena of racial representation has been tellingly illustrated in the continuing Mapplethorpe debate. The controversy surrounding the photographs of the late Robert Mapplethorpe, culminating in the much publicized denunciation of Mapplethorpe by the United States Congress in 1989, has inspired a second debate among cultural critics about Mapplethorpe's representations of African-American men. A particular critic's position on the degree of racism, the possible transgression of racial and sexual norms, and the discovery of a contestation of racism in these photographs has often turned on that critic's understanding of Mapplethorpe's own relationship to his material. Those critics who see the photographs as unambiguously racist usually assume that in the photographs' truncations and objectifications Mapplethorpe is uncritically celebrating his own fetishistic desire for black men. Others who see a transgressive politics in Mapplethorpe's work, or who at least see the work ambivalently or as ambivalent (as Kobena Mercer does in his rereading of his own earlier response to Mapplethorpe) find Mapplethorpe's own subjectivity less easily locatable in the work, which is seen as possibly exposing, critiquing, and even reversing racist desire, whether consciously or unconsciously.[14] Mercer suggests that rather than merely reproducing and endorsing racist representations of black men, Mapplethorpe is problematizing such representations by dramatizing the questions that such representations raise.[15] Similar arguments could be made about the fetishistic homoerotic representations of men of color in the fiction of Gray, Hollinghurst, and Spanbauer.

V

Other representations of gay interracial desire have a more benign appearance. In one such discourse, a racialized erotic attraction is acknowledged, but racist stereotypes are less overtly present, or are sanitized or even disowned and criticized. As with the white men who claim that their exclusive attraction to white men is based on compatibility rather than racism, here the erotic attraction is often presented as an appreciative aesthetic predilection unconnected to social stereotypes and unconnected to privileges associated with specific racial groups. Hence a man of color might openly desire white men sexually without articulating this desire in terms of a desire to have or be associated with socially constructed white privilege, white desirability, etc. Similarly, a white man might claim an attraction to the beauty or culture of black men without invoking other primitivist, exoticizing, pathologizing, or otherwise stereotypical discourses. The desiring subject will claim that the preference is personal rather than political, and of the same order as preferences for any other characteristics in a desired sex partner that mark people's erotic tastes (gender, class, specific physical attributes, age, and so on).

Thus in Edmund White's Foreword to Michael Grumley's *Life Drawing,* a novel treating, in part, a relationship between an African-American man and the white US narrator, White takes pains to recount his interactions with Grumley and Grumley's lover, Robert Ferro, so that he can assure readers that in their erotic preferences Grumley and Ferro were men of conscience rather than racist dinge queens: "And Robert and Michael had both told me they had black and Puerto Rican lovers. Not *lots* of lovers, not commodities or fetishes. Robert, for instance, had one lover for many years. He had his lover, and he had his husband, Michael."[16] But White's efforts to allay suspicions of racist desire seem to contradict his description of Grumley's home life:

> All he needed was his marriage to Robert and his adventures with those black men he and Robert both loved but seldom talked about. They lived on the Upper West Side in a big, comfortable apartment within easy striking distance of Harlem. . . . If they were serious about sexual love (not with each other but with those lovers we never met), they were equally serious about only one other thing: art, their artistic life together.[17]

Why did Grumley and Ferro seldom talk about those black men they loved? Why did we never meet them? Why is the Grumley-Ferro relationship a marriage while the relationships with black men (which White had assured us were few and long lasting) are adventures? Why are the black men suitable only for sexual love? Why were the black men not a part of art? Doesn't this scenario repeat a familiar white racist trope that constructs people of color only as sex objects (good enough to fuck, but not lover material)? And doesn't White's phrase "easy striking distance of Harlem" suggest precisely the kind of sexual predatoriness and anthropological imperialism that he is disavowing?

In his Afterword to *Life Drawing*, George Stambolion similarly attempts to forestall readings of racist fetishism when he describes Grumley's room in the New York City apartment Grumley shared with Ferro:

> What struck me most when I entered Michael's room was that it was a shrine or rather the site of two shrines for two extraordinary beings—the Buddha and the Afro-American Male. . . . Pictures of Afro-American men covered the four panels of the screen and surrounded the single windows. There were photographs, drawings, images cut from newspapers and magazines of men of every physical type and skin color and from a variety of occupations—athletes, workers, businessmen, models, poets. Most were clothed, a few naked, none anonymous. Not only did Michael have several photographs that were signed and dedicated to him, but he knew the names and biographies of every man there.
>
> That afternoon I realized the source of Michael's remarkable sensitivity to people of color and his ability to portray them so convincingly in his work. From downtrodden workers to fancy gamblers, the black characters in *Life Drawing* are as richly diverse as their white counterparts. Utterly real yet endowed with wonder, they assume exemplary positions of wretchedness and dignity, violence and order, dissipation and morality. Like gays in a straight world, they are at once similar to the rest of society and different because of an Otherness that is less a form of alienation than an invitation to adventure and knowledge. They, too, are guides and truthsayers.[18]

Needless to say, celebratory stereotypes are often as racist as demonizing ones, and Stambolion's efforts here to rescue Grumley only serve to implicate Stambolion himself in a problematic discourse of racial and cultural Othering. In the tradition of Faulkner's famous platitude that concludes the *The Sound and the Fury*, "DILSEY. They endured," but in an even grander homogenization, Stambolion here concatenates all people of color into timeless symbols of truth for the enrichment of white society ("They, too, are guides and truthsayers").[19] It's difficult to imagine Stambolion even considering writing a similar epigrammatic characterization of white characters and cultures.[20] My point here is that there is continuity between many of these apparently benign representations of interracial relationships and the more overt invocation of racist stereotypes I discussed in the previous sections of this chapter. While the benign representations may admit the determining power of race in society at large, their binary understanding of power often compels them to go to great lengths to distance their particular cases from racist practices, a denial that only emphasizes their inscription in racist power relations.

VI

On the opposite end of the representational spectrum of interracial desire are those discourses that claim to be color-blind; they are, however, no less amenable to be read as racist. While the exoticizing blurbs for the videos I cited in section III obsessively reify race in men of color, the race-blind representations completely ignore race and racism according to the humanistic premise that all people are really the same and the bourgeois construction of romantic love as somehow transcending and/or conquering the social inscriptions, physical sensations, and cultural conditioning of its participants. According to this world view, race is not or should not be a factor in any relationship. In this category of representation we find the sentiment expressed on the popular t-shirt, "Love Sees No Color," and the testimonies of people in interracial relationships that race is not inscribed in the relationship. In his entry on "African-American Literature, Gay Male," in *The Gay and Lesbian Literary Heritage*, Emmanuel Nelson writes a nostalgic description of Canaan Parker's novel *The Color of Trees* as affirming "the possibility of love that transcends cultural and class differences."[21] Nelson's synopsis both points to and embodies an ideology that pervades the collective consciousness of wistful bourgeois culture but that is also invoked as the legitimating raison d'être for white backlashes against antiracist legislative and educational programs, and, more specifically, for recent attacks on affirmative action programs in the United States—all of these campaigns rely on a logic of universal humanness and a teleological narrative of racism transcended.[22] In Parker's novel, the African-American narrator is derided by his radicalized black schoolmates and called an Uncle Tom by his white lover—these reminders of racial conflict are merely forgotten rather than resolved at the novel's "transcendent" end.

Larry Duplechan's novel, *Blackbird*, makes readers privy to the consciousness of an African-American narrator who is well aware of cultural and institutional racism in the United States (for instance, he understands that his drama teacher's failure to cast him as the lead in the school play, despite his clearly superior acting ability, is an act of racist discrimination), but who nevertheless exhibits no such awareness of the dynamics of racism in the sexual and romantic relationships of his peers and himself. He states that he likes blonds, and seems only to be attracted to white men in the course of the novel. The one exception that could interrogate the narrator's desire, where the object of his affections turns out—much to his surprise—to be part Cherokee, does not lead him to comment on his attraction to white men, or to find it problematic or politically resonant, and when his best friend ends up with a black lover the narrator mentions the man's blackness without further commentary. Racism and desire, conveniently, never seem to interconnect.

If racial difference and race itself is hardly acknowledged in these depictions of interracial relationships, it is not surprising that such representations would distance these relationships from the apparatuses of racism as well. While some interracial representations in this category might admit to the general existence of racism, and might even document incidents of racism directed against the parties in these relationships, the possibility of the existence of racism in the relationship itself or in one or more of the partners in the relationship is almost always denied. Often the question of racism is subsumed under the euphemistic, bland, and depoliticizing rhetoric of difference. Thus institutionalized privilege and socially constructed power relations are reduced to noncommittal differences. Larry Duplechan's novel *Eight Days a Week*, featuring another of Duplechan's black narrators who is almost exclusively attracted to white men, presents race as only one of several differences between the narrator and his black lover; this difference is no different from any other difference, and is not depicted as in any way shaped by the contexts of institutional racism. Revealingly, when Nelson's *Gay and Lesbian Literary Heritage* entry treats those writers who "sound far less sanguine about the durability of cross-racial connections,"[23] Nelson does cite racial difference as the significant axis of difference in this relationship in *Eight Days a Week*, but synecdochically replaces racism with difference in his synopsis of the novel: "Their racial difference, which is the basis of their desire for each other, ironically proves to be too disruptive."[24]

VII

There is a more explicitly racially aware reading of interracial relationships that often acknowledges the magnitude and effects of racism, and while probably inclined to condemn the more obvious kinds of racial fetishizing like the blurbs for the *HIS* videos, nevertheless denies a continuity between these representations and racially specific desire in general, usually, in fact, arguing or assuming that racially marked desire and interracial relationships signal antiracist sentiment. The reasoning here is that the racist white man is the one who won't sleep with black men (as in the "G/W/M seeks same" personals, or the G/W/M ads that end with "no blacks"), not the one who wants to sleep with black men; the potential racism of the also familiar "G/W/M seeks G/B/M" ads seems to be beyond purview.[25] Again, the *Gay and Lesbian Literary Heritage* is instructive: Emmanuel Nelson's description of Melvin Dixon's novel *Vanishing Rooms* as suggesting "that a white man, even when he is very much in love with a black man, can remain fundamentally racist"[26] exemplifies the assumption that one would expect a white man's love for a black man to be antiracist; the contrary scenario, that a white man's love for a black man should be assumed to be racist, is unimaginable, and so the racism here must be adduced as extraordinary (as indicated by Nelson's "even").

Stambolion's Afterword to Grumley's *Life Drawing* is again telling, as it embodies a more subtle formulation of this false causality that nevertheless symptomizes the unreflective popular wisdom of (mainly white) lay people and intellectuals alike. In addition to the recitation of Grumley's sensitivity to people of color in the passage already quoted, the Afterword also observes, after mentioning Grumley's shrine to "the Afro-American male," that over time Grumley and Ferro "had become politically committed to justice for people of color everywhere," and describes a dinner where Stambolion had seen Grumley and Ferro "verbally demolish a man who had dared support the white view on apartheid." Stambolion continues, "And in his column, 'Uptown,' Michael had written so naturally about black and Hispanic cultural events in Harlem that many of his readers when first meeting him were surprised to see he was Caucasian,"[27] before describing the shrine, as if to insist that far from indicating a racist fetish, the shrine in some way produced or was the product of Grumley's supposedly antiracist sensibility. (Stambolion does not say what exactly a "natural" writing of "black and Hispanic cultural events" comprises, why such a writing is an antiracist practice, and why it might be presumed not to emanate from a white writer—his use of the euphemistic word "Caucasian" rather than "white" to describe Grumley does, however, suggest some embarrassment about the racial dynamics of Grumley's work and desire, and re-enforces the sense that Stambolion's own work is the preemptive redemption of Grumley from accusations of racism.)

From the default assumption of the inherently transgressive power of interracial relationships, and the humanistic conception of the transcendent power of love that I mentioned earlier, comes the less reformist imperative to use love as a way of overcoming racial difference. As Jackie Goldsby puts it in her delineation of the undertheorization of race among gay men, the problem with the dynamics of interracial gay desire is that "Difference must be enforced, not transformed, and the privilege accorded it reinscribed if the sex is to keep its charge."[28] Goldsby's call to transform difference is, however, problematic, not only in its presupposition that difference itself is politically undesirable, but also in its unelaborated claim that difference can indeed be transformed into something else, that there is something outside of difference, a difficulty exemplified in James Earl Hardy's novel *B-Boy Blues*, a text that tries precisely to circumvent the kind of racial difference that Goldsby criticizes. I discuss Hardy's novel at length in the following sections.

VIII

The most trenchant and productive critique of and response to these recent discourses of interracial gay relationships has been the political debate, communal organizing, and individual self-reflections galvanized by the idea of "black men loving black men." This slogan and the political imperatives that have come to be associated with it—however erroneously[29]—were first popularized in Joseph Beam's ground-breaking anthology *In the Life* and Marlon Riggs's 1989 video *Tongues Untied*, and subsequently relatively widely disseminated and discussed. According to the popular interpretations of the slogan, a black man who loves white men in general, or who loves a particular white man, has only two possible, and closely connected, points of identification: either he is white-identified in that he accepts and aspires to whiteness or at least to be associated with white privilege or to be elevated by his association with it, and concomitantly looks down on other black people (and on himself) and so will not consider a black man as a sexual partner or lover, or he accepts the dominant culture's denigration of his blackness and humanness and thus identifies with an abject representation of blackness and seeks to reproduce this denigration in a relationship with a racist white lover. In either case the black man has internalized the dominant culture's racist ideologies, and is filled with self-hatred. He is a victim of false consciousness.[30] To contest this internalization of racism, black men are enjoined to expend their sexual, emotional, intellectual, and caretaking energies on the embattled "black community," and, specifically, on a black lover.

This enjoinder represents an important intervention into the politics of desire: it disrupts the black gay/gay black binary that positions black gay men as either happily gay but white-identified or proudly black but closetedly gay, by addressing a black gay community in which neither blackness nor gayness needs to be prioritized over the other.[31] Its argument for a politicized sexual separatism implies not only that desire is always politicized but also that ideology can revision desire. The desire that it advocates is thus very different from the all black desire in the porn video blurbs I described. In Hardy's *B-Boy Blues*, for instance, a narrative of all black gay desire, this desire is not appropriable by white subjectivity precisely because it is presented within an antiracist politics, in a context explicitly addressing white gay racism and the politics of interracial desire (this kind of self-reflection, is, of course, completely suppressed in the video blurbs), and framed by derogatory comments about white gay men and white gay culture. Unlike the self-deprecatory postures of some of the white characters in the porn video blurbs, here this contempt is the occasion for sexual revulsion rather than sexual arousal. Responding to the attempts of white men to proposition him, the narrator of *B-Boy Blues* comments, "I love color *au naturel*, not sun-soaked cancer-causing tans."[32] Because this separatism arises out of and as a contestation of a political context of racial subordination and aesthetic marginalization, it is also not equivalent to racist white separatism, which re-enforces rather than challenges existing racial hierarchies, resource allocations, and access to physical and discursive space, an equivalence implied by Darieck Scott in his article challenging the black men loving black men imperative: "I . . . do not believe that the revolution has arrived when people of all colors sleep together any more than I think it has when every sex act is between partners of the same race."[33] In addition to failing to account for the very different hegemonic and oppositional contexts and impetuses that gave rise to these separatisms, the ahistorical conflation of white separatism with antiwhite separatisms ignores the profoundly different effects and ramifications of each as it impacts political organizing and the power to challenge or consolidate the political status quo.[34]

B-Boy Blues dramatizes the force of the black men loving black men imperative by juxtaposing it with the humanist commonplace that true love transcends race. The second position is presented when the narrator and his friends are discussing gay relationships between black and white men. The narrator and his best friend, Gene, are skeptical of such relationships in general, believing that they stem from black self-hatred, but are challenged by their friend, Babyface. Gene explains that he doesn't oppose all relationships between black and white men, given that some of these men are together for "the right reasons"[35] (for instance, if the black man isn't interested in the white man as a status symbol), but insists that a black man who has his heart set on "a Nubian king" shouldn't "settle for anything less." The narrator concurs, explaining that he is not an "equal-opportunity lover" because he wants a reflection of himself in his lover. After further debate, "Babyface shrugged. 'Well, all I'm saying is, if a brother finds something special with someone who is *not* a brother, I don't have a problem with that. I mean, people are not color-blind, but love is. That's my closing argument.'"[36] While Babyface cannot deny racism's saturation of US culture, and the inevitable racial marking in which individuals in this culture participate, whether they do so consciously or not, he also insists that "love" somehow (he doesn't say how) transcends racialization. It is not only as if love stands outside of this color-coded culture, but as if love is an individual actor in its own right ("love" is given the same grammatical agency as "people" in his statement), independent of human will, desire, culture, and contamination. Love may not inevitably be racist, but Babyface is deluded to imagine that love stands outside of material human relations (since it is produced by and produces these relations)—to that extent, it cannot be color-blind. The extrapolated delusion of individual exceptionality is expressed even by the narrator, who in general takes an uncompromisingly hostile view of all relationships between black and white men, but also seems to feel obliged to pay homage to the humanist subject by admitting in this scene the theoretical possibility that he might be attracted to an exceptional white man: "I guess I should never say never—I said that about B-boys not too long ago—but no white man has ever turned my head."[37]

The other pole in this discourse is represented in the views of the narrator in other parts of the novel. He keeps copies of *In the Life* and its sequel, *Brother to Brother*, on his desk, and gets his lover to read both books. Some time after the above conversation, he unexpectedly comes across two of his business colleagues, a closeted African-American gay man and a supposedly straight white man, neither of whom he particularly likes, having sex with each other:

> "Yeah, fuck me hard, darkie. Yeah, give me that big black cock . . . ," Elias laughed, jerking off with his right hand and slapping Phillip on his thigh and butt cheek with his left hand so hard it made me flinch.
> . . . Phillip picked up the pace. "Oh yeah, white boy, oh yeah, I'm gonna cum . . ."
> "Oh yes, cum in me, darkie, cum in me . . ."
> *That* I did not need to watch.
> After I was out of hearing distance, I ran to the bathroom. I knew I was going to be sick. This nightmarish scene certainly explained a lot.[38]

This scene is easy for the narrator to interpret because its participants use such explicitly racialized terminology to address each other. He assumes that the white man is evoking an archetypical relation of racist domination by calling upon and enacting racist stereotypes (Elias slaps Phillip and orders him to fuck him and cum in him; Phillip is the primitive "darkie" with the big black cock), and that the black man submits to the humiliation either because of his own internalized racism or as a calculated way to appease the white man in order to further his own career. Either way, there is no possibility that the black man might be willingly and nonabjectly having sex with the white man. The author gets Phillip to confirm the narrator's suspicions when the narrator and Phillip bump into each other later and Phillip seems to explain that his sexual liaison with Elias is indeed a regrettable but calculated career move: "we gotta go along to get along if we want to get ahead."[39] The narrator's position throughout the novel is much more politically aware than the views espoused by his friends and himself in the earlier conversation: he believes neither that love can transcend race nor that individuals can transcend racism. But his view also is undialectical to the extent that for him any relationship between a white man and a black man will always and only reproduce what he reads as the racist dynamic of the relationship between Phillip and Elias as illustrated in the metonymic scene quoted above. Hence the explicitly racist language used by Elias in the scene is not to be taken as extreme or unusual but rather as an articulation of the dynamic of any sexualized relationship or desire or representation of desire between a black man and a white man, as the narrator suggests by correlating Elias's sexual liaison with Phillip with the work of Mapplethorpe and Phillip's response to that work: "He, the Jesse Helms fanatic, had no problem with the work of Robert Mapplethorpe. 'I know it offends many people, but I like it. It does something for me.' Uh-huh. The objectification of Black men *does something for you*."[40]

Yet the meaning of the above scene of interracial sex witnessed by Hardy's narrator does not run the course of the novel quite as straightforwardly as the narrator's unambiguous reaction to it seems to imply. The racial separatism implied in the narrator's articulation of his own desire carries with it the problems that separatist and nationalist discourses in general engender, and we see these problems in the novel as well. These discourses find their political efficacy by constructing their own subject against something else, and thus necessarily by homogenizing and essentializing that subject, while demonizing any deviance. Because a person of color in a relationship with a white person is always and only a victim of false consciousness, she is denied any agency, and thus further subordinated in the social hierarchy of racial subjectivity.[41] In addition, in the case of *B-Boy Blues*, black-on-black desire is constructed not only in opposition to whiteness but also in opposition to femininity, which is then associated with whiteness, so that the logic of the novel creates a sexist and femphobic narrative that assumes the undesirability of femaleness and revillifies effeminate gay men of all colors in its celebration of hegemonic masculinity. The final chapters of the novel stage the triumph of unexamined masculinity when the narrator finally fucks his b-boy lover, as if only this act of penetration can guarantee his masculinity, fulfill his subjectivity, and signal the completeness of their relationship. This is not to say that all effeminate gay men are sexual bottoms, but that here the narrator's fucking of his lover marks his transcendence of all roles—as if such transcendence doesn't itself define another role—and his ascension into the hallowed halls of *b-boydom*, a masculinist ethic which he constantly counterposes to the representative effeminate and openly gay men who do not interest him sexually or in any other capacity.

Since the binary opposition generated by the nationalistic imperative of *B-Boy Blues* opposes white-black relationships to black-black relationships, it is hardly surprising that the narrative doesn't know what to do with Angel Lopez, the only character in the novel who is neither black nor white. As a Latino, Angel's character and desire stand outside the black-white racial binary. Thus, Angel is completely desexualized, neither a desiring subject nor the object of anyone's desire, an aporia that exposes another kind of erasure necessitated by the prescription to black men to love other black men in *B-Boy Blues*.[42]

Finally, although the cover of *B-Boy Blues* bills the book as "A seriously sexy fiercely funny, Black-on-Black love story," as if to suggest a space away from what is not black, the novel is also very much a part of the discourse of interracial desire, as is demonstrated by its comments on white gay men and interracial relationships that I have already referred to. But this is not the only way in which this black-on-black love story is also a story of white desire. In his essay on the prescription to black men to love (only) other black men, Darieck Scott points out that this prescription naively assumes that a black man's desire for another black man is automatically untainted by the dynamics and discourses of racism.[43] In a profoundly racist society no such uncontaminated space outside of racism can exist. Thus, not only does black-on-black desire often participate in the discourse of interracial relationships in its self-identification in opposition to whiteness and white-black desire, but it can also use the very parameters of racist categories of blackness in its own construction. In *B-Boy Blues*, the narrator's search for and validation of a b-boy—"or banjee/banji/banjie boy, or block boy, or homeboy, or homie, or, as MC Lyte tags 'em, 'ruffneck,'" as the narrator explains[44]—who has a penis large enough to be remarked on, might appropriate homogenizing stereotypes (e.g., of acceptable and attractive masculinity, of desirable black masculinity), but does nothing to question or deconstruct them either.[45]

IX

I have discussed *B-Boy Blues* at some length because I think the novel's narrative of black-on-black gay desire, while one of the very few novelistic representations of such desire, nevertheless dramatizes the impasses that typify most other incarnations of the antiracist ideological imperative against desire between white people and people of color as well. (To my knowledge this imperative has so far emanated only from and to people of color; I have yet to find a writer or politician of any race advocating white men loving white men as an antiracist practice.) While the discourse of black men loving black men can be an effective political counter to racist representations and fantasies of interracial desire, it is also highly problematic inasmuch as it relies on nationalist paradigms of community and unitary models of subjectivity. How, then, can we move beyond the two positions presented in *B-Boy Blues* (white-black love is always and only racist; love transcends race), and the kinds of binaries that seem to account for much of their reductiveness, without at the same time reinscribing the racist fetish or failing to acknowledge the workings of internalized racism?

Interlude: Some Axiomatic Questions

(i)

Are the instances of racism I have delineated in the various representations and discourses of interracial relationships and racialized desire important? Given the vast machineries of institutionalized and personal racisms worldwide and in the United States, and the devastating consequences of many of these representations and other practices, how significant are the kinds of representations I have discussed? What are the purposes and dangers of ranking instances or effects of racism?

(ii)

Is there any value in arguing that the apparently most obviously racist representations of race are not, in fact, the most racist representations, that a less obviously racist discourse might be more racist? Again, who has what stakes in designating degrees of racism?

This is not a question merely of attempting to justify racism, but rather an attempt to avoid a simplistic Political Correctness that fails to account for the complexities and potentialities of desire, and the multiple and often contradictory sites and processes of racial identification and subjectivity.

(iii)

Can or should any part of the racisms I have delineated be rescued? How can these racisms be used? Can we make something happen in (the representations of) these interracial relationships other than destructive racism? Is there a productive racism? Given that race-neutral interracial desire or love is not possible (or that race-neutral desire of any kind is not possible), is some part of interracial desire potentially nonracist? Is an antiracist interracial desire possible within racism?

I earlier quoted Emmanuel Nelson summing up the story of the gay lovers in Larry Duplechan's novel *Eight Days a Week*. Nelson notes that their relationship ultimately fails: "Their racial difference, which is the basis of their desire for each other, ironically proves to be too disruptive."[46] If this disruption is a result of racial difference (the novel does not explicitly say it is), might this disruption be a good thing, one of the ways in which the conflicts between race and desire can be brought to a productive political head? Might this kind of disruption cause a relationship not to fail, but to flourish as disruption?

(iv)

If it is problematic to assume that a person of color who eroticizes race (whiteness or a specific coloredness) is merely a victim of false consciousness, what other meanings does this eroticization have? What would it mean if its author is aware, reflective, and even radicalized around questions of race and racism? Most critical discussions of interracial relationships describe a person of color who uncritically worships whiteness. What of the man of color who is politicized to the extent that he hates white men, but yet is sexually attracted to them? What is the relationship of his desire to his politics? Should the two be brought into agreement? In what ways is his desire different from that of an unreflective person of color who is presumably only a victim of internalized racism? Can an Afrocentric black man desire white dick? Can an Afrocentric black man desire a white master?

It is easier to argue that a racially aware man of color can legitimately desire a specific white man when the superficial trappings of their relationship reverse or neutralize the outward signs of racist power relations, than it is to defend a man of color who desires white men specifically/only or a man of color who apparently wants to (re)enact racist stereotypes in an interracial relationship rather than resist them. Thus Martin

Manalansan's discussion of the subversive potential of gay Filipinos' personal ads seeking white men, finds such potential only in those cases where, inter alia, muscular, aggressive, or sexually top Filipinos transgress "the fixed image of the feminized and infantalized Asian gay male."[47] But is a gay Filipino who is unable or unwilling to present himself thus, or who for other reasons (re)produces himself as "feminized and infantalized," doomed to be interpreted singly and simplistically as a victim of false consciousness? How might he benefit from this (re)production? What of an African-American man who is the masochist in an S/M relationship with a white man? What of an African-American man who is the masochist in an S/M relationship with a white South African man?[48] How might the reclamation of the negativity of "queer" function racially for queers of color?

Might a man of color's desire to be exoticized or his positive response to or appropriation of racist white fetishistic desire for him be productive? Can such a response or appropriation make this desire, or its fulfillment, something other than racist? Gay sex guru Pat Califia suggests the potentially reciprocal benefits of such an active response to fetishistic desire in her advice to a disabled gay man:

> Q. I've got so much love to give and no one to share it with. I've answered ads and placed many. So far all I've had are kinky replies.
> A. Check the resource guide for support groups for disabled gay men and lesbians. It sounds like you have succeeded in making initial contact with other men by advertising, but you have rejected them because they were "kinky."
>
> Please reconsider. I know that you view your amputations as a misfortune. It isn't a fetish for you; it's made your life harder. But think about this. Would you rather have sex with someone who is doing you a favor, trying to overlook a handicap that they actually find upsetting, or would you rather have sex with someone who is attracted to you and finds that handicap exciting?
>
> Of course, you may eventually get lucky and meet someone who feels neutral about your disability because they are more interested in who you are as an individual than in your physical difference. That would be ideal. But in the meantime, why close yourself off from social or sexual interaction with men who have eroticized amputees? Some of them are decent, handsome, interesting guys.[49]

Why, though, should this man work his fetish only as a second-best option? Is it possible or necessarily desirable for someone else to feel neutral about his disability? If desire works, does everything else follow? Can my equivalence between race and disability be read as nonracist only when disability is not considered misfortune? Would a self-hating person of color (i.e., a person of color who sees her race as misfortune) be able to embrace white desire without acceding to that self-hatred? How would my adaptation of Califia's advice speak to white people, who often only think of their race as a disability in the context of a reactionary discourse against affirmative action, and whose reluctance to embrace a position as racialized object of desire is far more likely to stem from racist distaste than antiracist outrage?

(v)

To what extent can we educate or change desire? To what extent should we want to educate or change desire? Again, what is the relation between sexual desire and political conviction? Given the current predominance of social constructionist theory in intellectual narratives of sexual identity, how might this narrativization be deployed to hypothesize the (re)politicization and rearticulation of desire? Given the intransigence of desire, in fact given the perversity of desire (it often seems that the more one condemns a particular form of desire, or the more one tries to change or eradicate it, the more persistent is that desire), how can desire be harnessed for political ends?

Leo Bersani, in *Homos*, succinctly characterizes the complex relation of desire to politics by pointing to the frequent disjunctions between people's political alignments and fantasy identifications, and the role that culture plays in shaping personal tastes.[50] But Bersani only seems to see desire working against ideological convictions with social conditioning only negatively influencing desire (i.e., to repressive rather than liberating ends). He also seems to see desire as fixed once a process of socialization has taken effect. Bersani doesn't envision desire changing as a result of political conviction, certainly. What is the potential for desire to change? And what of the possibility of politics positively influencing desire, of desire changing for the better as a result of political conviction? Is such a harmonious confluence of politics and desire necessarily desirable, given the possible value of disruption suggested in question iii above?

(vi)

What if a politically radical white person fetishizes race? Is this possible? If so, does awareness make a difference? What can this white person do with/about her fetish? What if a politically radical white person does not fetishize race, but participates in an interracial relationship? Is this possible? Does it make any difference? Is thinking about someone's skin racist? Is thinking about someone's skin only racist? Is not thinking about someone's skin possible? Isn't thinking about someone's skin better than not thinking about someone's skin?

Cultural and political representations of relationships between white people and people of color uniformly present antiracist politics as an extrinsic factor in these relationships, whether the representations seek to defend or denounce a particular interracial relationship. Usually one or both partners in such a relationship is/are apolitical in the realm of racial politics. But what if the partners in an interracial couple are explicitly committed to contesting racism? How would this political commitment impact, enhance, contradict, and rework the partners' desire for one another?

The racist pornographies that I elaborated at the beginning of this chapter dominate white representations of the nexus of race and desire. While white people have written on antiracist queer politics (Mab Segrest's *Memoir of a Race Traitor* immediately comes to mind here), white men, in particular, have seldom addressed such a politics in the context of interracial relationships. Gay novels treating interracial relationships usually acknowledge race as a determining factor in these relationships (even white writers, while they might not treat the dynamics of racism, do tend to acknowledge the presence of race in these relationships, as in Hollinghurst's *The Swimming-Pool Library* and Gray's *Time of Our Darkness* and short story "The Building Site"). Often the white partner in a black-white relationship does or says something overtly racist (as in Steven Corbin's *Fragments That Remain*, Melvin Dixon's *Vanishing Rooms*, and Darieck Scott's *Traitor to the Race*).[51] Sometimes black-white relationships are presumed to be almost always already racist as in *B-Boy Blues*. But it is easier to see the manifestations of race and racism in these articulations of them than in a relationship between a black person and a white person who is an antiracist activist.[52] How, if at all, would racism be manifested in such a relationship? And if the *Men of South Africa* videos create a reactionary gay politics of all white race, what would a relationship between two antiracist white men look like? How would race figure in their desire?

(vii)

Could one argue that a G/B/M seeking, not a G/W/M, and not necessarily a G/B/M, but a man of color (M/O/C) — any M/O/C —, both politicizes desire and disavows racist stereotypes, a type of strategic essentialism? Or does this desire for an M/O/C merely produce a new kind of racist fetishization, albeit one that is not specific to one particular race? And what about the G/W/M seeking M/O/C? Why do representations of such a G/W/M not exist, and would the politics of this G/W/M's desire differ significantly from, say, the G/W/M seeking G/B/M? In either case, how formative are the desiring subject's motives in our reading of that desire? How, if at all, does one ascertain these motives?

(viii)

What if a person of color is making the kind of representations of race and desire that I have constructed as racist in section III? Surely there is a difference between a black subject's desire for other black men and a white subject's desire for black men, even when both seem to reproduce dominant stereotypes? Could the black subject's desire signal parody, appropriation, and subversion of those stereotypes? Could the white subject's desire turn on a parodic, appropriative, or subversive mimicry or repetition of those stereotypes?

Does the race of the representer make a Difference? Does the answer to this question depend on the motivation(s) behind the creation of the representation (money, apathy, transgression, coercion, false consciousness, the mere drive to document a response or experience—i.e., impressionistic or anecdotal verisimilitude)? Does the answer depend on who the representer's real and imagined audience is? Who the representer's boss is? Is to predetermine answers to these questions to racially essentialize everyone, precisely the practice that the exposure of racist representations supposedly is designed to contest?

Is the insistence on authorial authenticity not also collaboration with white racist representations that capitalize on such discourses of origin and authority to reap more orgasms, more money, etc.? Thus *Machismo*, the US magazine featuring naked Latino men for the benefit of white gay readers, advertises some of the videos it promotes as coming "FROM LATINO FILMMAKER *FRANCISCO FRANCO*," as if to assure readers that these videos are the real thing, that is, really "Other." As one complimentary reader's letter to the magazine puts it, "Finally a magazine with flawless Latin men. And it is their real *ethnic* looks that make them SO sexy!"[53]

(ix)

Does gayness make a difference? How does the gayness of a particular representation of race, or of the creator or consumer of a particular representation, affect the impact and interpretation of that representation?

In Kobena Mercer's reevaluation of his own earlier reading of Mapplethorpe, Mercer concludes that Mapplethorpe's representation of black men is different from racist representations because Mapplethorpe was gay. Yet while Mercer's argument here turns on Mapplethorpe's gayness, he argues against racial essentialism in insisting that Mapplethorpe's whiteness should not determine our response to the photographs of African-American men.[54] Why is Mapplethorpe's gayness crucial, but not his whiteness? What is the relationship between racial essentialism and sexual essentialism? Could a heterosexual artist's depictions of African-American men be given the same reading that Mercer accords Mapplethorpe? Are the racist fetishes in the *HIS* catalogs or in the fantasies of gay interracialists special because they are gay?

(x)

Is there a difference between fetishizing race and the fetishisms of gender, age, class, specific physical attributes, or sexual practices that define a person's sexual orientation(s), preferences, and desires, and that are as much inscribed by social hierarchies and cultural propaganda as is race-specific desire? If a white person's attraction to black people is racist, is a gay man's attraction to other men sexist? Is there a difference between sexual specificity and political generality?

(xi)

If, as Jackie Goldsby writes, gay men eroticize (racial) difference while lesbians politicize it,[55] what are the significant differences among the various tropes of representation of lesbian, gay, bisexual, gendered heterosexual, and other interracial desires, and how would a feminist critique inform the racial politics of gay male desire? Darieck Scott quotes Paul Gilroy suggesting that "gender conflict . . . might establish the intensity with which racial identities are held."[56] Does the recuperation of hegemonic gender differentiation and validation account for the inability to transform dominant discourses of race and desire in B-Boy Blues? Is there a continuum between gendered antiracist discourses such as those played out in B-Boy Blues and Edmund White's assurance of Michael Grumley's manliness in his defense of Grumley's raced desires?[57] What is the relation of these narratives of gendered racialization to the analysis of interracial relationships in Manalansan's allowance of only reactionary agency for the gay male fem? And how do these narratives (dis)connect in Darieck Scott's essay that only can account for gay men who identify with hegemonic inscriptions of gender difference and conventional imperatives of masculinity as his theorization of the "worshipful hypermasculinity" of "the White Phallus" re-erases and re-marginalizes effeminate gay men?[58] Isaac Julien's film Looking for Langston has been widely applauded for its ground-breaking representations of black male subjectivities, but the film also associates gay male effeminacy with despicable whiteness (appropriately enough, the narrator of B-Boy Blues has a poster for Looking for Langston over his sofa, though he admits "I didn't care for the movie"[59]). How does this association implicate feminist discourses and gendered identifications with or against dominant representations of race?

(xii)

In his photo-essay, "Revenge of a Snow Queen," Lyle Ashton Harris suggests that black subjectivity finds agency in acknowledging and celebrating rather than denying or negating black desire and contradiction. Harris writes of himself, "My current work continues this claiming of radical Black gay subjectivity through the process of self interrogation and furthermore through the interrogation of location. For me transgression begins not by going beyond, but by inhabiting that racially and sexually fetishized space, and by exploring our relationship to it."[60] In a 1992 interview with OUT/LOOK, Isaac Julien suggests a similar strategy of emergence into the public sphere for the snow queen: "it's something I really think I need to come out about. DB: About being a snow queen? IJ: Yes! DB: Oh, me too. Let's come out!"[61] (At this point, the interview ends without further explanation of what the benefits or ramifications of this coming out might be.) Given the invisibility of black desire in US culture, and of black gay desire, in particular, black gay (and other) representations of black gay desire are important interventions into hegemonic discourses of race, power, and sexuality. Does it follow, then, that any black gay representation of black gay desire is politically transgressive? What about other representations of black gay desire? Analyzing the pathologizing logic of the Spanner Case Ruling in Britain, Julien asks, "[W]here do black gay men stand? Do we revert to a similar kind of moralism (i.e., black gay men should not practice s/m)? Or are the questions of race and slavery to remain always in erasure when s/m representations are discussed in white queer discourse, and thus kept in the closet?"[62] In a similar vein, Kobena Mercer argues that the white Robert Mapplethorpe's photographs of black men are valuable because of their representations of previously marginalized subjects.[63] Could the fetishistic all black video blurbs from HIS be said to make black (gay) desire visible, too? And given the voyeuristic nature of reading and spectatorship and the unstable and unpredictable identifications and cross-identifications that these activities proliferate, can one distinguish between the racist all black videos and Hardy's (anti)racist all black novel? Isn't each genre as likely to create identificatory and voyeuristic possibilities for subjects of all colors? (Some lesbians appropriate the lesbian scenes in heterosexual male pornography for their own arousal.)

X

In the concluding sections of this chapter I address some of the above questions via a brief treatment of Darieck Scott's 1995 US novel, *Traitor to the Race*, an account of interracial gay desire that avoids some of the problematic reductions I have delineated as so characteristic of explorations of this topic. Scott's text conceptualizes and materializes interracial gay relationships in a critical dialogue not only with dominant discourses on race and sexuality, but also with other representations of interraciality, and so fulfills some of the demands I have made of representations of such relationships to do justice to the identificatory complexity and political potential of interracial gay desire. This is not to say that *Traitor to the Race* solves all the problems and answers all the questions around the vexed impasses of interracial relationships, or that it is unproblematic in its representation of interracial and intraracial desire. Indeed, its very inscription in and reliance on the existing tradition of popular representation of race and sex are what position it to engage with these other texts. Thus *Traitor to the Race* gives us moments where a different possibility of conceptualizing interracial desire is pointed to. But these moments dramatize the productive possibilities of an increasingly qualificatory theorization of queer race, and also the absolute fragility of any utopian resolution of race's relation to desire in an age where the historical legacies and continuing practices of racism and imperialism in the West mark that utopianism as itself a reactionary politicized intervention into the debate about the meaning of race in queer desire.

XI

In his article "Jungle Fever? Black Gay Identity Politics, White Dick, and the Utopian Bedroom," Darieck Scott wants to explode current meanings of interracial relationships[64] but doesn't go on to say what new meanings they might take on. I want to suggest, however, that some of this work is undertaken in Scott's novel *Traitor to the Race* In this book, Kenneth and Evan, the black and white participants in an interracial relationship, find the dynamics of their relationship brought to a head by their intersecting and conflicting involvement and noninvolvement in various arenas of community politics, and the novel ends with an apocalyptic cultural conflagration in the form of an ACT UP dance-riot. Kenneth, the black character in the novel, is the visible political activist in conventional terms. Evan, the white character, gradually comes round to Kenneth's way of thinking and acting by abandoning his earlier fears and finally joining in the ACT UP dance-riot. But although Kenneth is the principle agent in *Traitor to the Race*, as his own cynical commentary on his involvement in the kind of white gay politics represented by ACT UP suggests, this agency is neither conceptualized essentially nor idealistically.

In his article Scott also complains about the regularity with which narratives of desire between black and white men are taken to their limit by a paradigmatic racist outburst on the part of the white character, usually including a reference to his lover as a "nigger," that is too easy a way out of grappling with the complexities of racism within desire. Yet Scott's *Traitor to the Race* seems to follow within the same parameters in its construction of two specific symbolic moments of betrayal of Kenneth by Evan: Evan's racist bonding with an old school friend when the subject of Kenneth comes up and Evan's cowardly flight from the site of a mainly black gay protest march which Kenneth had asked him to join. In its implication that these paradigmatic moments stand for the ramifications of Evan's rather obvious lack of a developed consciousness about racism, Scott's novel plays into the humanist quest to understand why a particular person is racist rather than to interrogate the structures that produce such individuals, and in this sense Hardy's *B-Boy Blues* is more politically relentless because of its insistence on the systemic and institutional nature of racism.

But *Traitor to the Race* is ultimately more disruptive of entrenched economies of identity than *B-Boy Blues* because *Traitor* irretrievably complicates notions of racial identity, racial loyalty, and raced desire with the layers of performativity that structure it qua novel and that inform its action. The title "Traitor to the Race" comes to suggest not so much a linear betrayal or a conclusive sense of race as it points to the slippery and multisignifying nature both of betrayal and of racial identity not in order to depoliticize the politics of desire, but to open up its political possibilities by engaging with the exigencies of fantasy and so constructing a black gay subjectivity that is constrained neither by unauthorizing prescriptions of essentialism nor by the stereotyping of white desire.

While the title "Traitor to the Race" refers superficially to the novel's central character, Kenneth, an African-American man with a white US lover and an apparent sexual distaste for other African-American men, it also points to notions of betrayal and of race that are much more complex and more difficult to adjudicate because of their ambiguous meanings and results. Although Kenneth's primary mode of political activism is with a white gay organization, he is not apolitical or unthoughtful about race relations. He continually identifies the institutional forces that favor his blond lover and discriminate against himself in their careers as actors and in their everyday subjectivities, a process that makes his relationship to Evan much more layered than would be the case if he were simply unthinking around the politics of race (the liberal humanist model of transcendent individuality) or simply filled with self-hatred (the Fanonian model of internalized racism). Kenneth seems to hate his lover both politically and personally even though he is sexually attracted to him and seems to love him as well. Kenneth attempts to work through his investment of Evan with so much representative potential in the sex scene that concludes the second of the novel's three parts, but this working through also becomes a working through of the inscription of Kenneth's desire, a working through as re-inscription, and a re-evaluation of that re-inscription.

Earlier, Kenneth's Afrocentric friend, Cyrus, had attempted to soothe some of Kenneth's guilt and anxiety by assuring him, "You don't love white *men*; you happen—as much as anything can just happen, I suppose—to be in love with one white *man*."[65] In the sex scene later on,[66] after Kenneth asks and demands that Evan fuck him, he answers Evan's question, "Who am I?" with a refrain that echoes Cyrus: "You . . . Just you. . . . Just a man. . . . Only a man." The sense that Kenneth is reducing Evan from representative whiteness to a white individual whom he happens to love is re-enforced by Scott's parenthetical and theatrical interjection of Kenneth's thoughts into the action. These thoughts seem to be moving cathartically to conjure up and then destroy the debilitating cultural icons with which Kenneth's sex with Evan is saturated. Kenneth recalls the rape and murder of his African-American gay male cousin, Hammett, by a group of white men at the beginning of the novel. Hammett had apparently attempted to intervene in the white men's assault on a white woman prostitute, and Kenneth yokes that scene to his sex with Evan in the dramatic present:

(KENNETH WATCHES: Now. Now, see how it . . . *You like white dick, boy? Yeah, you want it. You like it. Get down there. Hold him down! Yeah, black bitch, I'm gonna give you just what I gave her.* I hate you I like it I hate you I hate you I like it I likes it not I hate it I hates you not I hate)
(KENNETH WATCHES: *Some big white dick, huh, boy? Big as y'all's, huh? Jack off in his ear, Jack, while I split his ass open.* . . . No. Like Cyrus said? He's just one white man)

These parenthetical interventions do more than merely mark Kenneth's exorcism of his racially configured desire, since they inextricably entangle his own voice and fantasies with those of Hammett, Hammett's attackers, the prostitute, Cyrus, etc. Indeed, one of the novel's repeated motifs is the merging of horror and desire—the ways in which each creates and becomes a part of the other—with a variety of effects that are difficult to predict and evaluate, and in this scene we see Kenneth as much aroused by the cultural baggage of racist desire as he is exorcizing it—in fact, his arousal becomes one way of exorcizing it. Kenneth "wonders if he is lying" when he tells Evan that Evan is just himself and questions rather than merely affirms Cyrus's like-minded pronouncement: "Like Cyrus said? He's just one white man." This scene, then, does not represent a simplistic disavowal of race as Kenneth somehow comes to see past the race of his lover (his teleology from whitewashed African-American to generic liberal humanist) but his coming to terms with his simultaneous hatred and love of Evan's whiteness. Kenneth does not exorcize Evan's representative whiteness but sees himself being fucked by that whiteness—and irrespective of whether that is acceptable or not, he politicizes the sex and his narrative of it in multiple and open-ended performances that not only allow for varied subject positions and meanings within the politics of interracial desire, but that also expose the contradictions within the existing discourses of and about that desire (as most manifestations of desire spring from conflict and contradiction). Most literally in this scene we see the supposed fixity of the racist stereotype straining as Scott juxtaposes racist mythologies of black male penis size with white racist wills to domination; the disunities of gay cultural conventions are exposed in the figure of the black man who has a gigantic penis, and so is the fucker in fetishistic gay white male sexual fantasy, and who must be fucked, in another type of more overtly gendered white gay male sexual fantasy that associates the *fucker* with power and the *fucked* with powerlessness and even humiliation. Here, as in the scene in *B-Boy Blues* where the narrator comes upon Elias and Phillip in flagrante delicto, the black man is both at once, but where Hardy's novel suppresses that contradiction, *Traitor to the Race* structures itself around it.

My use of the phrase "coming to terms" in the above paragraph is not meant to indicate some sort of happy resolution or dissipation of tension in Scott's narrative of interracial desire; rather, it is a coming to terms with irreconcilability. Indeed, the novel ends on a note of hate, when Kenneth reads a letter written to Hammett by Warren, the man who was with Hammett on the night that Hammett was murdered. Referring to the publicity Kenneth was complicit in creating around Hammett and Hammett's gayness after his death, Warren writes, "*P.S. I saw your cousin. He didn't remember me at all. I hate him. I know you thought of him as close. But he betrayed you. He put your name out in the streets. He put what you were out there so that everybody could see.*"[67] Whether the reader is sympathetic to Warren's point of view or not, the force of this letter at the end of the novel emphasizes irreconciliation within race, family, relationship, and within Kenneth himself, an example of the kind of productive disruption I mentioned in question iii above.

XII

The stage-like directions, "KENNETH WATCHES," in the sex scene, are merely one instance of a pervasive pattern of performative discourses, structures, and practices in the novel; that is, in the action within the novel, and in the novel itself as an action. Kenneth and Evan are both actors. The television soap opera that finally makes Evan a star moves in and out of his other identities in the course of the novel. Kenneth spends much of his time inhabiting words, scenes, and people, both around him and imagined. Evan and Kenneth tell each other stories and act out a variety of roles in their own scripted sexual games in public and private. When Kenneth finally finds work as an actor, the play-reading becomes a play within the novel. Stage directions and other dramatic devices throughout the novel heighten the fusion of fiction and reality in the text; the narrative movement between different first and third person narrators, interspersed with commentary on the process of writing itself implicates Scott as author in the performance of the book and the thematics it conjures up. Finally, the text suggests that there is nothing outside of the performance as even Kenneth's outbursts about racism are retroactively evaluated as scripted set pieces, and, moreover, as scripted set pieces designed as sexual foreplay, making it yet more difficult to disentangle the dynamics of rape and racism from the production of fantasy and desire. Because the relationship between Kenneth and Evan is itself a performance in every sense of the word, their relationship and the political world "outside" of it become readings of each other, and the interplay between them an opportunity for individual self-reflection and re-invention as much as it is an inspiration for political transformation. To say that every interaction between Kenneth and Evan is a performance is not to deny the reality of the material consequences of racism, but to ascribe power to the abilities of catharsis, recreation, repetition, and release to articulate agency in an always contaminated but critically contestable context.

Chapter 4

Gloria Anzaldúa's Queer Mestisaje

I

You are entering a gay and lesbian-free zone. . . . Effective immediately, *BIMBOX* is at war against lesbians and gays. A war in which modern queer boys and queer girls are united against the prehistoric thinking and demented self-serving politics of the above-mentioned scum. *BIMBOX* hereby renounces *its* past use of the term lesbian and/or gay in a positive manner. This is a civil war against the ultimate evil, and consequently we must identify us and them in no uncertain terms. . . . So, dear lesbian womon or gay man to whom perhaps *BIMBOX* has been inappropriately posted . . . prepare to pay dearly for the way you and your kind have fucked things up.[1]

Thus Johnny Noxzema and Rex Boy characterize their Canadian 'zine, *BIM-BOX*. Readers unfamiliar with recent debacles within lesbian and gay political circles might be forgiven for at first assuming this to be a particularly scurrilous instance of violent homophobia. But, of course, the *BIMBOX* editors are themselves queer, and antihomophobic activists, and theirs is actually a fairly typical articulation of what has by now become a relatively familiar opposition in political and cultural realms between lesbian and gay activists and queer militants and, in academia, between lesbian and gay studies and queer theory.

The *queer* sensibility and aesthetic embodied in *BIMBOX* has been articulated and flaunted in the queer 'zines of the 1980s and 1990s: alternative lesbian, gay, bisexual, and transgender periodicals, often relatively cheaply produced and locally distributed, and usually espousing and embodying a militantly nonassimilationist ideology.[2] *BIM-BOX* suggests its contempt for the orthodox procedures of publication and distribution employed around much lesbian and gay writing that has attained corporate legitimacy by advertising itself as "free to those who deserve it."[3] The titles alone of some of the other 'zines suggest their oppositional relationship not only to mainstream straight publishing and politics, but also to mainstream lesbian and gay publishing and politics: *Pansy Beat; Not Your Bitch; The nighttime, sniffling, sneezing, coughing, aching, stuffy-head, fever, so you can rest zine.* One of the lesbian 'zines calls itself *Up Our Butts*, a particularly rich title for readers who have followed the feminist sex wars between the journals *Off Our Backs* and *On Our Backs*, and the lawsuit between the two.[4] To clarify its distance from the categories lesbian and gay, the Minneapolis 'zine *Holy Titclamps* comes stamped with the instructions "file under 'queer'" on its cover—presumably for the benefit of perplexed bookstore clerks. Destabilizations of and attacks on lesbian and gay identity abound in the 'zines. *QT*, for instance, promises an article on "the faggot who thought she was a lesbian," while the contents of *Scab #2* are described in a blurb for the 'zine as "Bitch Nation, anti-William Burroughs stuff, pro-gaybashing with map of gay areas, anti-SPEW convention article."[5]

The prevalence of sexism, racism, and classism in official lesbian and gay culture and politics as much as in the hegemonic heterosexual establishments is a frequent subject of the queer 'zines. In the September/October 1992 issue of the 'zine *Infected Faggot Perspectives*, Christian Salvador, described as "a short, left-handed, 18 year old, Pilipino, cross-dressing, pimpleless whore who's been entertaining the idea of watersports; part-time queer activist" writes,

> Early this last year I was introduced to west Hollywood—What is it?! It's two blocks of 21 and over white fags who don't even notice the existence of women standing two inches from them, much less a little thing like me. . . . Well, West Hollywood don't look like where and how I'd like to celebrate my queerness.[6]

This dissatisfaction with identity politics highlights what is one of the most striking characteristics of the 'zines, and this is, perhaps, what sets them most apart from glossier, more mainstream lesbian and gay publications: their difference from each other, their appeal to and identification with a very specialized readership *within* the lesbian and gay community—indeed, their contestation of the very idea that there is such an entity as a unified and unitary "lesbian and gay community," a totalization that has been repeatedly questioned for a over a decade by white lesbians, and by queer people of color of all genders. The 'zine *Swish*, for example, deals exclusively with gay (primarily white) punk rockers, while *Thing* focuses on gay African-American drag queens—there is no pretense that there is something for everyone here and there is no pluralist delusion that this is for or about "most people" or "everyone" (claims made by most of the mainstream publications, despite the fact that they are just as exclusive and limited as any of the 'zines are).[7] As each 'zine irreversibly invokes a queer specificity, so too do the 'zines' multiple voices illustrate that queer is not one thing. They smash the myth of the gay community.

In what follows, I locate the stakes at play in the politics of community and identity through a reading of the work of Gloria Anzaldúa. I focus on the antiracist critique of the articulation of a homogenous lesbian and gay community by showing how Anzaldúa, writing just before the queer 'zine explosion of the 1990s, prefigures, enables, and develops the kinds of arguments implied and insisted on in the 'zines, both in her exemplification of a colored queer identity, and in her fracturing of all kinds of communities.

II

In Chapter 1 I submitted the potential of queer to pluralize, disperse, interrogate, oppose, and fragment a politics that is organized solely around sexuality as identity. Queerness could also problematize the kind of single issue activism that has caused further undelineated lesbian and gay articulations to assume a default whiteness, middle-classness, and US Americanness, because queerness is so slippery to define, often connotes a politicization of identity, and does not depend on a binary opposite for its signifying power (as I suggested in Chapter 1, nonqueer is no more easily contained than queer is). In her article, "To(o) Queer the Writer—Loca, escritora y chicana," Gloria Anzaldúa contrasts the symbolizing power of the words "lesbian" and "queer":

> "lesbian" is a cerebral word, white and middle class, representing an English-only dominant culture, derived from the Greek word *lesbos*. I think of lesbians as predominantly white and middle-class women and a segment of women of color who acquired the term through osmosis much the same as Chicanas and Latinas assimilated the word "Hispanic." When a "lesbian" names me the same as her she subsumes me under her category. I am of her group but not as an equal part, not as a whole person—my color erased, my class ignored. *Soy una puta mala*, a phrase coined by Ariban, a *tejana tortillera* . . . Unlike the word "queer," "lesbian" came late into some of our lives.[8]

Although she expresses reservations about the word "queer," too, particularly in its embodiment in a white queer theory that seeks to unify queers or appropriate queers of color, Anzaldúa argues that the historically nongenteel connotations of queer allow more room to maneuver its definitional parameters.

In this chapter I develop queer's multiplying and re(de)specifying trajectory by exploring the uses that Anzaldúa puts queerness to, primarily in her book *Borderlands/La Frontera: The New Mestiza*, published in 1987 before "queer" gained its current academic chic, yet presaging many of the concerns of queer theory (though Anzaldúa seldom gets credit when queer theory's lineage is traced or its practitioners delineated). Whereas the substitutions I examined in Chapter 2 interchange whiteness and gayness so that queers of color disappear and gayness bolsters white supremacy across imperial divides, mirroring the many white writers and activists who disappear queers of color by analogizing race and sexuality, the kinds of racial and sexual exchanges effected by

Anzaldúa centralize queers of color by interpolating queerness from coloredness in a context that explicitly politicizes queerness as an anti-imperialist and antiracist (anti-) identity. (This is a narrative of gayness that I suggested might unsettle rigid binaries for some of the writers on interracial relationships in Chapter 3.) This is not to say that Anzaldúa uncritically posits a utopic ethnic or racial identity as a counterpoint to whiteness and gayness—she is as impatient with Mexican and Chicano nationalism as she is critical of white arrogance, and skeptical of the very idea of identitarianism—but that her oscillation between discourses of race and sexuality itself models a politicized, empowering, and nonidealistic elaboration of queer race.

III

In an essay in the anthology *The Lesbian Postmodern*, Judith Raiskin argues that Anzaldúa reworks nineteenth and early twentieth century scientific and sexological discourses bolstering teleologies of racial decadence with categories of sexual perversion, and vice versa. Anzaldúa does so, Raiskin maintains, by constructing mestiza and queer subjectivities as privileged consciousnesses. Here I want to extend the implications of Raiskin's analysis by suggesting that what Anzaldúa's work achieves is not merely an inversion of hierarchies (from queer/mestiza = degenerate to queer/mestiza = transcendent), but also a reconceptualization of the relationship of the categories to each other, and of the ways in which meaning is assigned to and between categorizations.

The multi-vocal title of *Borderlands/La Frontera* hints at the psychic and physical borders that Anzaldúa's narrative voices traverse, inhabit, and undermine: her border(ing) (non)identities are concretized by the border culture to which Anzaldúa's own work has been such an enormous contribution. The geographic border between Mexico and the United States creates Chicana/o identity and is the site for the continued persecution of Mexicans. Anzaldúa challenges linguistic frontiers in her use of Tex-Mex in the text. The book also works the borders between genders, genres, disciplines, and within/between identity/identities itself/themselves.[9] Yvonne Yarbro-Bejarano has argued that the writing of Cherríe Moraga "enacts an impossible scenario: to give voice and visibility to that which has been erased and silenced."[10] Anzaldúa is likewise engaged in the paradoxical reclamation of a neo-subject: the new mestiza. The act of writing is Anzaldúa's writing of herself into being (a celebratory counterpoint to the despair that informs much of the book; the process of writing itself here becomes its own justification) and points to the crucial role that texts, literature, and culture play in theorizing and enabling identities: "Being a writer feels very much like being a Chicana, or being queer—a lot of squirming, coming up against all sorts of walls. Or its opposite: nothing defined or definite, a boundless, floating state of limbo."[11] Writing is also a border inhabitant in *Borderlands/La Frontera*.

Anzaldúa begins the Preface to *Borderlands/La Frontera* by using writing to initiate a complex relationality between the physical and the psychical, the historical and the metaphysical, the context-specific and the universal, that will inform the entire book in various transformations, substitutions, and displacements of the "original" relation itself a homologization of abstractions and concretizations of different registers and media:

> The actual physical borderland that I'm dealing with in this book is the Texas-U.S. Southwest/Mexican border. The psychological borderlands, the sexual borderlands and the spiritual borderlands are not particular to the Southwest. In fact, the Borderlands are physically present wherever two or more cultures edge each other, where people of different races occupy the same territory, where under, lower, middle and upper classes touch, where the space between two individuals shrinks with intimacy.[12]

Anzaldúa's opening two sentences establish a contrast enforced in the formal division of labor between their symmetry. The first invokes the specific, the historical, the political, and the material (the Texas-US Southwest/Mexican border). The second gestures towards the universal although its inclusion of "sexual borderlands" also suggests more explicitly the kinds of sensual confrontations evoked by the first sentence. The final sentence of the above quoted paragraph further unsettles the binary, elaborating the framing imputation that each meaning of the borderland is to be seen as standing for all its other meanings. If the universal and the historically specific inform each other to such a degree that the one cannot mean without the other, then each has been indelibly inf(l)ected to the extent that it immediately brings the other to mind, and, as such, has undergone a transformation of its own (particular) meaning. The beginning of the third sentence, "In fact, the Borderlands are physically present wherever two or more cultures edge each other," retrieves the geography of the first sentence to emphasize it in the second. Psychological, sexual, and spiritual borderlands that are not particular to the Southwest are yet as *physically* present as is the geographic border between Mexico and the United States. Anzaldúa's text invites us to break down the borders between the physical and the abstract to see the latter informed and contextualized by the former.

I have discussed this opening paragraph of *Borderlands/La Frontera* in some detail because of the pattern it establishes for the book as a whole, and especially, because of the model it implies for thinking about racial identity, sexual identity, and queer race. By inviting us to transpose our knowledge and understanding in one realm to another apparently unconnected and alien one of a very different order, Anzaldúa displaces and defers any final or single meaning from a particular identification, and, indeed, from identity itself, and imbues each identifying moment with specific new meanings as a result of the transpositions.

These new meanings, insofar as they impact racial and gender categories, are displayed in Anzaldúa's attention to the politics of language in the book. In the last paragraph of the preface, Anzaldúa discusses the language "code switching" in the text, and the position of "Chicano Spanish" as a language "not approved by any society" (as she later explains, it is reviled both by Spanish-speaking purists and racist English-speaking monolinguals). She concludes, "[W]e Chicanos no longer feel that we need to beg entrance, that we need always to make the first overture—to translate to Anglos, Mexicans and Latinos, apology blurting out of our mouths with every step. Today we ask to be met halfway. This book is our invitation to you—from the new mestizas."[13] I am particularly interested in Anzaldúa's use of gendering and racing pronouns and noun endings in this sentence, again because her strategy here is paradigmatic of a process of (anti-)identity formation/dissolution and a series of transferences and switches that pattern the entire text, but that Anzaldúa never explicitly discusses when she does mention code switching and cross-identifications. In the sentence cited above, the enclosing Chicanos and mestizas appear to be synonymous in their identification of the "our" and the "we" that makes "you" of Anglos, Mexicans, and Latinos (in itself an uneasy opposition that fractures the conventionalized white/nonwhite duality). But there is also a teleological transformation in the course of the sentence as the generic masculine (the conventionalized universal) Chicanos becomes what is to be an unconventional universal in the text that follows, the feminine mestizas, paralleling the shift from uppercase nationalism to lowercase hybridity/bastardization. Not only, as I shall argue, does Anzaldúa's mestiza reflect the anti-identitarian, antinationalistic potential of the Queer Nation, but as queer comes to stand for mestiza in the text, so the metamorphosis into the mestiza also traces the transformation/(re)definition of the queer, and the paradoxical nature of the writing-into-being of both identities and transubstantiations (as the moniker "Queer Nation" itself points to the paradoxical notion of an anticategorical nationalism).

The feminist politics of Anzaldúa's project shapes her transgender identifications and appropriations. Anzaldúa's development of a female universal might be explained with reference to Wittig and Zeig's perverse feminization of classical heroes in *Lesbian Peoples: Materials for a Dictionary*, or Wittig's elaboration of conflict and fragmentation within a female universality in *The Lesbian Body*. *Lesbian Peoples* does not carry an entry for "man," and the entry for "woman" notes, "Obsolete since the beginning of the Glorious Age."[14] Using *Lesbian Peoples* to gloss *The Lesbian Body*, we could say that Wittig's universal woman is not so much a separatist being as a transformed separatist; men are not dead, but have been incorporated into the generic "she" in a reversal of the myth of the gender-neutral "he"—a reversal both in the sense of a change in political value and in the usurpation of gender hierarchies.[15]

In Anzaldúa's book the new universal is further specified by being raced, but the racialization works (as is characteristic of this text) not merely to emphasize a binary but to multiply its terms and poles (thus racial, ethnic, and linguistic difference is called on to distinguish mestizas and Chicanos from Anglos, Mexicans, and Latinos, rather than to distinguish men from women, mestizas from Chicanos). In one of the poems in the latter part of her book, Anzaldúa writes of her role of dragging integrity out of those who engage with her. She describes being repeatedly chosen to "pick at the masks" of "Colored, poor white, latent queer / passing for white."[16] The process of substitution here, in addition to suggesting a continuity between colored, poor white, and latent queer, makes poor white and latent queer as much the subject of passing for white as colored is. How does a latent queer or poor white pass for white? How does one even begin to find or construct a meaning out of this possibility? Other than simply finding experiences of class, race, and sexuality to be analogous, or seeing all the terms of identity here as highly metaphorical (readings which I am not inclined to follow, and which I do not believe would be amenable to Anzaldúa, either, as will become apparent later) one has to think of these terms as carrying enlarged meanings. Class is raced and sexualized. Sexuality must carry racial content, as race implies sexuality, and so on.

The "new language—the language of the Borderlands," that Anzaldúa invokes in her preface, refers, then, to more than the English/Spanish linguistic border, or even the boundaries between various Spanish and English languages, dialects, and registers. It also describes a new way of (un)gendering language, and of thinking through the meanings of race, gender, and sexuality. In her reading of the work of Cherríe Moraga, Norma Alarcón suggests how the conjoining of sexist, homophobic, and nationalist discourses in metaphorical re-presentations of Malinche allows for the negative versions of this kind of substitution: "not only is the lesbian in the Chicano imagination *una Malinchista*, but vice versa. Feminism, which questions patriarchal tradition by representing women's subjectivity and/or interjecting it into extant discursive modes, thereby revising them, may be equated with *malinchismo* or lesbianism."[17] The switch from the heterosexualized figure of Cortez's mistress and translator to the lesbian hinges on the (feminist?) betrayal that both supposedly inflict on a putatively unitary *raza*. Anzaldúa's witty naming of the "Fear of Going Home" as "Homophobia" in *Borderlands/La Frontera* recognizes and appropriates this intrication, and extends what in another context might be more conventionally feminist sexual overtones in lines of poetry like "splits me splits me" (describing the US-Mexico border) and "His hands tore cabbages from their nests, / ripping the ribbed leaves covering tenderer leaves" (describing a field worker) to hint at the ways in which meanings, including the meaning of identity, cross identities.[18]

This process is explicitly corporealized in the section of *Borderlands/La Frontera* entitled "How to Tame a Wild Tongue," where Anzaldúa quotes Melanie Kaye/Kantrowitz: "My fingers / move sly against your palm / Like women everywhere we speak in code."[19] This quotation is surrounded by Anzaldúa's discussion of the ways in which Chicano (Anzaldúa uses the masculine ending) culture and speech has historically been punished, marginalized, and misnamed. The insertion of the lines from Kaye/Kantrowitz acts as an intervention into one-dimensional political history by suggesting additional meanings of "women" and "code" here, not only by paralleling lesbian invisibility with Chicana/o marginalization, but also by deploying race and gender metonymically to stand for one another so that transcategorical intertextuality and interpretation becomes itself an extension of the queer's penchant for cross-identifying and eluding identity. In his *Making Things Perfectly Queer: Interpreting Mass Culture*, Alexander Doty figures the exemplary queer identification as cross-identification (a gay man making a lesbian identification, a straight man making a gay male identification, etc.). Anzaldúa's queer methodology constructs cross-identifications between race and gender, and, as I shall explain below, between race and sexuality. She uses "queer" to make queer identifications and to make identification queer and to queer identity.

IV

Anzaldúa makes an analogy between queers and mestizas in her provocative claim that all marginalized peoples are mestizas,[20] and in her discussion in *Borderlands/La Frontera* of what she calls "a mestiza consciousness."[21] She says that as mestizas cross all kinds of borders, so queers exist in every culture, and yet are also outcasts in each one. Anzaldúa thus generates a politicized queer identity, using queer to denote oppositionality toward political and social norms (in striking contrast to the proposition, encouraged by many mainstream activist groups, that lesbians and gay men are "just like everyone else") and as analogous with other marginal identities, when she writes of the "borderlands" between the United States and Mexico, between and within cultures, between genders, genres, languages, and within the self, "The prohibited and forbidden are its inhabitants. *Los atravesados* live here: the squint-eyed, the perverse, the queer, the troublesome, the mongrel, the mulatto, the half-breed, the half dead; in short, those who cross over, pass over, or go through the confines of the 'normal.'"[22]

Anzaldúa politicizes the terms/categories queer and mestiza in a trajectory similar to the development of the words Chicano and Chicana, as delineated by Norma Alarcón. Alarcón notes the emergence of "Chicano" from oral usage and the working class in the 1960s to designate a new politicization by some people of Mexican descent in the United States, and feminist interventions into Chicanoness in the 1980s under the sign of Chicana: "By including feminist and gender analysis into the emergent political class, Chicanas are reconfiguring the meanings of cultural and political resistance and redefining the hyphen in the name Mexican-American."[23] The deployment of Chicana as "the name of resistance" indicates an identity "consciously and critically assumed" rather than "a name that women (or men) are born to or with." Alarcón notes, by contrast, that "Mexico constructs its own ideological version of the notorious Anglo-American 'melting pot,' under the sign of *mestizo(a)*."[24] Alarcón's parenthetical men suggests the potential for "Chicana" to function as a feminist universal similar to Anzaldúa's deployment of "mestiza." Anzaldúa's innovation, however, is to use "queer" and "mestiza" against and toward each other to particularize each term and thus to rescue "queer" from its potential to become toothless in the United States, and "mestiza" from its bland neutrality in Mexico. "Mestiza," then, lesbianizes "Chicana," a subject on which Alarcón's article is tellingly silent, despite its numerous references to Anzaldúa.

Anzaldúa politically disperses the category queer so that it resists the kind of appropriations that white lesbians and gay men might want to make in order to conform Anzaldúa to their own fixed lesbian and gay (and even queer) preconceptions. Paradoxically, Anzaldúa's queerness also returns to the radical politics of the first lesbian and gay activists in the United States and Europe, and prefigures contemporary queer politics, for instance, by rejecting the limits of binary gender in her reclamation of the "berdache" tradition of some native American cultures. Rather than assimilating into hegemonic delineations of gender (i.e., dualistic prescriptions of appropriate maleness and femaleness), as is the wont among more conservative lesbians and gay men in the United States, she formulates the border inhabitant as "forerunner of a new race,/ half and half—both woman and man, neither—/ a new gender."[25]

Out of its context, Anzaldúa's metaphorization of mestiza identity could authorize a colonizing appropriation: those white lesbians and gay men, for instance, who are already overly eager to claim that because they suffer from (homophobic) discrimination they know what it feels like to be a person of color, do not need further encouragement to conflate these very different kinds of oppression and so to avoid having to recognize and confront their own racism, and to own their own inevitable imbrication in racist power structures. Anzaldúa might be seen as inviting the renewed erasure of the lives and bodies and voices of mestizas by, in the name of anti-essentialism and alliance building, apparently legitimating a following of white lesbians and gay men identifying as mestizas.[26] In *Borderlands/La Frontera* she makes a similar universalizing claim for queer:

> As a *mestiza* I have no country, my homeland cast me out; yet all countries are mine because I am every woman's sister or potential lover. (As a lesbian I have no race, my own people disclaim me; but I am all races because there is the queer of me in all races.)[27]

Anzaldúa's postulation that she is all races because there is the queer of her in all races would be suspect if made from a white perspective or from within a Western history. However, her metaphoric mestiza speaks clearly from an experience and understanding of sexism, racism, and US imperialism as personal, but also systemic and institutional. She thus establishes the queer's claim as a multilayered one. Not only does she situate *Borderlands/La Frontera* within feminism and Mexican, Mexican-American, and Chicana/o history, and suffuse the text with references and allusions to a mestiza/o and (female) Indian cultural heritage, but she also embodies her anti-Eurocentrism in the actual language of her book by extensively using various forms of English and Spanish in it, as well as smatterings of Nahuatl. These specific and political details cannot be analogized or transferred onto a bland white identity the way that the discourse of multiculturalism in its ritual popular invocation in the United States has erased the materiality of political conflict by skimming culture off the top of the work and lives of people of color.

The essays that comprise the first half of Anzaldúa's book chronicle the European genocide against Native Americans, the history of US imperialism in Mexico, the lynchings of Mexicans in the United States, and the development of various institutions of racism and economic exploitation like the maquiladores on the US-Mexican border. Such foundational contexts ensure that Anzaldúa's dissolutions of identity and multiplications of the signification of identity achieve their effect precisely because they are working from within an already established network of experiential and political affiliations. These dissolutions and multiplications, in fact, rely for their effectivity on the very knowledge that they work to undo, and as such are not synonymous with attacks on these identities emanating from a racist, sexist, or homophobic politics. The narrator explains this point of departure in terms of her contestation of hegemonic cultural norms, but it is equally true of her processes of undermining and resignifying identity/identities: "I feel perfectly free to rebel and to rail against my culture. I fear no betrayal on my part because, unlike Chicanas and other women of color who grew up white or who have only recently returned to their native cultural roots, I was totally immersed in mine."[28]

The later essays and many of the poems that make up the second half of the volume treat what by convention are more metaphysical concerns (the exploration of a disavowed part of the self), but these concerns become politically constructed and indelibly political (as metaphors and as themselves) by the histories that contextualize them in the book's opening sections. As Kate Adams notes, Anzaldúa's framing of her poetry in *Borderlands/La Frontera* is fairly unique: contemporary poetry is almost always published in chap book form or as part of a book anthologizing several poets. The elaborate preface to the poetry (Adams points out that Anzaldúa originally conceived of the book as a ten page prose preface preceding a volume of poetry, rather than the present 200 pages equally divided between essays and poetry) politicizes the poems in much the same way that the political histories delineated by Anzaldúa foreclose a pluralistic reading of her queers or mestizas or queer mestizas.[29]

V

As I have already suggested, Anzaldúa's contexts function in contradictory ways in the book. These contexts are critiqued, yet used to interrogate some of their opponents: "Her culture, though oppressive, also grounds her resistance."[30] In addition, they illustrate a larger process of unraveling at work in the book. While they serve to establish the text's antiracist and anti-imperialist politics, and to ground Anzaldúa's for(mul)ation of mestiza and queer subjects, they also become the objects of the motif of self-critique and subject-dissolution that shapes the book's structure and thematics. Anzaldúa explains that her "Chicana identity is grounded in the Indian woman's history of resistance."[31] That tradition of resistance is transposable across cultures and identifications, so that, finally and ironically, it is also the grounds for a resistance to the grounds itself, for a resistance to itself. Anzaldúa refuses to reify any single/singular identity. Just as the mestiza will demand the recognition of all her heritages, and the queer will traverse and inhabit all of these heritages, so the narrator will not give in to cultural purists or univocal nationalists who want her to "return" to an uncontaminated Mexican past. She insists on her Americanness also. She insistently claims the English language, too. She isn't satisfied with any stable identity. Perhaps the most courageous and empowering facet of the book is Anzaldúa's refusal to idealize any mythically good Indian past or Chicano present. She critiques the historical and contemporary sexism and homophobia in the cultures which find their confluence in her body and experience at the same time that she indicts white racism and US imperialism: "But I will not glorify those aspects of my culture which have injured me and which have injured me in the name of protecting me."[32]

Contradiction radiates throughout the book. Anzaldúa uses her various heritages to provide a counter-identity to the values of Anglo-America. She deploys these apparently stable identities to critique racism and imperialism, but also destabilizes and deconstructs these enabling grounds of counter-identification as she finds identity itself more and more elusive. She both defends and criticizes her culture in a series of gestures that establish the text's elliptical trajectory. Culture itself is intermittently constructed (like Alarcón's explanation of "Chicana" as "not a name that women [or men] are born to or with, as is often the case with 'Mexican,' but rather it is consciously and critically assumed") and essential (as Chicana is still tied to race and nationality). Anzaldúa unfixes the sign "Mexican" from its literal meaning to deconstruct race: "Deep in our hearts we believe that being Mexican has nothing to do with which country one lives in. Being Mexican is a state of soul—not one of mind, not one of citizenship."[33] Yet the very word "Mexican" is specific enough, grounded enough, that it resists appropriation by anyone who merely desires that identity (hence it is not a state of mind as much as it is not a state of citizenship). At times the voice in the text seems to long for a unity that implies an essentialist and nostalgic understanding of human subjectivity and history,[34] and, specifically, to insist on the singularity and homogeneity of "the Mexican way of life"[35] and "the Mexican culture."[36] Yet we are shown equally insistently that "[t]here is no one Chicano language just as there is no one Chicano experience,"[37] where the movement from Mexican to Chicano represents not only an ethnic, historical, and political rupture/evolution, but also a refiguring of the terms of subjectivity. No sooner has the narrator informed us of her quest to find her "own intrinsic nature buried under the personality that had been imposed on" her than she asserts, "Culture forms our beliefs,"[38] as if to deny that any such beliefless intrinsic nature exists. She forecloses any utopian impulse to retrieve a matriarchal historical originality by pointing to the hegemonic patriarchal ideologies of pre-Columbia America,[39] only to locate foundational gender symmetry in early Aztec society.[40] While the

Shadow-Beast of her/our fears seems to be an essentialist being who signals our true selves that have been repressed, and who might break out of its cage and shatter our masks of conformity,[41] in the more explicitly concretized realm of racial power relations, "The only 'legitimate' inhabitants are those in power, the white *and those who align themselves with whites*"[42]—where we might expect a racially essentialist demarcation, we find that race breaks down in the shifting sands of political affiliation.

The entire book seems to be at odds with itself as it mourns the loss of a putative wholeness[43] and seeks to overcome division, while also recognizing the inevitability of this multivocality, and even celebrating fragmentation as the enabling scene of the mestiza consciousness that Anzaldúa advocates. Anzaldúa does not lament her homelessness or statelessness, or non-identity as a Chicana lesbian who feels excluded from her homophobic and sexist Chicano home and reviled by the racist culture of her geographical homeland. Instead, her text becomes a bittersweet celebration of bastardization, of the richness of her border queer-mestiza identity.

Indeed, *Borderlands/La Frontera* is enabled precisely by contradictory movements such as these, and I believe that to see them as weaknesses in Anzaldúa's argument would be to miss the originality of her vision.[44] Instead, I read these movements as complementing the kinds of switches and transferrals that I have been elaborating, since they elude the epistemological and political linearity that hypostatizes a final or core identity (either as resistance or as domination), and questions our very understandings and articulations of identity and processes of identification. Judith Raiskin and Inderpal Grewal have suggested that Anzaldúa's work combines political commitment with a postmodern critique of identity. Thus the tensions between Anzaldúa's reclamation of a nonsexist Aztec heritage and her critique of the unified subject would testify to her adept negotiations between the insights of poststructuralist theory and the political and epistemological claims of communities devalued by patriarchal values and Western imperialism and racism. I think we can further understand these and other inconsistencies in the book as more than the clash of a politically strategic essentialism with skepticism of humanist ideologies, because they also invite us to reformulate our understandings of and responses to notions of contradiction and ambiguity. In the section of *Borderlands/La Frontera* entitled "*La herencia de Coatlicue*/The Coatlicue State," Anzaldúa writes that *Coatlicue*, the Serpent goddess who was divided and disempowered by a male-dominated Azteca-Mexica culture,[45]

> depicts the contradictory. In her figure, all the symbols important to the religion and philosophy of the Aztecs are integrated. Like Medusa, the Gorgon, she is a symbol of the fusion of opposites: the eagle and the serpent, heaven and the underworld, life and death, mobility and immobility, beauty and horror.[46]

Later she writes of the new mestiza consciousness that is flexible and plural, and that tolerates ambiguity and contradiction. This ambiguity extends to the nature and role of the new mestiza herself. While she may resolve ambivalence, she does not resolve contradictions. She is not ambivalent about contradiction. Her charge is to keep "breaking down the unitary aspect of each new paradigm," but also to heal the splits in our lives, cultures, and languages.[47] She is to fragment paradigms and proliferate contradiction, even as she multiplies her own contradictory imbrications in the apparatuses of contradiction—this is what it means to live in the borderlands/la frontera.

VI

As a literary text, *Borderlands/La Frontera* further shatters any notion of identity as unitary, fixed, stable, or comfortable, in its resistance to the categories of genre that inform traditional literature courses in the United States, and the disciplinary demarcations that constitute US academic institutions in general. It seems to encompass, for instance, poetry, theory, autobiography, mythology, criticism, narrative, history, and political science, while revealing the limitations of these delimitations, and, ultimately, of the notion of delimitation itself. Rather than substituting one identity for another, then, Anzaldúa's text presents a fundamental critique and reformulation of the very notion of identity, albeit—crucially—from a politicized Chicana lesbian perspective.

Chicana/o literature has itself occupied a border position in academia, between national literatures, between ethnicities, between the languages that demarcate fields of study. Héctor Calderón sees this literature demanding the interrogation of such boundaries: "We should eliminate both national departmental and disciplinary barriers that have marginalized Chicana and Chicano writers and critics and affirm that any American literary history from either side of the border must account for . . . the contributions of Chicana/o writers."[48] But Yvonne Yarbro-Bejarano notes that sexuality has been systematically excluded from academic ethnic studies, and, in particular, has been erased in Chicana theory. (Yarbro-Bejarano specifically discusses Norma Alarcón's article, "The Theoretical Subject[s] of *This Bridge Called My Back* and Anglo-American Feminism.")[49] Except for the few but important texts dealing specifically with lesbians or sexuality,[50] the most prominent books of Chicana/o criticism generally continue to pass over Anzaldúa completely, relegate her to a few footnotes, or ignore her lesbianism. University courses in Chicana/o literature follow suit. So Anzaldúa's work also challenges Chicano Studies curricula that continue mostly to either dismiss her or remain homophobically silent on the question of sexuality that punctuates her writing. Fittingly enough, perhaps, Anzaldúa's book thus inhabits the borderlands of Chicana/o Studies as much as it documents the political marginalization that this discipline supposedly teaches and studies.

Anzaldúa's text explodes open the categories America and American Literature, too. The extent to which her book challenges literary canons was illustrated to me by written student evaluations of a course on "Modern American Fiction" in which I taught *Borderlands/La Frontera*. One typical student, for instance, when asked to comment on the readings that I assigned for the course, wrote, "hate [David] Wojnarowicz, did not like reading Anzaldúa because I only speak English, [Robert] Coover was great." A later question on the evaluation form asked "What was most valuable about this course? What recommendations would you make for improvement?" The same student responded, "I don't think you should need to understand Spanish to read a book in a Modern American Fiction course." This student's ethnocentric conception of what constitutes "Modern American Fiction" is a reflection of hegemonic constructions of literary canons in educational institutions, and of efforts by conservative political figures to mobilize racist, sexist, classist, and homophobic prejudices in the service of a phantasmatic monolithic "American culture" with its English-only family values. The irony, of course, is that it is these blinkered views that constitute the true "American fiction," while Anzaldúa's text is a representative analysis par excellence of contemporary US cultures and experiences. Her new mestiza is the archetypal American.

That Anzaldúa goes further than merely challenging white hegemony was exemplified by the evaluation of one of the Chicana students in the class (although the evaluations were anonymous, this respondent identified herself as a Chicana). This student appeared to be equally offended by Anzaldúa's book, not because it used Spanish, but because of the "poor" Spanish and "bad words" that the student felt Anzaldúa used. The student explained that she had been taught not to "speak like that." She felt that Anzaldúa's text was disgracing Chicanas and Chicanos. Apparently, she wanted an uncontaminated space for her Chicana identity; she wanted a space Anzaldúa offers no-one.

Because Anzaldúa's book refuses on many fronts the kinds of identifications that readers are accustomed to looking for in texts they value (often readers see their ability to "relate to" a particular text as an indication of that text's success), it also eludes hegemonic paradigms of reading and teaching in the academic institutions and disciplines that are now starting to teach and study it. In a 1987 article on "Intelligibility and Meaningfulness in Multicultural Literature in English," Reed Way Dasenbrock argued that what he referred to as multicultural writers like Maxine Hong Kingston and Rudolfo Anaya used specific rhetorical strategies in their texts to bridge the gaps between their various constituencies of readers. Commenting specifically on the problems that a monolingual reader might have with these texts as compared to a bilingual-bicultural reader, and the calculated disconcertions that writers feed these monocultural readers, Dasenbrock nevertheless concluded, "No matter where one starts, the difference between the two reading experiences should be eliminated or at least reduced by the books' ends, as the monocultural reader should be that much less monocultural than at the start."[51] I want to reconfigure Dasenbrock's thesis in order to apply it to Anzaldúa's book, and to suggest that *Borderlands/La Frontera*, also published in 1987, actually goes even further in its construction and confounding of a multiple readership. Not only does the text undermine the kind of us/them dichotomy implied in Dasenbrock's analysis by positing an apparently infinite number of identities and constituencies in its possible audience, and thus bypassing any impetus to pander to the perplexities of a white readership that is constituted in binary opposition to a readership of color, but it also doesn't seem to move toward resolution, reconciliation, truth, or knowledge for any of those readerships (as neither of my student respondents felt that the book spoke sufficiently closely to their own experiences).

No matter now many historical contexts any reader knows or studies, complete mastery of this text will always be elusive. As one reads Anzaldúa's book, it becomes apparent that it needs to be understood within specific contexts, but each context in turn suggests others. Because the identities that Anzaldúa elaborates resist stabilization, there is no bottom line context that reveals a final truth. Context is infinite. *Borderlands/La Frontera* intersects with many histories: Chicana/o history requires an understanding of Mexican/United States relations, an understanding that in turn points to Mexican history, and a history that, in turn, invites an examination of Latin American history as a whole, and so on. Chicana/o history also intersects with the history of the labor movement in the United States, and with Chicana feminism, and white feminism. Anzaldúa's queerness is intricated with the struggle for lesbian and gay rights in the United States, and with a specifically Chicana/o lesbian and gay history.

Anzaldúa's text explicitly demonstrates what poststructuralist theorists have been arguing for three decades: there can be no mastery of a text; there can be no all-knowing teacher. No single reader will be able to understand every addressed identity of *Borderlands/La Frontera*. A heterosexual Chicana might feel excluded from the queer identity elaborated in the text, while a white lesbian might feel alienated from the book's mestiza consciousness or its use of Spanish. A Chicana lesbian who does speak Spanish and English might find some of Anzaldúa's specific border colloquialisms unintelligible (because Anzaldúa deploys so many kinds and registers of Spanish and Spanish-English mixtures in the text, as well as English and Nahuatl, even most bilingual readers are frustrated by some or other moment in the book). Understanding is always partial and fragmented. While it is important for us to do our research, it is also important that as readers we stop feeling frustrated because of our inability to understand everything in the text, and that as teachers we undermine impetuses to present ourselves as all-knowing. We need to emphasize that it's OK not to have access to everything in a text, that, in fact, it is worthwhile for teachers and students to recognize and cultivate and become comfortable with this partiality and fragmentation. This is the best lesson in identity, politics, and difference that we can teach and learn.

VII

I have illustrated how the logic of *Borderlands/La Frontera* works to dismantle categorizations and derail predictable outcomes, both in the delineation of a new kind of consciousness, and in the actual structure and vocabulary of the book. This process functions at all the levels of identity formulated in the text and shapes the articulation of queer race. It instigates a politicizing slippage between the marks of race and queerness that racializes queerness and queers race in the body, in the meetings of bodies, and in the theorizations of these bodies and meetings. The demarcations of race and sexuality are ultimately reinvented to such an extent that they are torn from their conventional meanings and reworked into an inextricable, co-dependent, mutually informing, yet polysignifying cluster of understandings and associations, both intimately material and infinitely metaphorical.

Part of what "queer," as Anzaldúa uses it, allows for, is a conceptualization of identity that is different from definitions of lesbianness and gayness revolving around sexual orientation only, and thus normalizing middle-class white (often male) experience. In her article about coalition building among women, "Bridge, Drawbridge, Sandbar or Island: Lesbians-of-Color Hacienda Alianzas," Anzaldúa insists, "All parties involved in coalitions need to recognize the necessity that women-of-color and lesbians define the terms of engagement."[52] The same principle holds true for queer activism and queer theory: feminism and antiracism, queers of color and white female queers and their experiences, and colored female queer theory must set the agendas and delineate the parameters of these agendas if queer is not to become a synonym for gay white men. And just as a cross-cultural queer theory must lead to a multiplication and interrogation of the methodological and categorical epistemologies that describe sexuality, so this centralizing of colored female queerness implies a radical revisioning of white male queer agendas, rather than the token addition of queers of color and/or female queers. The tokenistic thinking underlying such attempts to display diversity reflects the poverty of much white-sponsored multiculturalism in political, educational, and cultural organizing. Just as liberal pluralism consolidates its singularity by *adding to* the variety it has on offer, so white political organizers secure their empire by inviting people of color to join their organization. The organizers are usually hurt when people of color are not grateful for these invitations, and show little interest in being added to an organizational structure that is already irrevocably white, with a white agenda. As Angela Davis says, these white organizers must completely dismantle their groups and build new ones from scratch *with* people of color.[53] Few white people are willing to do this.

Certainly, as I indicated in Chapter 1, queer doesn't always function as multivocally as Anzaldúa deploys the term, and multivalent queernesses can generate new anxieties as well. Anzaldúa's consistent juxtaposition of queerness and coloredness can encourage the kind of collapsing of distinctions between different kinds of identities that I discussed in Chapter 1, especially when this juxtaposition does not attend to the race(s) in queerness and the queerness of particular races, but rather parallels the large and unspecified category of coloredness with a universal queerness that seems to be raceless (or all races) but is in effect white when it is couterposed or analogized with coloredness.

In Chapter 1 I also hinted at the unlikelihood and possible undesirability of queer's multiplying and re(de)specifying trajectory. As I have illustrated in the present chapter, the kind of play with identities performed by Anzaldúa can disperse the queer foregrounding of the sexual component of identity. Queer can come to no longer denote sexual orientation. It is not unheard of for people to claim membership in the Queer Nation for reasons completely unrelated to their sexuality: in one instance that I know of a heterosexual man identified as queer because he had been stigmatized as a nerd in high school. In this way, queer can be said to undermine the monarchy of sex that uses a discourse of sexual liberation to police and prohibit bodies and delimit relationships.[54] Certainly, revolutionary strategies are necessary to combat the racism and sexism of mainstream lesbian and gay organizing, and of the academic discipline (I use this word very deliberately) of Lesbian and Gay Studies as it is becoming institutionalized in the US. But if queer does come to stand for identifications of, for instance, race and gender, as much as those around sexual orientation, is there not a danger that questions of sexuality will once again be subordinated to other *seemingly* more important, more influential, or more definitive questions, and that lesbian and gay existences will be (re)rendered invisible? Is this not precisely what queer militancy has had to contest — the relegation of queer concerns to the realm of the personal, the private, the secondary, and the trivial by other progressive political movements? Contrarily, is wanting queer to be everything, not just a new kind of Western white male imperialism, another instance of white (in this case, gay) male desire to be everywhere, talk about everything (including Chicana lesbian writing), and be *essentially* everything? On the other hand, isn't queer irretrievably contaminated by the sexual? Isn't its primary meaning tied to the colloquial understanding of queer as connoting homosexuality, and isn't it a delusion to imagine that the category can come to stand equally for those who are marginalized by racism, sexism, and classism?

I don't think these questions are necessarily answerable, or even that answers are desirable. But I do believe that the strength of queer theory lies exactly in its insistent posing of these questions. The project of queer theory may be precisely to bring an end to a specifically queer theory. This possibility should not worry those of us who have a personal-political investment in queer theory—who work in this field—because the irony, of course, is that we desperately need queer theory to theorize the end of queer theory. For me this paradoxical dialectic resonates with the words of Johnny Noxzema and Rex Boy with which I began this chapter because it describes their own (and my own) very conflicted imbrication both in lesbian and gay politics and in queer theory. In Chapter 5 I will exacerbate this conflictedness by arguing for the most uncomfortable understandings of queerness in order to theorize queer race even in the context of a political agenda that works in counterposition to that elaborated by Anzaldúa.

Chapter 5

Jeff Dahmer

I

This chapter charts a confluence of the problematics explored in the previous chapters by asking how, if at all, queer might be useful in a discussion of Jeffrey Dahmer. In the first place, it returns to the difficulty of defining queer. If the hermeneutic manifestation of the slogan "gay is good" allows, by counterpoint, for an articulation and celebration of negativity in queer, in academic queer theory this negativity is nevertheless implicitly taken to enact a progressive political understanding of identity and opposition (certainly, this is an understanding of queer for which I have been arguing, and which, in the preceding chapter, I have taken Gloria Anzaldúa to be delineating and enacting), then where does that leave a homoerotic serial killer? Jeffrey Dahmer is apparently as inappropriate a hook for this queer campaign as he is ineligible a mascot for a "gay is good" agenda. Sharon Stone, after all, killed obnoxious straight white men in *Basic Instinct*; Dahmer killed mostly poor gay men of color in real life. The shame of Dahmer has led to a disavowal of his possible gayness by all but the most rabid of homophobes, unless that gayness is used to indict institutional homophobia (this is rare); it has also led to a strategic forgetting of his apparent whiteness both by rabid homophobes and by antihomophobic activists.

In the second, and related place, these omissions separate discussions of race from those about sexuality in connection with Dahmer, a separation that also erases the racialized sexual subjectivity of those he murdered. In the preceding chapters I have shown how diverse strategies produce this kind of separation, and suggested what kinds of theoretical consequences result; here we see the very material and human destruction that such theoretical foreclosures can wreak—I am referring to the ways in which Dahmer's violence has been reproduced not only in the discourse about his killings, but also in the ensuing conflicts in Milwaukee, and in the 1994 prison killing of Dahmer himself. In addition to mimicking the kind of mindset that might have enabled a Dahmer, many representations of the Dahmer case restage the particular horrors of Dahmer in a predictable plethora of phobic displacements of identity and identification.

My third strand of hypostatization turns around the scene of interracial desire that I have staged in Chapters 2 and 3. I suspect that the neat separation of race from sexuality in analyses of the events around Dahmer's 1991 arrest and insanity trial can be partly attributed to the reluctance of commentators to take on the question of interracial desire (both on the part of Dahmer and those he killed). In fact, those who do consider the subject can only think of it in its inverse form (Dahmer must have hated people of color) or express bafflement as to why someone who held white people in low regard—supposedly a trait of some of the men Dahmer killed—would consent to have sex with a white person, as some of Dahmer's victims apparently did. Anne E Schwartz, reports, for instance, that Curtis Straughter's "friends were puzzled when they heard he was one of Jeffrey Dahmer's victims because of Straughter's open hostility toward white men."[1] Both Schwartz and Straughter's friends seem to assume that political/racial hostility translates into sexual revulsion. In Chapter 3 I asked, "What of the man of color who is politicized to the extent that he hates white men, but yet is sexually attracted to them?" This is a seemingly nonexistent possibility to those involved with and commenting on the Dahmer case. Likewise, Dahmer is taken to have lured men of color to his home only because he hated them and wanted to kill them. Desire drops from a picture that would become too convoluted otherwise. These critics don't ask why Dahmer might have had such strong desires for those he supposedly hated, or how desire and prejudice might produce one another. They do not ask how desire might override or reconfigure prejudice or principle (and vice versa), and how desire might produce its own cancellation.

I want to extend my analysis of interracial gay desire in Chapter 3 by complicating dominant Dahmer discourse in order to suggest both how racial fetishization can lead to literal death and how the denial of such fetishization reinvents the erasure of the fetishized subject. My aim is not to answer the question of whether Dahmer's killings were racist or not (in any case, I do not believe that they need be only racist or only not racist), but rather to show how both those professional writers and lay commentators who see the killings as racist and those who do not ground their positions in a pivotal and ominous denial of the ways in which race and sexuality form particular and nonfactorizable identities. Thus, they deny queer race.

I am also interested, in this chapter, in multiplying and destabilizing the content of sexual identities, the categories of sexual practices, and their nomenclatures (gay, queer, homosexual, etc.), as I suggested the value of the simultaneous deployment of different—and even conflicting—but specifically purposeful understandings of queer in Chapter 1. Here, for instance, I perversely give Jeffrey Dahmer a gay identity to counter the gay commentators who have insisted that he was not gay, presumably for fear of homophobic public reaction to a gay Dahmer. I leave my own insistence on

Jeffrey Dahmer's gayness polemically and strategically unproblematized at the same time that I move toward a definition of sexuality that can never stand on its own, as a way of indicating how competing discourses of identity and politics need not be seen only as indicative of conflict in need of resolution, but can also work in concert to mark the very disjunctions of identity from political effectivity that characterize the absence of or impoverished nature of current intellectual and social epistemologies of queer race.

II

Media coverage of the Dahmer case was imbricated in a sustained and complex logic of homophobia at the same time that it actively disavowed any homophobic intentions and effects. Initial references to the Dahmer murders as "homosexual overkill" by public officials and in the mainstream press were vigorously protested by lesbian and gay activists in Milwaukee and elsewhere, who pointed out that Dahmer's actions were no more representatively homosexual than a heterosexual serial killer's killings would be representatively heterosexual, but that those who used the phrase "homosexual overkill" would never have used the term "heterosexual overkill" to characterize a heterosexual mass murderer.[2] The phrase "homosexual overkill" was thus, once more, naturalizing heterosexuality and pathologizing homosexuality. Members of the media responded to the protests surprisingly quickly, and the term "homosexual overkill" was soon dropped from reports on the case. In fact, the media seemed to become so concerned that their reports not appear homophobic, that all references to Dahmer's sexual orientation also disappeared from most coverage of the case. Dahmer's gayness was also hardly mentioned at his trial.

This change was welcomed by those espousing a liberal politics of assimilation. Dahmer's sexual orientation had nothing to do with his becoming a serial killer, the argument went, so references to his sexual orientation were inappropriate in media coverage of the killings. But if Dahmer's sexual orientation could not be mentioned, neither could institutional homophobia. Liberal celebrations of individualism generally identify prejudice and success as manifestations of personal achievements or failings, and so can only look at individuals as repositories of humanistic or anti-egalitarian values, rather than at the formation of these individuals through socially constructed and institutionally enforced power relations. The result, then, of media attempts at liberal tolerance was that the occlusion of Dahmer's gayness also occluded the identification and discussion of societal homophobia in general, and specifically of the external and internalized homophobia that might have contributed to Dahmer's development as a serial killer, Dahmer's own homophobia that might have led him to kill gay men, the possible effects of homophobia on the men whom Dahmer killed, and of the possibility that institutional homophobia might have made them more accessible to the murderous Dahmer. Of course, I cannot say that Dahmer's homosexuality definitely turned him into a serial killer, but such a teleology is certainly possible given the overwhelming evidence that Dahmer had internalized societal homophobia to such an extent that he felt guilt, shame, discomfort, and hatred about his own homosexuality, and that a logical result of these feelings could have been the urge to destroy those with whom he attempted to satisfy his proscribed sexual desires.[3] However, with gayness out of the way, Dahmer could be constructed as an inexcusable monster, and the society around him could escape being implicated in his crimes.[4]

While a few writers lamented the fact that homophobia had not been put on trial with Jeffrey Dahmer,[5] during and after Dahmer's trial the reporters who did discuss homophobia and Dahmer's gayness (primarily the gay media) tended to ignore the fact that Dahmer was white and that all but three of the seventeen men he murdered were of color. This reticence was presumably a sign of embarrassment, a dread of having gayness associated with racism, or a fear of talking about interracial sex in the context of the Dahmer murders. The habit of partializing identity or of assigning individuals separate racial and sexual identities makes it impossible for people to speak of Dahmer as white and gay or of those he murdered as gay people of color. Usually the lineaments of white gayness are not difficult to identify. As I have indicated in previous chapters, even though the racial component of this identity is often assumed rather than articulated, gay whiteness is nevertheless normalized to such an extent that queer identities of color become literally unthinkable. In the case of Dahmer, though, the specification of whiteness becomes much harder because of the immediately and explicitly monstrous and racist connotations that whiteness takes on in this context. The embarrassment accompanying such a specification points to the incoherence of a liberal discourse of individual responsibility threatened by the contaminating truth of generality. Dahmer's own apparent insistence that the races—and sexualities—of those he murdered were irrelevant, and that he chose his victims because of their physical features ("My only objective was to find the best-looking guy I could"[6]), does not bracket race and racism, given the prevalent association of particular physical features with specific racial identifications. In any case, Dahmer might not have realized that his murderous desires were racialized, or he might have been lying. He might have been as interested in political correctness as the media was, and there is much evidence to suggest that Dahmer was not as nonchalant about race as he claimed to be.

Many of Dahmer's acquaintances report that he seemed to hate black people (and black gay men, in particular), and frequently referred to black people with racist slurs. Dahmer's racial consciousness was demonstrated in his claim that he thought that Jamie Doxtator, whom he had lured to his grandmother's house in 1988 and killed, was "Hispanic." This particular victim was, in fact, Native American. Doxtator's mother later told reporters that she was initially relieved to hear that those Dahmer had killed were "black, Hispanic, and Laotian,"[7] since she then mistakenly believed that her Native American son was safe. Both Dahmer's and Doxtator's mother's accounts suggest that race was very much at issue, and that Dahmer was actively thinking of race when he brought men of color to his home prior to killing them. In addition, it seems that Dahmer's victims were mostly poor and might have felt neglected and vulnerable in other ways, too: institutional racism produces a disproportionately high ratio of poverty, neglect, and vulnerability among people of color in the United States, and thus even the class status and degree of self-esteem of Dahmer's victims cannot be said to be extrinsic to race. Although Dahmer's attorney insisted in his opening statement at Dahmer's trial that the case was not about race, the race of each of Dahmer's victims was mentioned several times in the course of the trial, an indication of the impossibility, on the part of both the prosecution and defense camps, of not seeing race in the case.[8]

III

While legal and media figures learnt not to explicitly remark on Dahmer's gayness in their official representations of him, Dahmer himself invoked what we might think of as gay rights strategies (i.e., strategies that share discursive space with the liberal logic of gay civil rights and identity politics) in the course of his growing momentum as a serial killer and his consequent run-ins with and escapes from the law. As with the media's belated ignoring of Dahmer's gayness, these practices suggest the limitations and dangers of a liberal gay rights discourse.[9]

Commentators have bemoaned the fact that Dahmer had so many brushes with an incompetent or unobservant legal system and with other state officials (a probation officer, for instance) prior to his final arrest, and yet was able to continue killing. If the law and the others had been more vigilant and more conscientious, this argument goes, Dahmer might have been caught sooner, and several lives might have been saved. In one such early encounter, Dahmer was convicted of sexual assault and of enticing a child for immoral purposes in 1989.[10] In his remarks to Judge Gardner successfully soliciting the latter's leniency, Dahmer came out to the judge: he told him that he was gay.[11] In a chillingly magnified version of this plea two years later, Dahmer came out to two police officers who were summoned by neighbors when a drugged fourteen year old Konerak Sinthasomphone escaped from Dahmer's apartment. The policemen returned Sinthasomphone to Dahmer's custody and left the scene after Dahmer convinced them that Sinthasomphone was his adult lover.[12] Dahmer killed Sinthasomphone shortly afterwards.

What is particularly remarkable about these scenes is that before and after each of them Dahmer had on many occasions indicated that he felt shame and guilt about his gayness, and was loathe to accept his gayness, let alone admit it to others or matter-of-factly assume it in their presence. In the Gardner and Sinthasomphone incidents, then, whether consciously or not, Dahmer came out only for his own murderous advantage.

These coming outs enabled him to kill again because they played on the sympathies of others trained to be good civil libertarians. In June of 1990, Dahmer's probation officer, Donna Chester, had suggested to Dahmer that he contact "a gay rights organization" in connection with what she perceived to be his problems with his sexuality.[13] Dahmer's matter-of-fact proclamation of his gayness to the two police officers in 1991 might have been the logical result of such a contact, had it occurred, but the context in which it was uttered and the purpose for which it was deployed could hardly have been what Chester had anticipated or hoped for.

We can read the police officers as similarly confounded. Antiracist and antihomophobia activists have assumed that the police officers who delivered Konerak Sinthasomphone back to Dahmer acted out of racist and homophobic impulses,[14] but we might equally argue that they were acting out of racist and antihomophobic impulses or antiracist and antihomophobic impulses. They may have dismissed the concern of bystanders because these bystanders were not white. They may have felt less compassion for Sinthasomphone because he was Laotian and apparently gay. They might have suspected nothing was amiss because they ignorantly assumed that gay male relationships are typically violent and degraded. However, they might also have felt a pressure to honor interracial relationships, or to honor gay relationships, and to not assume that a sexual liaison between two males was criminal or immoral, or even to not presume to interfere in an order of sexual conduct that was alien or perhaps offensive to them. After all, one of the police officers[15] did respond to what he might have thought was homophobic (and miscegenaphobic?) anxiety about Sinthasomphone's relationship with Dahmer by telling one of the (African-American) women who, still concerned, had summoned him to the scene again, "Ma'am, I can't make it any more clear. It's all taken care of. He's with his boyfriend and in his boyfriend's apartment, where he's got his belongings also . . . It's as positive as I can be . . . I can't do anything about somebody's sexual preferences in life."[16] Given the notorious homophobia of police departments, it is ironic that in a newspaper interview months later, another of the officers would defend their actions with recourse to a similar invocation of the very imperative for tolerance that the police department's critics might have insisted on:

> I can't believe the community would believe that I would leave a young boy bleeding and just turn him over to someone, just leave without having administered any care. That just wasn't the case. We thought there was a caring relationship between these two individuals. Being homosexual is not against the law . . . and I don't base any decision on that.[17]

What concerns me here, in addition to the fact that these words were apparently uttered by officers from a police department with a reputation for racism and homophobia, is the uses to which they have been put by those who reported on the incident. Anne Schwartz, from whose Dahmer book I have taken the quote "I can't do anything about somebody's sexual preferences," makes every effort in her book to exonerate the police officers (and the Milwaukee police department in general) from any imputation that they acted inappropriately in returning Sinthasomphone to Dahmer's custody, and in the Dahmer case in general. She uses diverse strategies to achieve this goal: publishing the criminal records of those Dahmer murdered in order to make them less sympathetic and the police, by contrast, more sympathetic; representing homosexuality in a demeaning way for a presumptively homophobic readership so as to further demonize the men Dahmer murdered; and, in contradistinction, using the "I can't do anything about somebody's sexual preferences" quote to present the police officers as models of understanding and tolerance. Schwartz manipulates the mutually dependent discourses of gay rights and homophobia in the service of a racist and homophobic agenda as well as Dahmer himself did for a time.

Contrarily, we see racism enabling homophobia and homosexuality while reproducing racism in Dahmer's probation officer's failure to visit Dahmer in person because he lived in a "bad area." Phrases like "bad area" are usually racialized codes used by white people or middle- and upper-class people of color to indicate neighborhoods populated predominantly by (usually poor) people of color, but in the case of Dahmer, it was one of the few white people—the person Chester was supposed to visit—living in an area inhabited by people of color who was the bad element.

IV

To point to particular deployments of a gay rights discourse in the Dahmer case, is not, of course, to say that public commentators, media reporters, and police officers had suddenly renounced their homophobia, but rather to illustrate the inadequacy of that kind of rights discourse to contest institutionalized homophobia and other power structures—these discourses don't appear to have slowed down the killings that might have been, in part, an expression of Dahmer's internalized homophobia. Indeed, there is much evidence to suggest that no-one had reformed their homophobic attitudes, that they were all saying what they thought they were supposed to say, the contradictions in their positions and practices revealed by bumblings, slips, and plain ignorance.

In the first place, the mere absence of explicit mention of Dahmer's gayness does not guarantee that a particular representation of him will not be homophobic. Where Dahmer's homosexuality is not explicitly made issue of, oftentimes he is nevertheless homophobically coded as gay. Many magazine articles that do not explicitly dwell on Dahmer's gayness still use his gayness to sensationalize the case. A revealing article in the South African magazine *You*, on Dahmer's 1994 prison murder, illustrates how the complex interplay of racial and sexual identities in the Dahmer case have in some ways brought homophobia to a crisis, while at the same time drawing out the homophobic potential of racism. Andrew Burke, the article's author, comments on Dahmer's death,

"Brutal? Perhaps, but what about Dahmer's victims? The 17 gay men and youths he met in bars and shops over a period of 13 years? The people he invited home, committed all kinds of sick sexual acts with and then killed?"[18] What are the "sick sexual acts" alluded to but not specified here? The reference cannot be to Dahmer's necrophilia or cannibalism, since the phrase "and then killed" indicates that these "acts" were committed while the people Dahmer killed were still alive (Dahmer reportedly ate the bicep of one of the men after he had killed him). They might be the occasions on which Dahmer lay naked next to a drugged but living man. However, given the language used by Burke, and the context of the rest of the article, they can also be taken as any type of homosexual sex, including the consensual gay sex that was the predominant type of sexual activity that Dahmer probably engaged in with his victims while they were still alive. Burke's homophobia here is confused by his questionable identification of the men and youths Dahmer killed as gay. So much so that he has difficulty simultaneously expressing his homophobia, racism, and sympathy for those Dahmer murdered. Later in the article, Burke's inability to conceptualize a nonpathological gay identity emerges explicitly when he expresses shock that Dahmer ordered a subscription to *Playgirl* magazine while in prison. Is Burke's horror here due to his distaste for pornography, or at the gay desire asserted in the image of Dahmer looking at pictures of naked men? These men are adult and usually white, so it would be difficult to construct this looking as criminal, immoral, or continuous with Dahmer's murders unless it is gay desire itself that is seen as murderous and thought to be criminal. It is likely that Jeffrey Dahmer would have been gay even if he had not been a serial killer, but this possibility does not seem to occur to Burke, for whom the two identities go hand in hand—and for whom, no doubt, every other gay man with a subscription to *Playgirl* is Dahmeresque.

Burke's sinister representation of gay sex is typical of the way in which the numerous books on Dahmer also adumbrate gay sexuality by way of outraged connotation.[19] The conflation of Dahmer's crimes with his gay sexuality is shaped by a larger cultural demonization of homosexuality. Diana Fuss explains,

> In the history of Western psychoanalytic representations of the ravenously hungry, insatiably promiscuous male invert, *gay sex has always been cannibal murder*. . . . The psychoanalytic morbidification of homosexuality upholds and lends scientific legitimacy to a wider cultural view of gay sexual practices as inherently necrophilic.[20]

In his Dahmer book, Don Davis attempts to further demonize Dahmer by exploiting the story of the Konerak Sinthasomphone family's 1980 flight from Laos to the United States in his discussion of Sinthasomphone's fatal encounter with Dahmer (a route followed in several of the other Dahmer books as well). By referring to the "brutal" Communist "regimes that had taken over Saigon," in order to highlight the irony of Sinthasomphone's murder in Milwaukee, Davis also surreptitiously links Dahmer with these "Communists."[21] This kind of associational rhetoric recalls the familiarly homophobic and reactionary gay-baiting as Red-baiting/Red-baiting as gay-baiting tactics of social and political delegitimation that reached their apotheosis with McCarthyism, but that continue to be used today by conservatives and liberals of all sexual orientations to police queers of all political persuasions and to undermine socialists across the sexual spectrum.

In the second place, although most newspaper accounts of Dahmer did not usually mention his gayness after the initial flurry of homophobic coverage, virtually all the books that have been written about Dahmer, with the notable exception of his father's memoir, explicitly dwell on his homosexuality, and most do so with a homophobic logic that normalizes heterosexuality and pathologizes homosexuality, though all the authors would probably deny that their books are homophobic. Lionel Dahmer's *A Father's Story* often does not give the gender of those Jeffrey Dahmer killed, and only mentions the son's homosexuality halfway through the book, but much like the language of the trial (see below), the language Lionel Dahmer uses in discussing his son's "perversions" resonates with the homophobic discourses that have been used historically and continue to be used in the present to describe, pathologize, and dismiss lesbians and gay men.[22]

Third, merely saying that Dahmer's gayness is not at issue does not guarantee that one will not explicitly make it an issue. This kind of hypocrisy was particularly in evidence at Dahmer's trial. At the beginning of the trial Dahmer's attorney stressed that this was not a case about homosexuality, but much of the language in the trial seemed to function as a code for homosexuality, and Dahmer was frequently explicitly homosexualized as well. The police officer who was called upon to read Dahmer's confession in the course of the trial exemplified the normalization of heterosexuality in the trial by using the phrases "homosexual sex" and "homosexual activity" to describe Dahmer's sexual encounters with the men he murdered[23]—this witness would not have referred to heterosexual sex as "heterosexual sex" or "heterosexual activity." This is another common practice in most of the Dahmer books as well. As is the case with whiteness in the arena of race, here a sexuality that is presumed to be normal and universal need not be specified or named. Ed Baumann uses the technique to homophobically pathologize Dahmer in his book, *Step into My Parlor*, by referring to Dahmer's murders as "homosexual slayings." If the adjective "homosexual" here normalizes heterosexuality (heterosexual slayings would just be slayings), it also reduces homosexuality to momentary eventfulness. Baumann further forecloses the possibility of a gay subjectivity by conflating gay identity with gay sex in his continual designation of Dahmer's sexual contacts with those he murdered (including sex that was consensual) as "homosexual acts." Clearly, a gay trip to the grocery store would not constitute a "homosexual act" for Baumann.

Homophobic representations of Dahmer mirror the homophobic contexts of his family homes, and the homophobia of the larger society in which Dahmer grew up. These homophobic and probably homophobic surroundings could have affected Dahmer's thinking about his sexuality and his crimes, and could have created a link between the two. Dahmer's statement to the court before sentence was passed on him could refer as much to his homosexuality as it could to his crimes: "I knew I was sick or evil or both. Now I believe I was sick. The doctors have told me about my sickness, and now I have some peace." Dahmer also claimed in this statement that he had not pleaded insane in order to get off, "but for trying to study me in the hopes of helping me and learning to help others who might have problems," an eerie reminder of the kinds of institutional surveillances and categorizations that have long been used to violently normalize lesbians and gay men.[24] The judge in the trial re-enforced the representational slippage between Dahmer's criminality, homosexuality, and alleged insanity, in the context of that historical constitution of deviance, by ordering that Dahmer undergo a brain scan, ostensibly to determine if Dahmer was criminally insane when he committed the murders to which he confessed.[25] Such an examination reverberates with historical and contemporary brain and other scientific studies of lesbians and gay men. The interpretation of these diagnoses, prescriptions, and procedures as the discursive legacy of medical and psychiatric pathologizations of homosexuality until only a few decades ago in the United States is also enabled by the fruits of that legacy in the homophobic discourses around Jeffrey Dahmer throughout his life, and the evangelical language in which it is couched: "I should have stayed with God," Dahmer told the court shortly after the above explanation of his actions.[26]

Ironically, the families of Dahmer's (gay) victims used the same language to denounce Dahmer at the trial before sentence was passed on him. Although none said anything explicitly homophobic, homophobia could certainly be construed in their comments. One quoted the Bible, another thanked God for the verdict, while another called Dahmer "El Diablo."[27] My point here is not to guess at what these speakers were thinking or intending, but rather to demonstrate how their language is constructed, represented, interpreted, and analogizable within phobic parameters and to point to the limited availability and uses of linguistic and other resources for generating an oppositional discourse to racialized sexual violence when that oppositional discourse itself fails to account for the multiple imbrications of racial identity with sexual identity for Dahmer and those he killed.

V

While the (mostly unsuccessful) efforts of writers, reporters, and lawyers to degay Dahmer are undertaken in the name of antihomophobic altruism, in fact, they have the opposite effect, not only because homophobic values and assumptions continually break through them, but also because they are used to further demonize Dahmer. Even though everyone knows he is gay, if he isn't represented as gay, liberals don't have to feel bad about bashing him. An influential consequence of these multiple homophobic undercurrents of Dahmer discourse is the erasure of the gayness of those Dahmer killed.

If Dahmer is the monster gay killer, then his innocent victims must be the opposite of him (i.e., they can't also be gay). The multiple efforts to hide and deny the gayness/bisexuality/queerness of many of those Dahmer murdered[28] are not only testimony to the continuing homophobia that might have partly caused Dahmer to kill in the first place, but also to the reality that the degaying of Dahmer is nothing of the sort. If, as I have suggested, the families of those Dahmer murdered use an evangelical and homophobically coded language to denounce Dahmer, then their efforts to present their sons, brothers, etc. as diametrically different from the demonized Dahmer inevitably involve some degree of homosexual panic, often accompanied by varied, sometimes unconscious, and incessantly confused efforts to deny any gayness in their loved ones. As is true for many of those reporting on the case, much of the time these families seemed to be caught between their own homophobia and their need to present those Dahmer murdered as "innocent victims." Like Andrew Burke in the *You* article discussed above they often found that their own homophobia seemed to preclude them from imagining a gay man as an "innocent victim."

Journalists and other writers on the Dahmer case frequently went to some length to heterosexualize those Dahmer murdered. Baumann's book displays the densest signs of homosexual panic in his attempts to heterosexualize as many of Dahmer's victims as he can. For instance, Baumann comments on Konerak Sinthasomphone, "Like many of his American friends, the bright-eyed smiling teenager even had a girlfriend," as if to insinuate Sinthasomphone's heterosexuality is to make him more innocent, and Dahmer, by contrast, more monstrous.[29] The exception to this trend is Anne E. Schwartz, who is so eager to exonerate the police in the Dahmer case that she attempts to demonize those Dahmer murdered by dwelling on their homosexuality and concluding her book with the table of their criminal records. In Schwartz's case, homophobia functions as much to demonize those Dahmer murdered as it functions to normalize them in other accounts.

Many of the families of those Dahmer murdered followed the example of most of the writers, in their attempts to heteronormatize their queer family members. Several of Dahmer's victims were reportedly estranged from families who did not approve of their gayness; several hid their gayness from their families; in one case a victim who escaped did not want to report Dahmer to the police for fear that the publicity would lead to his family's discovery of his queerness.[30] The victims sometimes denied their own queerness. Dahmer's final victim, the man who escaped and lead police to Dahmer, was reputedly heard yelling "I got six kids. I love women. I aint no fag." when police officers arrested Dahmer.[31] After the details of Richard Guerrero's murder were made public, the Guerrero family continued to refuse to believe that Guerrero was gay, or, in any case, to claim not to believe that he was gay. His sister told a reporter,

> I don't believe he had a secret life . . . He was always broke. He never had any money. He had three girlfriends. He spent time with Mom and helped her clean the house and ran

errands for her. Where in the world could he do this secret stuff? Maybe he went in that bar because it was cold and he wanted to wait for the bus. You can't make me believe he was gay. The only way I think Dahmer could have got him was by luring him with money or a party.[32]

In an appearance on a television talk show, the mother of Anthony Hughes, another of the men Dahmer murdered, insisted that her son was not a "homosexual out on the street."[33] It is difficult to tell if the denial here turned on Anthony Hughes not being a homosexual or not being out on the street, or both, but given that Shirley Hughes is "a deeply religious woman who taught a Bible class at Garden Homes Evangelical Lutheran Church in Milwaukee,"[34] it is quite possible that contextual and discursive limitations make it impossible to separate homosexual from out on the street, and that Shirley Hughes herself might be hard-pressed to say exactly which of the terms she was hoping to disidentify from her deceased son. Later on in the same talk show, when Hart D. Fisher, the creator of a controversial Dahmer comic book, defended his representation of Anthony Hughes and of Dahmer's killings on the grounds that his comic was merely presenting the facts of the case, Shirley Hughes interjected, "It's not fact!" Here again the object of her denial is not clear. Was she pointing out that all representation carries a perspective with it, and in that sense cannot be factual or objective, or was she passing judgment on comics as a genre (she admitted to not having seen Fisher's text, but said that a comic book representation of her son was by definition degrading), or was she denying the "fact" that her son was gay (a point that the comic does not make, but that it can be taken to imply in its depiction of the sexual liaisons between Dahmer and those he murdered), or was she denying that he performed specific actions attributed to him, or that he was gay in a certain way? I am suggesting that it is precisely the confusion among these different possibilities, the difficulty of disentangling them from one another, that is symptomatic—for those directly involved in the Dahmer case and for those capitalizing on it and attempting to make sense of it later—of the ways in which Dahmer discourse has brought homophobic and homoerotic representation to an interlocking crisis.

VI

Most accounts of the Dahmer case that do acknowledge the gayness of some of the men Dahmer murdered do so in order to emphasize their victimhood—they are presented as the victims of racist and anti-gay hate crimes. In these accounts, then, there is silence about Dahmer's own gayness so as to polarize Dahmer and his victims, but still the mechanisms of institutional homophobia that demand closetedness, deny gay existence, and normalize heterosexuality are re-enforced in this invisible-making of Dahmer's sexuality. As I suggested with Schwartz above, however, the denial of

Dahmer's gayness can also be used homophobically to pathologize those he murdered. For some right-wing hate groups and individuals, the occlusion of Dahmer's gayness had been so complete that they could praise Dahmer for performing a service to society by killing homosexuals, apparently blissfully unaware that it was another homosexual whom they were celebrating. Martha Schmidt, in her article, "Dahmer Discourse and Gay Identity," cites several instances where gay activists, editors, and publishers in Milwaukee were harassed by homophobic letters and phone calls lionizing Dahmer after the Dahmer story broke. One such caller told a gay newspaper publisher, "[T]oo bad Dahmer got caught when he did. He should have killed more of you faggots. He did a service to the community."[35] Physical assaults against Milwaukee queers also multiplied following news of Dahmer's arrest—whether these homophobic acts were homages to Dahmer or protests against Dahmer is not always clear.[36] Either way, it seems, queer Milwaukeeans lost out: if a queer-basher approved of Dahmer's actions he might bash other queers in imitation of Dahmer (here Dahmer's gayness is conveniently forgotten); if a queer-basher disapproved of Dahmer's actions he might bash other queers as a form of retaliation (here the gayness of those Dahmer murdered is conveniently forgotten). Whereas one set of homophobic representations of Dahmer sees him as a homosexual killer (and not as a killer of homosexuals), in this other set of homophobic representations, Dahmer is a praiseworthy homophobe (and, often, a praiseworthy racist) and nothing else. It is the coming together of homosexuality and homophobia in Dahmer that makes conservative commentary on him incoherent, that makes Dahmer so confusing for many liberal heterosexual commentators, and that makes him so difficult for queer commentators.

The way in which Dahmer confused received wisdom about the discourses of rights, identity, subjectivity, and marginalization, is succinctly illustrated in Don Davis's description of the process of jury selection for Dahmer's trial: "Like a couple of farmers, McCann and Boyle picked through the crop, the D.A. weeding out anyone with a bias against homosexuals, while Boyle discarded those who did not like psychiatrists."[37] McCann, the D.A., weeds out anyone with a bias against homosexuals, presumably in order to generate maximum sympathy for the homosexuals Dahmer murdered—but this tactic can only have meaning if Dahmer's homosexuality is suppressed. Davis's own nonchalant description of the jury selection process surely indicates how successful this strategic suppression was, since it doesn't seem to occur to Davis that Dahmer's own homosexuality might complicate the simplistic binary Davis narrativizes—indeed, he seems to have forgotten, for the moment, that Dahmer himself was gay. Thus Dahmer's gayness was erased as much from the minds of right-wing moralists who saw him as the force of avenging heterosexuality as from the understanding of liberal lawyers apparently outraged by Dahmer's murders of gay men.

The denial of Dahmer's gayness may seem to be more benign than the explicit homophobia that usually accompanies representations of him as gay, but, in fact this denial is very much a part of the fabric of the institutional homophobia that might have been partly to blame for Dahmer's murders in the first place. In a *Chicago Tribune* article on Dahmer, Robert Blau and Jean Latz Griffin quote Bill Williams, a gay activist and music instructor at Columbia College in Chicago: "No one, especially not parents, sits down with a young gay man and says, 'You're starting to date men now. This is how you do it. This is what to be careful of. These are the kind of men to watch out for.'"[38] It is particularly ironic that the writers of this article use this quote to point to the lack of gay mentoring for the men Dahmer murdered, an absence that denied them role models and that may have made it easier for Dahmer to kill them, while the writers fail to acknowledge that Dahmer, too, was gay, and, as accounts of his internalized homophobia suggest, might have benefited from such mentoring. Other representations of Dahmer re-enforce this absence by assuming that Dahmer was heterosexual. Assumptions of universal heterosexuality are common enough, but it is particularly amazing that such assumptions about Dahmer should persist even after his arrest and trial had made his sexual orientation quite clear. Often these assumptions result from a complete inability to imagine the realities of gay identity. In "A Beer and Some Chips with Jeffrey Dahmer," published in *Esquire* magazine in 1995, Vernell Bass recounts a visit he paid Dahmer when he was Dahmer's neighbor years earlier. During his visit with Dahmer, he recalls, he asked Dahmer about his single status and listened to Dahmer mention an ex-girlfriend. He comments, "The only thing that made me wonder about him was the fact that I never saw him with a woman or anyone, but I thought that he could be grieving over his ex-girlfriend." Bass believes that in Dahmer he had a friend with whom he could converse "man to man" whenever he felt like "just talking to another guy away from the wife."[39]

Whether Bass's hindsight is intended to cast critical light on his earlier assumption that Dahmer was heterosexual or whether in 1995 he remained completely uncritical of that assumption is unclear. However, his comments do point in the direction of a myriad of even more stubbornly heterosexual representations of Dahmer. This tendency to assume the universality of a very limited type of heterosexuality develops from the kind of heterocentric naïveté that characterizes many retrospective Dahmer narratives. In a representative instance, Joel Norris's book unquestioningly recapitulates the reports of Dahmer's army buddies in Germany: "Dahmer didn't talk about girlfriends either, friends said, even though they remember that he would sometimes go into town to frequent one of the local female prostitutes."[40] A blinkered reading of what should by now be a familiar narrative of the ways in which many gay men have had to and continue to have to hide their homosexuality and feign heterosexuality in homophobic societies, must ignore the evidence of hindsight suggesting that Dahmer was gay. Norris and Dahmer's "friends" either assume that Dahmer visited female prostitutes or take at face value Dahmer's apparent claim that he did. Whether Dahmer did or not is beside the point; it is the inability here to conceptualize a nonheterosexual subjectivity that is telling. Finally, logically, and most alarmingly, we see the results of the keeping (open) secret of Dahmer's homosexuality in the prison murder of Dahmer himself, and in the way the murder was reported. Because Dahmer's murderer was apparently a black man who hated white people and/or who was enraged by Dahmer's murder of so many men of color [41] the killing is usually seen only as a racial murder. It is seldom spoken of as a possible gay-bashing as well as a racially inflected killing, despite the evidence that Dahmer was subjected to homophobic taunts in prison,[42] and that Dahmer's killer apparently claimed to be the son of God,[43] a chilling throwback to the homophobic evangelical rhetoric around which Dahmer grew up and was sentenced.

VII

The various discourses that highlighted the race of Dahmer and the races of those he murdered, as well as of the person accused of murdering Dahmer himself, while downplaying or denying their sexual orientation, constructed the Dahmer case as racially overdetermined, or, more subtly, as a case of white gay murderousness. This logic implicitly points to Dahmer's gayness by denying or remaining silent about the gayness or bisexuality of most of the men he murdered. On the day that the Dahmer verdict was announced, Rita Isbell, the sister of Errol Lindsey, one of the people Dahmer had murdered, wore a shirt to court with the words 100% BLACK printed on it, as if not only to distance herself from Dahmer's race (and sexuality) with her claim to racial absoluteness, but also to assert race over any other identification. Isbell addressed the court prior to Dahmer's sentencing:

> Whatever your name is, Satan. I'm mad. This is how you act when you are out of control. [*Voice rising*] I don't ever want to see my mother have to go through this again. Never Jeffrey! [*Screaming*] I hate you motherfucker! I hate you![44]

Isbell then charged the defense table and lunged at Dahmer. Ironically, Isbell was demonstrating the possibility of a shared rage with Dahmer ("This is how you act when you are out of control") that, given the legend on her shirt, and Dahmer's internalized homophobia that was not mentioned in court but that may have partly led to his murders, would connect, however crudely, white gay identity with black heterosexual identity, once again at the expense of an inarticulable colored queer identity.

This erasure was exacerbated in the ways in which sexuality as an explicitly named category of identity and analysis fell completely out of the binary in other contexts related to the Dahmer case, as if the difficulty of conceptualizing queer race—conveniently enough—made impossible any kind of conflictual subject positionality (i.e., a situation in which one finds oneself at odds with someone with whom one might in some way identify). The racial polarization was symptomatically re-enacted after Dahmer's trial in the ruckus that erupted around the Dahmer comic book produced by Hart Fisher. While those protesting the comic book on TV talk shows and in a street demonstration outside Fisher's house were overwhelmingly black and presumptively heterosexual, those defending the comic book on TV and in shows of solidarity at Fisher's home were overwhelmingly white and presumptively heterosexual.[45] It was as if not only the media and others responsible for representing the story needed to circumscribe the conflict around one clear set of opposing identities, but also the protestors and counter-protestors themselves were unable to imagine any other way of making politics. That the liberal discourses of identity had learnt nothing from the horrible chain of denials and violence in the Dahmer case was well illustrated by Wisconsin State Representative Gwen Moore's pat reflection on the aftermath: "Everybody was mad at somebody else. It really elucidated the kinds of division that exist within the community, black versus white, homosexual versus heterosexual, the community versus the police, the police chief versus the police union."[46] Once again we are left with discrete oppositions of race and oppositions of sexuality that fail to recognize each other in each other, and that reproduce the understandings of identity that relegated Dahmer's victims to shadow lives long before they met Dahmer himself. The "black versus white" figure also erases other racial identifications and re-centers whiteness by foreclosing any discussion of racial conflict between different peoples of color. This is a familiar collapse in US culture, as has been illustrated in the reduction of the intersecting and competing interests of Korean Americans, Latinas, Whites, and African Americans to a black/white conflict in rhetorical retrospectives of the 1992 Los Angeles uprising.

VIII

Because of the particular (racial and sexual) identities associated with Dahmer and the men he murdered, it is difficult to intervene into dominant Dahmer discourse without restaging racist and/or homophobic desires, fears, loathing, and prejudices. When such interventions are attempted, they inevitably privilege a particular set of alliances over others, thus showing how the inability to think through queer race has drastically limited the kinds of queernesses that can be imagined, and reduced the political potentialities of any identity in which racial and sexual identifications are overdetermined. It is usually clear how the rare right-wing celebrations of Dahmer are racist and/or homophobic, yet it is also true that straight white counter-cultural appeals to Dahmer are compromised insofar as the politics of race and the politics of sexuality make any such appeals transparently suspect, and that white queer Dahmer apologists must be problematized to the extent that an articulation of racial identity will interrogate particular understandings of queerness, queer theory, and queer politics. In this sense, to think through race in the context of queer theory is also to profoundly undermine any singular understanding of the productive negativity in queer.

Given that Dahmer was white and that 14 of the 17 men he murdered were not, and all observations or conclusions about the murders and the case have been racially overdetermined, it is far easier to make a case that Catherine Trammel is an oppositional figure in *Basic Instinct* than it is to read subversion in Dahmer because the men she kills are apparently white, and, to a lesser extent, because they appear to be heterosexual (as I have indicated, there has been a reluctance in various quarters to dwell on the sexuality of the men Dahmer killed, so sexual orientation has become less a site of political significance than race has in the Dahmer case). The cult around Dahmer that has developed in various political and cultural arenas is thus constituted almost exclusively by those who appear to be white and heterosexual. Dahmer received numerous supportive letters and gifts in prison[47] (much of the mail was from women;[48] I have no information on the races of the senders of the letters and gifts). In addition, a more public Dahmer cult developed between the time of his imprisonment and death, and in some cases continues today. Dahmer's Diner, a band from San Diego, California, explains its fascination with Dahmer as a strategy for shocking people: "The thing I think is great is that it just goes against society so hard," one of the band members explains.[49] Whether the "it" here refers to Dahmer's doings or the band's own relationship to Dahmer is unclear, but either way the sentiment seems to be specifically white and heterosexual.[50] To celebrate Dahmer or denigrate those whom such a celebration outrages might be to critique various networks of social hypocrisy and political simplicity, but at the expense of appearing insensitive to already-existing social apparatuses of racism and homophobia. The "Dahmer's Diner" t-shirts that have been sold at the band's performance venues take on a similarly problematic character in the context of the "100% BLACK" shirt worn by Rita Isbell at Dahmer's trial. Despite protestations to the contrary (one band member insisted "It's not that we don't care about the people he killed . . . It's not like, 'They were fags, they deserved it'"[51]), these Dahmer representations cannot escape black/white gay/straight race/sexuality polar inscriptions. They are taken to stand for whiteness against blackness, straightness against gayness, sexuality against race, or race against sexuality, and not, for instance, whiteness against straightness, or straightness against whiteness. Similarly, Jeffrey Dahmer t-shirts bearing the legend "Milwaukee's Best," sold by Boneyard Press, the publisher of the controversial Dahmer comic, could equally be read as a satiric indictment of racism and homophobia in Milwaukee as they could be seen as a celebration of this racism and homophobia.[52]

The difficulty with any kind of Dahmer worship, then, is that while it might contest particular complacencies and bigotries, it is also inevitably racist (and homophobic?). This racial coding is complicated rather than merely re-enforced by the (homo)erotic nature of Dahmer's killings. An exceptional gay celebration of Dahmer is Andrew Holleran's *Christopher Street* article, "Abandoned," in which Holleran argues that Dahmer exemplifies a refusal to tolerate the dominant codes of gay male culture that normalize uncommitted sex and mandate the acceptance of abandonment. Dahmer refused to be abandoned by killing those who would abandon him. Holleran views Dahmer as a subversive figure who refused to play by the rules.[53] Here race and a sexuality that is itself conflictedly politicized override each other. It is difficult to imagine anyone who is not white celebrating Dahmer in this way. In this sense what could potentially be celebrated as a queer perversity is limited by racial specificity.

The notorious Dahmer comic complicates the questions raised by Holleran's article because it is not framed from a gay perspective, and thus cannot be assumed to speak from an antihomophobic politics. A panel in the comic depicts Dahmer performing oral sex on Ricky Beeks, one of the people he murdered.[54] The picture disturbs me not only because I find it erotic, but also because the racial codings of the two figures are so undeniable, emphasized by the sharp color opposition of the black and white drawing. In fact, it is the combination of gay eroticism and racialization that particularly disturbs me. Is this picture merely a depiction of fact, as Fisher claims of the entire comic? Is it an attempt to make Dahmer's crimes attractive? Is it the inextricable intrication of racism with eroticism that is disturbing, or the apparent invitation to separate the two out from each other? Is eroticism even eroticism in this context?

Similar questions could be asked of the intrication of homophobia with homoeroticism in Dahmer's crimes. In an interview with *The Advocate*'s Lance Loud, the director of an independent film on the Dahmer story highlights the unsettling nature of this intrication by referring, perhaps satirically or sarcastically, to the "love scenes" and "cute guys" that are supposed to be a draw in his film.[55] To refer to love scenes in this context is bound to outrage many, and especially anyone associated with those Dahmer murdered, as the reference seems to romanticize the murders and thus see them from Dahmer's perspective. Similarly what is otherwise (probably) mistakenly taken to be a harmless phrase, "cute guys," here seems to see Dahmer's victims from his predatory perspective, or alternately, to see Dahmer himself as an attractive figure, as if he is one of the "cute guys." The shock effect of these phrases depends simultaneously on an ability to separate race from sexuality, and sexuality from other (social, economic, political, cultural) contexts, as well as a discomfort with such a separation. For while the phrases, on their most literal level, speak only to sexuality, as if desire were independent of race or class or politics, they are read as being about race, so the discomfort they create is around racism as much as it is around homoeroticism and/or mass murder. This double bind illustrates the crisis of identity that marks an historical moment in which the politicization of desire (though marking an elusive trajectory) nevertheless is consistently misread, misunderstood, and made impossible demands of.

One of the taboos surrounding the Dahmer case involves the sexual attraction that many white gay men feel toward Dahmer. I have yet to hear a man of color admit to such an attraction. Usually this is something that cannot be spoken publicly, and only with difficulty in private. Holleran's article, in which he describes Dahmer as handsome and confesses, "I'd have gone home with him in a second," is unusual in its public confession of white gay desire for Dahmer.[56] Other kinds of identifications with the Dahmer case point to the ways in which the divergent imbrication of homoeroticism in Dahmer discourse is connected to and symptomatic of apparently anomalous processes of identification and denial. In this sense the logic of queer race not only makes queer identities central to discussions of culture in general, but also metonymically and synecdochically analyzes the coming to political identity of subjectivity in general. For instance, what is a familiar refrain in the representation of serial killers—their ordinariness—has become in the Dahmer case a racially determined identification that gestures to the underlying but even less apparent racial meaning of the familiar theme. To point to the normalcy or everydayness of a serial killer has become part of the chill of and fascination with serial killers. "The lesson from Jeffrey Dahmer's life is that he is no monster at all. He is all too human," Forrest Sawyer concludes his 1993 *Day One* television program on Dahmer.[57] This type of representation of serial killers also allows critique of the social institutions that produced the killer or that symbolically permit their actions, or that the killer is taken to exemplify in her or his everydayness. To claim some connection to a notorious murderer (or any other celebrity) is a commonplace way of attempting to find some fame of one's own. But in the Dahmer case this convention becomes increasingly suspect as the slew of connections and identifications around it points to the racially and often sexually specific permutations of this universalizing logic in other contexts, too.

Processes of identification and disidentification around Dahmer not only have emphasized the precarious nature of ever-anxious distinctions between the normal and the abnormal, but also have closed the gap between the queer and the nonqueer, as queerness comes to stand for the perverse, and as Dahmer fallout queers the ever widening circle of subjects associated with Dahmer as a person, media event, and social phenomenon. What Dahmer's lawyer did unconsciously by attempting to distance himself from Dahmer, other commentators on the case do quite openly. In the trial, the more Dahmer's attorney, Gerald Boyle, attempted to show how abnormal Dahmer was, the more normal Dahmer became. In one particularly disjunctive moment in his closing argument, Boyle tried to prove Dahmer insane by way of contrast with himself: after he used a star chart to adumbrate Dahmer's perverse qualities, explaining that Dahmer's insanity included "masturbating four, three four times a day, two three times a day as youngster ... masturbating all over the place," Boyle continued, "This is Jeffrey Dahmer. My little star, my little circle, would say lawyer, father, sports, happy. I have only positives."[58] Some of Boyle's listeners would no doubt outwardly share his disgust about Dahmer masturbating "all over the place" or "two three times a day" as a youngster, but nevertheless be aware that their own sexual obsessions, and masturbatory desires and practices mark them more like than *un*like Dahmer in this respect. Others might wonder exactly what about masturbating frequently and in various locations is insane, or might quite happily admit that they do so, and question the normalcy of someone who has only "positives." Boyle makes the distinction even more slippery by interspersing the normal ("masturbating ... two three times a day ... masturbating all over the place") with the abnormal ("masturbating into the open parts of a human being's body") in his list of Dahmer's perversities.

The rush to claim kinship with Dahmer has also been more overt. As newspaper reporters remark on how normal Jeffrey Dahmer was, so old acquaintances of Dahmer speak out on their supposed perceptions of him. An academic writer mentions that Dahmer was her friend,[59] and a journalist turned book writer insists on meticulously recounting her own personal involvement in the unfolding Dahmer case.[60] In his book about his son, Lionel Dahmer agonizes over the qualities he shares with Jeff, asking if he might in some way be responsible for his son's crimes.[61] White gay novelist Dale Peck makes the problematic nature of these attractions and identifications more explicit in an article on the aftermath of Dahmer in Milwaukee's lesbian and gay communities he wrote for *Out* magazine. Whether courageously, maliciously, or just rebelliously, Peck continually reminds readers of ways in which he identifies with Dahmer. He mentions the anonymous men he tricked with at the same time that details of Dahmer's crimes were first being made public, he notes that neither he nor Dahmer had a driver's license,[62] and he imagines gay men in Milwaukee "making their way from one kind of ghetto to another, the same way that my tricks and I once made our way to the Folsom."[63] "Jeffrey Dahmer, I remember, seemed quite close to me," he says.[64] As part of his research for the article, Peck visits Milwaukee. He reports on a visit to a "hustler bar":

> There were a couple of black men, one sitting, one leaning against a wall, both waiting. There were a couple of old, drunk, white men, waiting. And there was one young Latino boy who thought his wait was over when I walked into the bar: When I looked at him, he was already looking at me, staring without blinking, and he continued staring until I left the bar. He was handsome but thin, a frail body topped by big, dark eyes. Hatred filled those eyes, I felt, but need overshadowed the hatred, and as I returned his stare I also felt the emotional reality of Jeffrey Dahmer's actions for the first time.[65]

Peck's arrogant assumptions about himself as a white man (the "young Latino boy" must be waiting for him) lead to an identification with Dahmer that allows white ethnocentrism to reproduce itself under the guise of antiracist analysis. Peck is supposedly exposing the racist apparatuses that underlay Dahmer's killings and that foreclosed a vigorous police search for the missing victims. We see here how the various racist dynamics of interracial white gay desire that I explicated in Chapter 3 can even appropriate the kind of antiracist discourse that I suggested was necessary but lacking in those representations of interracial desire. This is not to say that an antiracist interracial desire is not possible, but that race and desire can not be separated from one another insofar as both are always already interlocked in a series of polarities that defines their very existences.

Are these claims to personal acquaintanceship and kinship in sensibility, and these insistences on Dahmer's normalcy, shaped by Dahmer's whiteness and middle-class upbringing where his gayness must, again, be erased? Would these white reporters be so quick to see Dahmer as an Everyman if he were a person of color or a white person from a working or lower-class family? And do the claims of his representativeness also suggest an understanding of normative whiteness as racist whiteness? I wrote in Chapter 2 of the difficulty white people, in particular, experience in delineating the contents of whiteness. When whiteness is delineated it is usually to chart racism. Does whiteness have a content beyond or besides racism?[66] In that chapter I also suggested whiteness was more easily definable in terms of something else, and that whiteness could be substituted for other identities, in that case gayness, in order to link these identities and maintain a reconstituted white hegemony. In the case of Dahmer, if whiteness is to be understood as racist whiteness, then this racism and whiteness are displaced onto a serial killer whose gayness is well-known but little mentioned. Thus, in a reversal of the process of substitution whose workings I illustrated in Chapter 2, where gayness constructs itself in terms of racist whiteness, here racist whiteness envisages itself in terms of gayness. But because race and sexuality are never articulated simultaneously, racism is conflated with gayness itself, rather than with white gayness in particular, and gayness is blamed for racism.

IX

The Dahmer case helps us to redefine queer in several ways. While it suggests the limitations of liberal gay political discourse, to the extent that we interrogate its racialization it also problematizes any easy gay/queer binary by showing the inadequacy of a queerness that is merely reactive to gayness or to anything else, or merely an inverse reclamation of negativity. Thus, whereas in Chapter 2 I pleaded strategically for a politicized understanding of gayness, here it is apparent that even queer, when it is not further elaborated, cannot rescue gay in this regard. Conversely, only to discern queer in terms of a conventional understanding of progressive politics is to impoverish the potential of queer theory to diagnose the function of codifications of desire precisely where such discourses are successively formative: the moments when the meanings of queer generated by the interstices of gay desire and racial identification are most elusive and disturbing. This is something like the invention or discovery of queer race. The queer in queer race is thus doubly queer both insofar as it queers queer and destabilizes the (dis)connection between queer and race.

Chapter 6

Your Picture Here

I

I send an email message to a gay man of color who, at the time, is an acquaintance of mine. (He and I are now lovers. He says he is queer, not gay.) I tell him about Dale Peck's Dahmer article and how I can't make up my mind if the article is very courageous or completely disgusting. (In retrospect I think that one shouldn't overestimate the functional potential of writing, but I assure myself that I would have expressed the same ambivalence to any colleague, no matter what her race might be.) My real conflict is between guilt and outrage. When I rent the Dahmer trial video, the white store clerk makes a comment about one not wanting to go home with Dahmer. I am surprised at how protective I feel about Dahmer. I tell the clerk tersely that since Dahmer is dead this is an impossible scenario. He attempts a mumbled response, but doesn't know what to say. I really want to tell him that Dahmer was gay-bashed (I assume the clerk is straight from what he tells me about his ex-wife). When I request Dahmer books and articles from the interlibrary loan office at the university where I work, the Latino librarian, who never otherwise comments on my orders (or even seems to notice their content), tells me what a monster Dahmer was. I am reminded again, now, of how easy it was for so many people in the United States to point to South African racism in the 1980s, as a way of feeling better about their own country. I wonder if they are disappointed that apartheid is "dead." Once more I feel resentful, and want to defend Dahmer. But on the bus I am trying to hide the cover of the Dahmer book I am reading. Someone on the bus who seems to me to be a straight black woman suddenly laughs. I imagine that she knows what I am reading and that she thinks she knows that I am a gay white man. On the homebound bus that afternoon I am reading the Dahmer book again (why?). A black man moves away from me. Does this have anything to do with the book? I am embarrassed when I buy Dahmer books at the used book store (even though I keep thinking to myself—as I do when I purchase pornography—that I could say that these are research purchases). Why is this? Many people must buy these types of books—every book store has a quite large "true crime" section—but still I wonder what the white clerk is thinking as she rings up my sale. What is so special about Dahmer? Or is this about me being white and gay? Or is it about something else for me? My desire for Jeffrey Dahmer? My desire for Jeffrey Dahmer's desire? I feel sorry for him. I was born in the same year that he was. He played the clarinet;[1] so do I. I am attracted to him, his voice, his glasses at his sentencing.

A reader of this section of this manuscript commends me for attempting to theorize my own identity in relation to this work. I worry that I might be essentializing biology and experience, somehow implying that one writes a certain way because of one's gender and race and sexuality, as if to suggest that an arbitrary list of facts of one's history reductively explain everything. Or hopping on the already-overused feminist/postmodern bandwagon toward self-critical/self-indulgent self-reflexivity.

II

Nevertheless, in the city where I lived just weeks before the verdict in O.J. Simpson's 1995 criminal trial was announced, an African-American woman challenger lost a city council race to an African-American male incumbent councilman. The man, militantly antiracist, was a vociferous homophobe. The woman, also (militantly?) antiracist, claimed to have antihomophobic sympathies. The race for theory.

III

Yom Kippur. Robert Shapiro tells Barbara Walters how offended he is that Johnnie Cochran compared Mark Furhman to Adolf Hitler, and racism to the Holocaust. He says that Cochran believes that everything is about race. He (Shapiro) does not. Much earlier in the trial, Shapiro had passed out fortune cookies to celebrate the discrediting of defense witness Dennis Fong.

Discussion of "the race card" and, later, of reactions to the verdict in the O.J. Simpson trial ignores all races other than whites and African Americans.

IV

The white victims get queerer. Gossip abounds. About white sex. Nicole supposedly had a lesbian relationship with Faye Resnick. Ronald Goldman is rumored to have been gay. My friends and I watch TV and conclude, "Of course he was."

V

In one of my classes I turn on the classroom television set for the announcement of the verdict. The white students are hysterical. An African-American feminist is angered by the verdict. Some of the students of color are shocked. Other students of color are subdued. Outside the classroom white boys are running around campus shouting "Kill O.J.!" Later I find the same words graffitied in the men's restroom near our classroom. Members of the Women's Resource Center march around campus to protest the verdict.

Meanwhile white people on the Oprah Winfrey Show claim that they have never heard white people talking the way Mark Furhman does.

VI

Selected demographics of my neighborhood in the city where, in a different neighborhood, the African-American woman lost the city council race to the African-American man: more men than women live here, more white people than people of color, proportionately more gay people than in most other neighborhoods in this city, more seniors than in most other neighborhoods. This doesn't mean that there isn't also a large population here of women of all genders, races, and sexual orientations, and of gay men of color (men of color of other sexual orientations are not as visible). Almost everyone who lives in a house or apartment here is middle and upper-middle class, though liaisons of passion also mean that some poor people live here with their wealthier lovers (are interclass relationships more common among queers?). One also needs to distinguish between the people who live here and those who come to visit, as tourists, as queerbashers, as diners, as dates, as lovers, as prostitutes, as sex-seekers, as fun-lovers, as "family," as family, as friends, and as fag hags. But, how does one name distinctions that are not necessarily congruent with class, race, gender, and sexual identifications and perceptions?

On the morning of October 4, 1995, the day after the verdict, the neighborhood in which I resided was already plastered with pro-O.J. propaganda. I stumbled across flyers stuck to the streets and sidewalks, and pasted on lamp poles, and on the windows and doors of stores. I tried to pry one off the tarmac, but it was affixed too securely; I only managed to pull away crumbs of paper.

This was not on television.

One of the flyers features a black-and-white photocopied photograph of O.J. Simpson, apparently arm-in-arm with someone else, except that the someone else has been removed—cut out, torn out, covered over—from the picture and replaced with a blank white spot and the legend written in pink on each copy of the flyer, "your picture here." The entire ensemble is framed in a heart, hand-drawn in the same pink marker pen.

Another of the flyers merely reproduces—rather poorly—a photograph of O.J. Simpson, but the pink marker pen has again been used to individuate the production: O.J.'s outline has been pinked, and his lips and eyelashes have also been colored in pink.

VII

Each of the two flyers could mark a queer appropriation of O.J. In the first, bisexual and gay male passers-by are apparently invited to take the place of the dead Nicole, thus fantasizing themselves as O.J.'s lover and articulating male desire for him. Are these men invited to fantasize themselves as women, too? Are men of color invited to fantasize themselves as white, too? In the second, no indirection is required: O.J. is simply pinked and queered. We want him to be queer so we will reveal his queerness—read his queerness—make him queer.

Now although I have called these texts "pro-O.J. Propaganda," a homophobic reading of them could just as easily construct them as anti-O.J. Propaganda. Here the queerification of O.J. Simpson would be seen as an insult to the man himself. An anti-O.J., antihomophobic reading could also see homophobia here; in this case it might be argued that the propagandist is queering O.J. in order to associate queers with murderers. And a racist or antiracist reading of the flyer could note the equation of black people, or black men, with murderers, as the pink in the flyer makes black people, or black men, queer, and can be read as antiracist and antihomophobic, or racist and homophobic. And even if O.J.'s guilt is not assumed, the substitution of a queer man for Nicole in the first flyer carries with it the shadow of homophobic violence: Nicole is dead, in the same way that her queer male replacement is or might be dead, no matter who does the killing. Given the steady stream of queerbashings, and several hate murders, in this neighborhood during my eight year residency here, these homophobic possibilities could carry the weight of urgent warnings or calls to action to resist and end homophobic violence and threats of further bashings.

A homophobic, sexist, and antiracist reading of the flyers could also construct them as anti-O.J., here inserting O.J. Simpson in a tradition of black men who have been either racially supermasculinized or, in this case, racistly feminized, in order to deny their individuality, humanity, and masculinity.

White supremacist readings of the flyers might also construct them as essentially about race, about O.J. as a killer of whites—though the whiteness of Ron Goldman and Nicole Brown-Simpson have not been dwelt on in public nearly as much as O.J.'s blackness has.[2]

An antiracist reading of the flyers might also turn on O.J.'s blackness, specifically O.J. as a killer of whites.

Any reading could associate black people, or black men, with queers, and/or see them as queer.

VIII

Queer gender.

In another setting, the message of the first flyer, "your picture here," could signify heterosexual female desire for O.J. Simpson, and/or would be more readily apparent as a feminist protest and warning against spousal abuse. In this latter case, the implication would be that O.J. was at least guilty of battering Nicole, and women passers-by might already be, or could easily become, like Nicole, victims of domestic violence. (Feminism has helped queers, too. The specter of domestic violence in gay male relationships is also raised if it is the battered Nicole who is imagined to be missing from the picture.) In addition, given the lesbianization of Nicole while O.J. Simpson's trial was in progress, the flyer could be about lesbian-bashing, in particular, or even about O.J. as a lesbian killer.[3] Or as a killer of white lesbians? Or as a killer of upper-class white lesbians?

These readings of the flyer, however, are not uppermost in my mind, given the flyer's multiple placements in a well-known gay male neighborhood, and given the campy trappings of the pink O.J. flyer, which seems to envisage him as a queer rather than a misogynist.

Or a queer misogynist?

The battered Nicole reading does suggest what kinds of appropriations and erasures are often effected in the service of a queer agenda, and how the potential misogyny of such an agenda might further caution against a too easy celebration of the binary-breaking potential of queer. For if the "your picture here" poster allows for the fantasy substitution for Nicole of a gay man of any color, is this substitution not, in fact, dependent on Nicole's murder for its fulfillment? And to what extent can the "your picture here" flyer critique O.J.'s woman-bashing at the same time that it represents gay male desire for O.J. Simpson? The queerifying move, then, allows a gay man to take the place of a woman, or, in a more theoretical vein, we can say that the poststructuralist strain of queer theory ushers in the death of the woman in its insistence on the instability of gender and sexual identities, and its infiltration of queerness into every subject.

The queer substitution in the "your picture here" poster thus not only celebrates the murder of a woman as the condition of its possibility, but also renders women irrelevant in the new gender supermarket, a procedure not unlike those that ignored, demeaned, and erased women in the androcentric gay male organizations, theories, and cultural products that queer is supposed to contest and succeed. Misogynistic queer films like *The Crying Game* illustrate the consequences of this takeover: who needs women, if a man can be as good—or better—a woman than any woman can? (In *The Crying Game*, the unsympathetic female villain is killed off, while the heroic "man" who fools both the audience and his lover into thinking that he is a "woman," stays around to effect more transformations.) The illustration on the cover of this book underscores some of the complexities of this problematic: if Joan Jett-Blakk's militant drag simultaneously undercuts violent masculinity, heterosexual presumption, and black nationalism, while also refiguring politics per se, I intend it, in addition, to signal the further discourses, bodies, dresses, and habits in which it is intricated. The figure of drag, here, draws attention to the production of race and sexuality, and the absence of women, as if its very embodiment of the mutually constitutive components of queer race also point to the infinity of other subjectivities already drawn and waiting to be drawn in their multivariable interdependencies.

Before a fortnight had gone by, the flyers had been defaced and torn up. Vandals? Homophobes? Antihomophobes? Racists? Antiracists? Feminists? Antifeminists? Vigilantes? City clean-up crews?

One of my students tells me that she is not able to turn in her paper because she is currently living in a shelter for battered women.

IX

Meanwhile, in its efforts to illustrate the worldwide attention generated by the O.J. Simpson criminal verdict, ABC News presents snippets from television news programs from around the world. The collage includes South African TV newscaster Riaan Cruywagen speaking in Afrikaans about the verdict (a photograph of O.J. in the corner of the South African TV screen presumably clues non-Afrikaans-speaking US viewers in on this). To show how worldwide reaction to the verdict illustrates racial polarization to the same extent that US reactions do, ABC News shows a group of black South African men cheering as the verdict is announced. To illustrate its claim that worldwide reaction is also mixed, ABC News shows two black South African men criticizing the verdict.

The theme of San Francisco's 1995 Lesbian, Gay, Bisexual, and Transgender Pride Celebration Parade and Festival is "A World Without Borders." Books and articles about "The Global Village of Gay/Lesbian Rights" are flourishing in the United States.[4] In a San Diego gay newspaper in June 1995, a picture from the recent pride parade in neighboring Tijuana, Mexico, is captioned "Reminiscent of the first San Diego Pride Parade in 1975, approximately 150 people gathered for the first ever Tijuana Gay Pride Parade on Saturday, June 15."[5] Clearly, the United States is the only model for anyone else to follow. In 1994, the 25th anniversary of Stonewall, pride parades around the United States were organized around the theme "A Global Celebration of Pride and Protest." A December 1995 capsule article in a Southern California gay newspaper is entitled "British Gays to Colonize Island." Apparently, gay activists plan to protest Britain's restrictive immigration laws by occupying the island of Lundy, erecting a gay flag, printing gay money, and issuing gay marriage licenses.[6] In 1996, the theme of the Los Angeles Gay and Lesbian Pride Celebration is "Pride Without Borders." I receive an email about a new book series from The University of Chicago Press: *Worlds of Desire*. In the meantime, US gay tourists and gay do-gooders, and, increasingly now, but still in smaller numbers, lesbian tourists and do-gooders from the United States, travel in record numbers to Third World countries to sightsee and to help establish gay organizations in those countries. Mexico continues to receive huge loans from the United States.

X

My encounters with queer O.J. and the routes to and from which these encounters have connected, reflect some of my adumbrations of queer race in this book, and gesture toward responses to some of the questions suggested by these. The queering of O.J. shows how the critical intervention of race as an analytic category queers queer theory to the extent that it makes it queerer. This is not to say that race is otherwise not present as an analytic category, for, as I have argued throughout this study, race is always present, at least in cultures that have been shaped by various histories of racism. But it is the interventive explicit-making of critical assumptions based on racially specific understandings, experiences, and agendas, that localizes, multiplies, fragments, and ultimately strengthens a theoretical enterprise seeking both to create and contest epistemologies of social identity and cultural interpretation. Nor is this to say, then, that race alone challenges queer theory to take itself seriously, for, as I have urged in the case of O.J. Simpson, distinctions of gender also make queer theory queerer inasmuch as they engender race and reshuffle racial alliances.

To the extent that queer race privileges some axes of analysis (sexuality, race) over others (gender or class, for instance), it will be limited by the same kinds of exclusions that it points to in critiquing contemporary discourses of race and sexuality. To the extent that the terms of queer race can be shown to stand for, depend on, and infer other terms, queer race is much queerer than that reading of its limitation suggests. My particular project in this book has been both to make specific arguments about the imaginative conjunction of race and sexuality as well as to derive general principles about the workings of culture in and through identity as it is constructed by political and intellectual discourses, and vice versa. It is deluded to think that one can talk about everything, though one hopes that one's local analysis will have theoretical significance. A book on queer gender, or queer class, or gendered class, or classed race, or gendered race (etc.), or on three or more of these overdetermined accumulations of power relations would obviously look different from this one, although its conclusions about the ways in which identity is constructed in culture might be similar, albeit that sexuality, race, class, gender, etc. function specifically and differently in configuring inside and outside, personal and political, and so on.

While my interest in this book has been in the racial permutations of particular theoretical lacunae, the racial inflections of selected cultural sites of queerness, and the implications of these permutations and inflections for the productive and interpretive project called queer theory, and while these implications speak to understandings and constructions of raced sexuality and sexualized race, queer race itself has also made it clear that there is no ultimate analytic axis that will once and for all stabilize the work of queer theory. (That is, of course, unless this instability itself is seen as a constant.) As each distinct, yet arbitrary, focus produces a particular set of conclusions and problems, so each will also overlay and point to an infinite multiplication of problems and conclusions activated by the categories it interrupts, contains, comprises, and those which critically contest the focus itself.

Thus I cannot say that questions about various constructions of Jewish identity or a commitment to the contestation of anti-Semitism are irrelevant to queer theory any more than I could imagine these apparently secondary concerns to be peripheral to O.J. discourse. In Chapter 2, I showed how gay desire in/for South Africa per se is contingent on a presumptively heterosexual regimen of imperialist and racist relations in and between the United States and South Africa. In the case of Dahmer discourse I argued that each effacement of the logics of race or sexuality created identifications and alliances that themselves spoke to a relation of power with the effaced dynamic (Chapter 5). The entire arena of desire in the interracial gay texts examined in Chapter 3 is also particularly masculinized. Each instance of racial desire is filtered through unique assumptions about the gendering effects of particular racial qualities; perfect "masculinity" is almost always the ultimate goal for the characters, authors, and intended readership of the texts of these representations. This is a race-gender effect whose collusive, genocidal consequences are charted in Anzaldúa's perverse invocation of a feminine/feminist universalism in *Borderlands/La Frontera* (Chapter 4). Queer theory must initiate the domino effect as part of its queerness.

What queer race does for queer theory, then, is to show how the "queer" of queer theory cannot stand alone, or at least how it cannot stand for sexuality alone. If queer theory challenges or should challenge globalizing impulses in sexuality studies to instead generate queer sexualities (i.e., sexualities that are as different from each other as they are different from a putative hegemonic norm), then queer race both undergirds and undermines this differential process by further fragmenting queerness, by unqueering queerness (i.e., by eroding sexuality as a unique ground of knowledge), and by pointing to the irretrievable interpenetration of queerness with "other" markers of identity and hence situating queerness and queer theory in their global contexts.

Concomitantly, as queer race transmutes queer theory, so queer theory resituates race as always already sexualized and potentially queer. The pink O.J. flyer is an attention-getter because of the ways in which it manipulates narrow understandings of race and sexuality: it draws attention to the fact that representations of O.J.'s blackness, masculinity, and heterosexuality, are as inextricably tied to one another as they are interdependent on Nicole's whiteness, and supposedly questionable femininity and heterosexuality. The probability that insinuations of Nicole's lesbianism sit far more easily than representations of O.J.'s gayness, can be read to explain as much about race as about gender, testifying not only to what I identified in Chapter 2 as sexuality and race's reliance on each other for mutually constitutive and sustaining compasses, but also to the lamentable consequence of monodirectional narratives of subjectivity, a consequence that I have variously identified and elaborated throughout this book: the erasure of queers of color from theoretical paradigms, cultural representations, and imagined identifications that rely on separately conceptualized components of subject formation, ranging from crude appeals to identity politics to poststructuralist articulations of desire. In addition, as anyone who was not black or white was excised from the polarized political and intellectual discourse about the 1992 Los Angeles uprising, and about the 1992 Dahmer trial, so here one set of oppositions must cancel out all others as the condition of its definition: black women disappear from the O.J. Simpson trial as completely as it renders any possibility of queer black men unthinkable.

XI

Over a year later, though, after the civil trial, just after his Rockingham mansion has been auctioned off, O.J. says faggily on television that he hopes to have as much fun wherever he goes as he had at Rockingham.

XII

Finally, then, the instabilities of queer theory produced by its collision with queer race might suggest that queer theory is forever relegated to a state of fragility, self-reflexivity, multiplication, and disintegration, with the crucial proviso that these qualities be seen as strengths rather than weaknesses in queer theory, at the same time that they also reconfigure queer theory itself. Rather than thinking of queer theory as challenged by or even transformed by queer race (this would already be to concede queer theory to whiteness), we might want to think of this reconstituted thing *as* queer theory, analogously to thinking of critiques of white feminism in the 1970s and 1980s by feminists of color as primary feminist practice rather than as an addendum to an already centered (white) feminism.

XIII

Queer race, therefore, cannot indicate a descriptive, resolutional, or finite theory of race, insofar as race itself must be deconstructed as much as sexuality is when the two collide. Rather than attempting to finesse a substantial, practical, or ingenious global closure to the multiplying subjects and multidirectional problems and possibilities posed by queer race, I have illustrated how the questions raised in specific cultural productions of queerness and in the enabling possibilities of reading culture queerly, open up the complexities of queer theory in general. This is not to deny the substantive explanatory potential of a race-sex breakdown of selected cultural phenomena: I have shown, for instance, how the silent articulation of whiteness as gayness attempts to disable an antiracist queer critique of racialized institutions and of the institutionalization of queerness, how the working through of racial difference, rather than its disavowal, generates a politically rich understanding of queer race, and how the displacement of feminism onto racial politics can re-imagine/realign queerness as an historicized but non-essentialist counter-identity-in-process. It is, rather, to understand these interventions into various cultural discourses as a methodology of cautionary and ongoing disruptions whose coherence lies not in generalizable empirical results but in the theoretical procedures they model.

The particular cultural texts that I have examined have been produced by, in, for, and against an English-speaking metropolitan West, and as such make the extension of queer theory's racial content to the politics of (post)colonial internationalism coterminous with queer theory's own constitution in the sites of knowledge that have informed and exposed that imperialist advance. In *Culture and Imperialism*, Edward Said points out that in the late twentieth century the Unites States became the preeminent imperial power. The subjects of my own study, centered there, necessarily speak of the imperialist projection in queer theory, even as this theory critiques an apparently heterosexual and sometimes homoerotic Western colonialism.

This personal/political analogous/conflictive collusion was exemplified in the timely tabloid queer-trashing of Manuel Noriega and Saddam Hussein[7] (each exposed as a transvestite who has sex with boys or men) soon after the United States attacked their countries in 1991, and in gay male desire for Dahmer and O.J. These two kinds of queer reading came together as "terrorism" irrupted in the domestic sphere: a May 1995 *Globe* report "revealed" suspected (since convicted) Oklahoma City bomber Timothy McVeigh's "kinky obsession" with fellow suspect Terry Nichols[8] at the same time that some gay men were infatuated by the white, boyish, crew-cut McVeigh's television images, an infatuation that had subversive potential in the context of the mainstream media's racist and imperialist first assumption that the bombing had been the work of Middle-Eastern terrorists.

That the 9/11 2001 attacks should not only generate worldwide interest, but that US news stations should laud this interest, is indicative of the ways in which cultural imperialism undergirds the production of calculated knowledge bases which, in turn, shape political aspirations and formations. Given the work of queer theory in rereading popular culture (i.e., the very antiseparatist ideology that distinguishes queer theory from some other paradigms of sexual identity), and my own suggestion of the cross-categorical formative relevance of anomalous axes of power, oppression, and resistance, queer reading must be understood, in addition to and by way of its other effects (including its scorn for simplistic First World–Third World binaries that envision knowledge and appropriation working only unidirectionally), as in some way underscoring that colonizing imperative.

Said also argues for the crucial role of culture in the West to fashion the understoodness of imperialism or in the Third World to disperse anti-imperialist counter-narratives (though Said's definition of culture is narrow and elitist in its traditionalism). These congruencies point to one of the possible characteristics of queer that I did not outline in my Chapter 1 definition of the term: its concern with culture and interest in style. Thus the theatrical and media-hungry antics of direct-action visibility groups in the United States like ACT UP, Queer Nation, and the Lesbian Avengers, that spurn a more traditional politics of rallies and marches,[9] and the supposedly narrow obsession of queer theorists with rhetoric and representation. In their argument for the contributions that sociology can make to queer theory, Arlene Stein and Ken Plummer recapitulate what has by now become a common complaint—especially by social scientists and humanists hostile to poststructuralism—against queer theory:

> Queer theorists . . . appreciate the extent to which the texts of literature and mass culture shape sexuality, but their weakness is that they rarely, if ever, move beyond the text. There is a dangerous tendency for the new queer theorists to ignore "real" queer life as it is materially experienced across the world, while they play with the free-floating signifiers of texts. What can the rereading of a nineteenth-century novel really tell us about the pains of gay Chicanos or West Indian lesbians now, for example? Indeed, such postmodern readings may well tell us more about the lives of middle-class radical intellectuals than about anything else![10]

I hope that this book has demonstrated that the multiply interlocking ways in which various discourses (i.e., those of race and sexuality, and those of text and reality) shape each other, make the distinction between text and what is beyond the text hard to sustain. Indeed, it is difficult not to suspect that Stein and Plummer's trite and reifying understanding of "the pains of gay Chicanos or West Indian lesbians" comes from text rather than fieldwork. This is not to say, of course, that fieldwork is unmediated, untextualized, or less prone to make colonizing assumptions than the reading of books. My own focus on culture is meant to show precisely that our "readings" of culture themselves entertain culture's reading(s) of the "real."

The texts of popular culture and high culture that I have examined reveal not only how discursive assumptions about race and sexuality transactively shape people's choices, actions, and beliefs but also that the "structures of attitude and reference"[11] informing productions of popular culture and the conclusions of intellectual work are much more contiguous than is commonly assumed. Theoretical aporia allow for derivative slips in compilations of community, and vice versa. Chapter 2 demonstrated how identity can mutate as it appropriates and replaces other identities: as specific understandings of race and sexuality can come to stand for each other, so both the arbitrariness of the delineations of these identities and the potential linkages between them point to the precariousness of all epistemologies of race and sexuality. In Chapter 4 I also identified a process of identity displacement, substitution, and hermeneutic crossing in Gloria Anzaldúa's *Borderlands/La Frontera*. But here the effect was to self-critically politicize and politically self-fashion subjectivity, unlike the monocausal freezing of sexuality into race discussed in Chapter 2. The crucial qualifications attached by other terms (gender, class) enables this connective refining of political desires, showing again how the meaning of queer identity and queer theory is always different and always dependent on the additional lenses through which its self-constitution and analysis is filtered. The ease with which queer O.J. can be read homophobically or antihomophobically is a product of conceptions of and agendas for particular racial identities and affiliations, as the significance of his gender depends on the situational relationship of queer theory to feminism, and in the same measure that racist and antiracist readings of O.J. depend unreductively on the sexual situatedness of O.J. Simpson, the reader, and the reading.

Contrarily, in Chapters 3 and 5 I argued that racialized gay desire is locked into predetermined parameters of meaning. But to concede that this desire is either always racist or never racist (see Chapter 3) or to evacuate race or sexuality from the scene in an attempt to circumvent these predeterminations (see Chapter 5) is only further to entrench the dichotomies that a discourse of queer race must unsettle. Politicizing desire, on the other hand, allows for a productive intervention of race-based analysis into queer desire, albeit at the expense of fracturing the utopian political dream of a coherently contestatory queer epistemology. In juxtaposing Chapters 4 and 5, then, we can see very different effects of a queer hermeneutics. In the first case, the skeptically anti-assimilationist and radically-connective sensibility of queer creates an understanding of political alliance and an experience of multiple subjectivity that could inform a postmodern democratic activism; in the second, this same skepticism is amenable to a monstrous devouring of difference within the very multiplications of identity that queer generates. Even as "queer" designates alterity, both in the sense of alterity signaled by categories like lesbian and gay, and in the sense of subaltern oppositionality to those categories, the force of that alterity (while epistemologically consistent) is not politically predictable. Queer theory must chart the logic of these different effects rather than assume an amenable outcome. Hence the queering of O.J. Simpson does not have a clear-cut re-evaluative effect: while it can act subversively to unsettle race/sex binaries, to contest heterocentric presumption in general, and to interrogate rigid assumptions about the appearance and performance possibilities of gender, it can also use racism and homophobia to mutually re-enforce one another as they are inflected by a misogynistic common ground. What is significant is the formative role that each pole plays in the understanding of the others, no matter what the outcome.

To think of the pink O.J. flyers as an in(ter)vention of queer race analogous to my own project in this book is to understand the uncomfortable context in which I situate such an undertaking. The pinking of O.J. Simpson, whether a reclamation or an instigation, is never amenable to a wholly benign reading given the gendered violence that enabled it (whether O.J. is guilty of the murders or not), the fraught race relations that color any interpretation of it, and the overt or subconscious racism that informs much anti-O.J. rhetoric. Commenting on a talk that Sister Souljah gave at Hampshire College, during the course of which Sister Souljah's homophobia caused some confusion among audience members, E. Frances White concludes,

> I have to say that while in some ways I was really upset by the homophobia that was revealed, I was also actually heartened by the way that sexuality disrupted something. It created a kind of mobilization, towards identifications across narrow boundaries. To me what is posed is a kind of almost negative tension between race and sexuality.[12]

I have set out to capitalize on this kind of negative tension in this book. My purpose has not been to entertain queer race as coming to the rescue of queer theory, as finally fixing inequities, or quelling voices of dissent and (out)rage. Rather, I have used queer race as an abrasive to intensify these conflictive intersections, for it would be politically naive, as well as intellectually dishonest and personally unsatisfying to me to wrap up queer. This would be to betray the very difference of queer—its refusal to ignore negativity, its distrust of happy endings, its renunciation of false unity, its retreat from finity.

Notes

Chapter 1

1. Steven Epstein's much-cited essay, "Gay Politics, Ethnic Identity: The Limits of Social Constructionism" (1987) is already the classic postulation of this analogy. More recently in his *Homos* (1995), Leo Bersani seems to be aware of the need to account for queers of color by explicitly discussing the positions of black gay men and lesbians, yet still lapses into binaries pitting "blacks" against "gays" and "black homophobia" against "gay racism" that once again erase the identities of queers of color (62). In a 1992 OUT/Write panel, Margaret Cerullo (Harper, White, and Cerullo, "Multi/Queer/Culture"), pointed to two topical places where this opposition erases queers of color by constructing gay as white: the question of whether lesbian/gay should be recognized as an affirmative action category (the question itself assumes that racial affirmative action categories do not include lesbians and gay men); and the separate categorizations of AIDS as a "gay epidemic" and an "epidemic among people of color" by "the mainstream" and by AIDS activists (32, 33). For further discussion of the ways in which gayness is constructed as white, see E. Francis White's contribution to the panel (34–36). Regarding the black gay vs. gay black debate, which pits gay identity against black identity in order to determine which is more formative, see L. Lloyd Jordan (1990). He is equally unable to conceptualize an independent subjectivity for queers of color. Commenting on the way in which lesbian sexuality has been theorized independently of coloredness, and vice versa, Sagri Dhairyam (1994) writes of the difficulty of articulating "a lesbian self over the complex resistance of a colored body" (25).
2. Siobhan Somerville (1994) has shown how, in fact, "the classification of bodies as either 'homosexual' or 'heterosexual' emerged at the same time that the United States was aggressively policing the imaginary boundary between 'black' and 'white' bodies" (245), and how ideologies of race and sexuality reflected each other in popular and scientific discourses in the late nineteenth and early twentieth centuries in the United States. For a description of the ways in which black culture constructed and influenced homosexuality in the United States, see Mumford (1996). Mumford notes that in the early twentieth century, homosexuality was conceptualized in terms of race. Black and homosexual geographic spaces blurred, and social scientists argued that color difference substituted for gender difference in homosexual relationships. I discuss this process of substitution, but of sexuality for race rather than of race for sexuality, in Chapter 2.

3. An important recent exception to this trend toward insulation is the collection edited by Blount and Cunningham, *Representing Black Men* (1996).
4. For critiques of white queer theorists who do not adequately treat race, see Yarbro-Bejarano (1995) and Muñoz (1999), 11.
5. De Lauretis, "Sexual Indifference and Lesbian Representation" (1993), 148.
6. Ibid.
7. For some accounts of this racism in political activism and cultural production, as well as in white lesbian and gay intellectual work, see the following: Hemphill (1991); Jordan (1990); Manalansan (1993, 1994); Alonso and Koreck (1989); Omosupe (1991); Gupta (1989); Ratti (1993); Hammonds (1994); Beam (1986); Goldsby (1990); Ma (1992); Chin (1991); Nguyen (1993, 1994); Fung (1991, 1993); Chee (1991); Anzaldúa, "Bridge, Drawbridge, Sandbar or Island: Lesbians-of-Color Hacienda Alianzas" (1990) and "To(o) Queer the Writer—Loca, escritora y chicana" (1991); Anzaldúa and Moraga (1983); Gomez (1988); Segrest (1993); Melvin Dixon, "Other Voices, Other Rooms: An Interview with Melvin Dixon"; Cornwell (1979); Dotton (1975); Dhairyam (1994); Fernández (1991); Roscoe (1988); Landers; Mackey, "Life Behind the Bars" (1990) and "A Promise" (1990); Vaid (1995), 274-306.
8. See Patton (1993).
9. In Sandra Tsing Loh's 1994 *Buzz* article on the lesbianization of the annual *Dinah Shore Golf Tournament* in Palm Springs, California, lesbian comic and entrepreneur Robin Tyler is quoted as saying,

> What's reflected in Dinah Shore is an international, global movement. Our space has moved from bars to festivals to cruises to international travel. Lesbian life has changed from movement to industry. Traditional business finally sees us as a market. After all, the average annual income of a gay household is forty-two thousand dollars, lesbian thirty-six thousand dollars. Compared with the average American household's thirty thousand dollars, we have a lot of disposable income! (64)

Tyler's words symptomatically reflect the uncritical acceptance on the part of lesbian and gay public figures of (sometimes homophobic) reports of lesbian and gay economic prosperity. These are reports that necessarily ignore the voices of closeted queers or queers who for other reasons do not have access to the reporters' figures. There is an equal complacency on the part of the avowedly heterosexual writer who quotes Tyler.
10. See Hammonds (1994), especially 128, for further discussion of the unspoken whiteness of the canonical categories of much queer theory.
11. As I wrote this introduction I contemplated characterizing *Update* for readers who might not be familiar with this publication. Given my agenda of exposing the exclusions that undergird most political and cultural work that presents itself as "lesbian and gay," I could not honestly describe *Update* as "a San Diego lesbian and gay newspaper." It was tempting, then, to try to identify and articulate its focus and exclusions. I could have attempted to name the narrowness of its scope by referring to *Update* as "a middle-class white gay male newspaper," but even this is an imprecise generalization, given the important differences in political and religious affiliation, age, citizenship status, physical and mental abilities, and so on, among middle-class white gay men. In fact, I realized that there is no finitely delimiting list of defining differences, and that my efforts to pin them down were symptomatic of the seductive promise of empowerment through communal identity and of the power of the politics of categorical unity that I am critiquing. I have resisted the urge to (unsuccessfully) delineate *Update*'s constituency, instead leaving that

marker "gay" which includes all the possibilities that that gay and those quotation marks invoke and exclude.

12. The title of the column itself points to the problematic I am identifying. Both the words "tribal" and "rites" (which the "Writes" alludes to) conjure up a fixed and self-contained community of identicality in the tradition of Western ethnographers and anthropologists who reify and reduce Third World peoples and cultures. The title "Tribal Writes" in Norman's column constructs the gay community's uniqueness by erasing the identifications and traditions from other "communities" that subjects might bring to queerness (for instance, communities of color, and lesbian feminism). This is a common conceit for many white gay men, and, to a lesser extent, for white lesbians, as the latest spate of books on so-called worldwide lesbian and gay cultures, and lesbian and gay communities in the United States attest. Frank Browning's *The Culture of Desire: Paradox and Perversity in Gay Lives Today* (1994) comes to mind here: even to ask the question, "Do the subculture and life-style of urban gay life in America . . . constitute an actual culture comparable to other ethnic and racial cultures . . . that make up the heterogeneity of modern American life?" (1) as Browning does to set out the agenda of his book, is to normalize middle-class white gay maleness and obliterate, inter alia, queers of color, in the same way that efforts to analogize gay/lesbian identity with ethnic identity must separate the categories in order to make analogy possible.

13. In describing Norman I faced difficulties similar to those enumerated in note 11 above with regard to my characterization of the newspaper *Update*. I have chosen to highlight those constructions of identity and those components of Norman's personal identity that I feel are most pertinent to the present discussion.

14. Norman (1992).

15. Seidman (1994), 172.

16. Seidman (1994), 173.

17. Ibid.

18. Epstein (1994), 196.

19. See Dev (1990-1991) and Gómez-Peña (1989) for some antiracist arguments against multiculturalism as the term is popularly deployed in the United States.

20. Gevisser, "A Different Fight for Freedom: A History of South African Lesbian and Gay Organisation—the 1950s to the 1990s" (1994), 29.

21. For additional general discussion of gay US imperialism, see Altman, "On Global Queering" (1996). The dangers of a lesbian and gay theory that seeks to discover the culturally constructed specificities of sexual identity but within the methodological framework of a Western epistemology, are discussed by Hanawa (1994), Almaguer (1993), and Gutíerrez (1989). Leyva (1996) specifically addresses the ways in which racing queer studies means questioning hegemonic lesbian and gay epistemologies, and critiques the "white people did it first" presupposition informing much lesbian and gay studies. For further criticism of universalizing tendencies in lesbian and gay studies see Smith and Bergmann (1995). Writing specifically about Spain and Spanish-speaking Latin America, Smith and Bergmann also point out that even queer theory, in its efforts to decolonize sexuality studies, may be instituting a neo-colonial order by first, questioning "the continuity and integrity of identity and community," and thereby undermining the already tenuous political agency of Spanish-speaking lesbians and gays (2-3), and second, launching a critique of an identity that has never existed in Spanish-speaking cultures in the first place (10). In the context of the United States, James Earl Hardy's novel *2nd Time Around* (1996) makes the point that black gayness may be so different from white gayness that the (white) word "gay" is inappropriate to describe black gayness ("queer" fares no better) (126-130).

22. Chris Berry, "Sexual DisOrientations" (1996), 173. See the following for refutations of the claims that "postmodernism" and "theory" are Western inventions: Bhabha (1988); hooks, "Feminist Theory: A Radical Agenda" (1989); Trinh (1985).
23. Chris Berry, "Sexual DisOrientations" (1996), 176.
24. As Haney López, "The Social Construction of Race" (1995), writes, "There are no genetic characteristics possessed by all Blacks but not by non-Blacks; similarly, there is no gene or cluster of genes common to all Whites but not to non-Whites" (194). See also his "White by Law" (1995). For further discussion and illustration of the construction of race in the United States, see also the following: Omi and Winant (1994); Gates (1992); Moraga (1983); Appiah (1992). For exemplary accounts of the textual and other effects of the discursive construction of race, see Gates (1986) and Said, *Orientalism* (1979). For a critique of Appiah's argument, see Jayne Chong-Soon Lee (1995). For a concatenated history of the concept of race, see Appiah (1995).
25. "Queer is not a Substitute for Gay" (1993).
26. For some other related definitions and discussions of queer, queer politics, and Queer Theory see the following: Seidman (1994); Stein and Plummer (1994); Savage and Julien (1994); Epstein (1994); Edelman (1995); Weston (1995); Abelove, "Critically Queer: Interview with Henry Abelove" (1995) and "The Queering of Lesbian/Gay History" (1995); Jagose (1996); Altman, "On Global Queering" (1996); (Charles) (1993); Smith and Bergmann (1995); Sedgwick, "QUEER SEX HABITS (Oh, no! I mean) SIX QUEER HABITS: Some Talking Points" (1995); Berry and Jagose (1996); Harper, White, and Cerullo, "Multi/Queer/Culture"; Anzaldúa (1991); Angelides and Bird (1995); Penn (1995); Butler (1993); de Lauretis (1991); Doty (1993); Duggan (1992); "Forum on the Political Implications of Using the Term 'Queer,' as in 'Queer Politics,' 'Queer Studies,' and 'Queer Pedagogy'" (1994); Warner, "Introduction: Fear of a Queer Planet" and "From Queer to Eternity: An Army of Theorists Cannot Fail" (1992); Halperin (1995), 62-67; Smyth (1992); Barry (1995), 143-48; Bianco (1996); Rashid (1995); Berlant and Warner (1995); Hall (2003), 1-111; Hawley (2001); "Queer is not a Substitute for Gay" (1993).

Various kinds of conflations of "queer" with "lesbian/gay" saturate popular and academic discourse. As I have indicated, this equation is not necessarily a bad thing, but its consistency does conceal the potential uniqueness of "queer," and forfeits the articulation of a specifically queer politics. For instance, Bill Stella's "Manifesto For Progressive Queers—A Pro-Active Agenda," *E-Directory of Lesbigay Scholars* (1994), seems to miss the opportunity to situate "queer" as a promiscuous radical corrective to assimilationist gay organizing by asserting, "Queer couplehood is a right." Except for two articles, the second Queer Theory special issue of *differences* collapses "queer" into "lesbian/gay." The two exceptions are Teresa de Lauretis, who renounces "queer" in favor of "lesbian," and Evelynn Hammonds, who writes about the possibility of "queer" articulating a racialized theory of sexuality that lesbian and gay studies has failed to do. In the queer theory issue of *Sociological Theory*, Steven Epstein's overview article sets up a queer/straight dichotomy, thus implicitly allowing "queer" to do the same work that "gay" would do in such a binary. John Champagne in *The Ethics of Marginality: A New Approach to Gay Studies* (1995), conflates gay and lesbian studies with queer theory/studies, often using the terms interchangeably, and even explicitly indicating this interchangeability in the phrase "gay and lesbian studies and/or 'queer theory'" (xlvi). Donald Morton, in his introduction to *The Material Queer: A LesBi-Gay Cultural Studies Reader* (1996), mentions queer as antagonistic to lesbian/gay, but goes on to conflate the categories when he attacks both discourses. In "Birth of the Cyberqueer" (1995), Morton also equates gay with queer in order to attack the latter. As part of this critique, Morton cites as prime examples of queer theory the work of Frank Browning and Dennis Cooper—but Browning's liberal rather than radical politics would make him more gay than queer, and Cooper, a poet and fiction writer, could hardly be thought of as an exemplary illustration of the category "theory." Morton goes on to criticize queer activists for protesting the supposed homophobia of the film *Basic Instinct*. While it is true that Queer Nation, as well as more conservative groups like the Gay and Lesbian Alliance Against Defamation criticized the film, Morton ignores cultural critics-activists identified with a "queer" sensibility who defended the film. See Barnard (1992), Halberstam (1992), and B. Ruby Rich, "Reflections on a Queer Screen" (1993).

Some writers do attempt to distinguish queer from lesbian/gay, but often only some distinctions are made, and other possible differences are ignored. For instance, while de Lauretis's introduction to the first Queer Theory issue of *differences* does articulate an important epistemological shift from lesbian and gay to queer, nevertheless, as the subtitle of the special issue indicates ("Lesbian and Gay Sexualities"), de Lauretis does not include sexualities other than lesbian and gay in her queer agenda. Similarly, in their introduction to the "Critically Queer" issue of *Critical Quarterly*, Jon Savage and Isaac Julien use "queer" to define a new post-gay aesthetics that embraces the negative, the marginal, and the radical, but in terms of the sexualities it encompasses queer is still short-hand for lesbian and gay here—only lesbian and gay identities and sexualities are at stake.

27. For discussion of gay male sexism, and other arguments for the unique and discrete theorizations of the categories "lesbian" and "gay," see the following: Frye, "Lesbian Feminism and the Gay Rights Movement: Another View of Male Supremacy, Another Separatism" (1983); Adrienne Rich (1980); John Morrison; Preston; Zimmerman (1993) For further discussion of the gender of queer theory, see Butler (1994).
28. For instance, the most visible protestors of the theme of San Francisco's 1993 Lesbian and Gay Pride Parade—"The Year of the Queer"—were middle-class white gay men. For further articulations of the intellectual and activist positions for and against "queer" see "Forum on the Political Implications" (1994) and the letters to the editor in the November 1993 and March 1994 issues of the *Lesbian and Gay Studies Newsletter*.
29. Andrew Parker, contributor to "Forum on the Political Implications" (1994), 55.
30. Cf. Foucault's insistence that "homosexuality is not a form of desire but something desirable" in "Friendship as a Way of Life" (1989), 204. Foucault is considered by many to be the immediate founding inspiration for much of what goes by queer theory today. For accounts of Foucault's role in this regard, see Warner (1992) and Sedgwick (1991).
31. Edelman (1995), 343.
32. Ibid.
33. Harper, "Multi/Queer/Culture," 29.
34. See Anzaldúa (1991, 1999)
35. Anzaldúa (1999), 25.
36. (Charles) (1993), 103.
37. See de Lauretis (1991), xvii, Note 2.
38. I am indebted to Bérubé and Escoffier's article "Queer/Nation" (1991) for this observation regarding Queer Nation's name.
39. Hall (2003), 86.
40. Anzaldúa (1991), 251.
41. Since this assumption is so pervasive, I will merely cite some paradigmatic examples here. Steven Epstein, in "A Queer Encounter" argues, "The challenge that queer theory poses to soci-

ological investigation is precisely in the strong claim that no facet of social life is fully comprehensible without an examination of how sexual meanings intersect with it" (197). Similarly, all the articles in the 1995 "queer issue" of *Radical History Review* envisage queer as a question of sexual meanings. Michael Warner's introduction to the 1991 "Fear of a Queer Planet" issue of *Social Text* is exemplary in the care it takes not to conflate "queer" with "lesbian/gay," but the term Warner uses to designate the hegemonic identities which queer contests—"reprosexuality"—does still privilege sexualities, sexual identities, and sexual practices as the sites of difference and conflict over which queer presides.

42. Quoted in Jagose (1996), 98.
43. *Constitutional Talk* (1995). A Bill of Rights is enshrined in Chapter 2 of the constitution approved by the South African Constitutional Assembly on 8 May 1996. Section 8 (3) of the Bill of Rights guarantees that "Neither the state nor any person may discriminate directly or indirectly against anyone on one or more grounds, including race, gender, sex, marital status, ethnic or social origin, colour, sexual orientation, age, disability, religion, conscience, belief, culture, language and birth."
44. Reid-Pharr (2001), 97. My attention was drawn to this point in Reid-Pharr's book by Hall (2003), 93.

Chapter 2

1. I use the gendered term "gay" in this chapter specifically to denote male homoerotic identities and representations, although some of my comments about gay US imperialism also apply to US lesbians.
2. Cindy Patton (1993) explains an additional way in which the specification of whiteness can be used in the service of a racist political agenda:

    While it may seem paradoxical to mark the unmarked category in this way, it is crucial for neo-fascist racist discourse to produce as a theoretical effect a white identity that sees itself as distinct from the unmarked nonidentity of the (white) hegemonic middle class. This racist white identity operates as importantly against the nonvigilant "race-mixing" white as it does against the "nonwhite." (151)

3. See, for instance, Frankenberg (1993); hooks (1992); Dyer (1988); Levine (1994); Coetzee (1988); Pratt (1988); Toni Morrison (1992); Bloom (1994); (Charles) (1993); Keating (1995); Haney López, "White by Law" (1995); Frye, "On Being White: Thinking Toward a Feminist Understanding of Race and Race Supremacy" (1983); and the 1997 "white issue" of *the minnesota review* (issue #47).

    To say that I will not rehearse these arguments for the ethnicizing of whiteness does not mean, unfortunately, that most conferences, journals, anthologies, and college courses have stopped equating ethnicity with nonwhite ethnicities. Even now pitifully few college courses in ethnic literature include work by white writers as white writers. The vast majority continue to imply that white people are unraced, thereby normalizing whiteness, and reproducing white racism. In his 1988 essay, "White," Richard Dyer points out that the drawback of "Images of" studies that look at groups defined as oppressed is that they reproduce "the sense of oddness, differentness, exceptionality of these groups, the feeling that they are departures from the norm.

Meanwhile the norm has carried on as if it is the natural, inevitable, ordinary way of being human" (44). Dyer quotes a participant in the video *Being White*, who notes that white domination is reproduced by the way that white people "colonise the definition of normal" (45). Dyer continues,

> The colourless multi-colouredness of whiteness secures white power by making it hard, especially for white people and their media, to "see" whiteness. This, of course, also makes it hard to analyse.... Any instance of white representation is always immediately something more specific—*Brief Encounter* is not about white people, it is about English middle-class people; *The Godfather* is not about white people, it is about Italian-American people; but *The Color Purple* is about black people, before it is about poor, Southern US people. (46)

Dyer urges that we must "see whiteness as whiteness" (48).

4. *International Wavelength News* (October 1993): 1.
5. Ibid.
6. Williams (1989), 185. For some further discussions of the conventions and demands of "realness" in pornography, see Dyer (1994) and Ross (1989).
7. For a brief discussion of the use of sound in porn films and videos see Williams (1989).
8. *Men of South Africa II: Boereseuns/Boer Boys*, Voortrekker Productions-International Wavelength, 1992.
9. For a definition and analysis of the "money shot" in porn films see Williams (1989).
10. *Men of South Africa*, Trekker Productions-International Wavelength, 1991.
11. *International Wavelength News* (December 1993) 2.
12. Most famously in recent years, the popular gay porn video *Carnaval in Rio* established the unspoiled beauty of Brazil conterminous with and containing the bustle and sophistication of Rio de Janeiro as a particularly accomplished nexus of romance, aesthetics, desire, and arousal for many gay men in the United States.
13. When we do see black people in the sequel video, they appear in long shots and in mixed-gendered groups, unlikely candidates for sexualized representation—as sexual subjects or objects—in the codes of gay pornography. As if to emphasize the white and endogamous character of gay desire, both videos sporadically show their performers masturbating over magazine pictures of naked men who always seem to be white. This is not, of course, to say that white gay sexualization of black men in itself is antiracist or engages the agency of queers of color, as I explain in Chapter 3.
14. For further discussion of the West's disavowal of its own enablement of apartheid by emphasizing the uniqueness of South Africa see Jolly (1995).
15. For a brief discussion of such criticisms, see Jack Kroll (1986). My use of the term "black" here follows the South African liberation movement's politicization of the term, rather than the ethnic model of racial appellation common in the United States. In South Africa under apartheid, peoples designated as "nonwhite" by the government often emphasized their solidarity in opposition to apartheid by identifying with the term "black" even if they were officially classified as "colored" or "Asian" in terms of the Population Registration Act enacted by the apartheid government in 1950.
16. Wolf (1991), 100.
17. Wolf (1991), 99.
18. Wolf (1991), 106.

19. Quoted by Wolf (1991), 106.
20. I have refrained from qualifying viewers in terms of race. While the videos' audience might be presumed to be white by the video-makers, one could also argue that national identifications might override racial ones for some viewers. It is thus conceivable that a US viewer of color would feel included in the videos' construction of their potential viewership by participating in the videos' imperialist US and imperialist gay US vision of South Africa.
21. "Gay Abandon" (1993).
22. "How About Us?" (1994).
23. For chronicles of the racism of official white gay organizing in South Africa, and the subsequent formation of multiracial gay groups, see Gevisser and Cameron (1994). This history came to a head with the 1984 expulsion of the white-run Gay Association of South Africa from the International Lesbian and Gay Association for its refusal to condemn apartheid and its failure to protest the arrest and detention of South African black gay anti-apartheid activist Simon Nkoli.
24. For instance, many of the characters do not attempt to perform the stereotypes of heterosexual masculinity, as is common in most gay porn videos, but instead present viewers with a variety of voices and mannerisms that mark them as gay.
25. *Men of South Africa*, Trekker Productions-International Wavelength, 1991.
26. See Williams (1989).
27. See Waugh (1995), 320.
28. See Fabian (1983), Mohanty (1984), and Said (1979).
29. For some documentations and histories of public prejudice and official government campaigns against lesbians and gay men in South Africa see the following: Cameron (1994); Gevisser, "A Different Fight for Freedom" (1994); Retief (1994); "Government Ban Gay Publication" (1992); "Gay Abandon" (1993): "S. Africa Ban on *Advocate* Remains" (1992).
30. While the video's work as tourist propaganda is most evident in the final scene, this scene merely culminates the ways in which porn conventions are used throughout the video to bolster the selling of apartheid South Africa. For instance, earlier in the video one of the performers, who identifies himself as living in "Johannesburg, South Africa," says to the camera, "Why don't you come along and pay me a visit?" Here the porn convention of presenting the characters as real people open and eager for real or fantasy sexual encounters with viewers neatly dovetails with efforts by the South African Tourism Bureau to lure overseas visitors to the country.
31. For an account of official white gay complicity with this appeal, see Davidson and Nerio (1994).
32. A variety of travel companies specializing in gay cruises and tours are now thriving in the United States, as are the specialized gay (and, to a lesser extent, lesbian) travel packages that are offered by many other travel agents. Recently one travel company even began advertising specifically gay tours to South Africa. Gay travel magazines and newsletters now complement the array of gay travel guides that have long been gay best sellers in the United States and Europe.
33. See Lane (1995) and Dyer (1988). In a more recent analysis of Virginia Woolf's *Orlando*, Jaime Hovey (1997) adds nationality to the equation, arguing that queerness is associated with and deployed as nonwhiteness so that the novel's (queer) white characters can be accepted as heterosexually English.
34. Here I would also distinguish my argument from Lee Edelman's analysis of Fanon and Baldwin. Edelman (1994) asserts that "a homophobic logic can conclude that 'white racism' equals 'homosexuality' insofar as each of these terms individually can be represented as equal to 'castration'" (55). I am making the case that it is neither a necessarily homophobic logic that

equates whiteness with homosexuality nor an inevitably racist whiteness that thus stands for homosexuality. Rather, the equation can proceed from an antihomophobic gay agenda and can identify whiteness itself with gayness (an identification that nevertheless is racist in effect).

35. Eve Kosofsky Sedgwick begins her influential *Epistemology of the Closet* (1990) with the following much-cited assertion of such a centrality:

> *Epistemology of the Closet* proposes that many of the major nodes of thought and knowledge in twentieth-century Western culture as a whole are structured—indeed, fractured—by a chronic, now endemic crisis of homo/heterosexual definition, indicatively male, dating from the end of the nineteenth century. The book will argue that an understanding of virtually any aspect of modern Western culture must be, not merely incomplete, but damaged in its central substance to the degree that it does not incorporate a critical analysis of modern homo/heterosexual definition. (1)

For other explications of heterosexuality's dependence on homosexuality, see Dollimore (1986), Farley (1980), and Beaver (1981).

36. Dyer (1988), 48.

37. Tellingly, gay porn videos by directors and distributors known for their "exotic" products are also now turning to white Australian and Eastern European subjects—as if, having run out of racial Others, they have found new lines of exoticization and domination. (The idea here is that Eastern Europeans are seemingly forever condemned to having lost the Cold War and white Australians are reminded not only of their history as a colonized and colonizing people, but also that they are a nation descended from criminals.)

38. See Fung (1991), Waugh (1995), and Jackson (1995), especially Chapter 4. I should add here that I do not necessarily agree with the assumption that heterosexual men identify singly and monolithically in the case of heterosexual porn, a doubt that Waugh does raise in his groundbreaking early 1980s article without pursuing it: "For further research: am I wrong in assuming that straight men's fantasies never flirt with the forbidden corners of the text? Do they never project on/identify with the female roles? I'm afraid to ask any" (318).

39. For discussions of this argument, see Patton (1993); and Lee, Murphy, and Ucelli (1993). For discussion of the Othering of homosexuality in East Asian cultures, see Chris Berry (1996), "Sexual DisOrientations."

40. For representative recent samples of these explicitly conservative gay voices in the United States, see Kirk and Madsen (1989), Miller (1994), and Bawer (1993, 1996). For discussion of the public explosion of gay neocons, see Warner (1997).

41. Analogous to my own insistence on the importance of deconstructing whiteness, queer theorists have emphasized that the interrogation of heterosexuality is as imperative a task as is the elaboration of nonheterosexual sexualities if the normalizing assumptions of heterosexuality are to be disrupted. Jonathan Ned Katz's *The Invention of Heterosexuality* (1995) exemplifies queer interest in such a project.

Chapter 3

1. The conflation of interracial relationships with relationships between white people and people of color ignores the fact that relationships between people of color of different races are also interracial relationships. The reduction homogenizes people of color and privileges white

124 | Queer Race: Cultural Interventions in the Racial Politics of Queer Theory

subjectivity by erasing the important differences, conflicts, and congruencies that might arise in a relationship between, say, a Latino and an African-American man. This kind of reduction is evident as much in popular assumptions about interracial relationships as in intellectual discourse around such relationships by white people and people of color. For instance, a recent newspaper article in a US gay weekly on "Gay and Lesbian Interracial and Inter-Ethnic Couples" discusses and interviews only interracial couples that include a white participant. See Diedoardo (1994). Similarly, none of the participants in the Forum on interracial gay male relationships in the Winter 1992 issue of OUT/LOOK even mentions relationships *between* gay men of color, despite the fact that the generic term "interracial relationships" is used throughout to characterize the topic of discussion. See Almaguer et al (1992). The same narrow definition of the term "interracial" is assumed in an article on interracial lesbian sex in a 1995 issue of *On Our Backs*. See Smyth (1995). Likewise, B. Ruby Rich, writing on representations of race in queer film uses the terms "cross-race" and "racial difference" only to designate a relationship between a white person and a (any) person of color. See Rich, "When Difference Is (More Than) Skin Deep (1993).
2. Rich, "When Difference Is (More Than) Skin Deep" (1993), 321.
3. This is the title of one of Bornstein's unpublished plays.
4. Rich, "When Difference Is (More Than) Skin Deep" (1993), 319, 335.
5. See Goldsby (1990) for a discussion of the relatively high degree of lesbian politicization in the United States on issues of race compared to gay men. Smyth (1995) has added, "It seems that lesbians glorify diversity to such an extent that it objectifies race in as problematic a way as gay men do when they sexualize it" (17).
6. See Saillant (1995).
7. For some brief descriptions and discussions of these stereotypes, see Fung (1991, 1993); Gupta (1989), 175; Almaguer (1993); Nguyen (1993); Chin (1991); and Manalansan (1994).
8. "Rice queens," "taco queens," and "dinge queens" are the terms, sometimes derogatory and often racist, used colloquially to indicate white gay men who are particularly and generically attracted to, respectively, Asian men or men of a specific Asian nationality, Mexican men, and black men. "Snow queens" refers to black men who are attracted to white men, and "matzo queens" to men who are attracted to Jewish men.
9. See Gaines (1998) and Mulvey (1975).
10. An explanation may be needed here for non US readers: "Oreo" (a registered trademark of Nabisco foods) refers to a cream-filled chocolate biscuit (made by the Nabisco Co.), hence to a sexual threesome with a white man "between" two black men. The word is also used—derogatorily and problematically—to indicate a white-identified black person, i.e., someone who is "black on the outside" but "white on the inside."
11. Most of the video blurbs I have quoted appeared in HIS mail order advertising flyers between 1990 and 1995 (a few of the flyers are from earlier and later dates).
12. *Adam Gay Video 1995 Directory.*
13. See Boone (1995) for a discussion of some homoerotic literary Orientalisms.
14. For further argument that Mapplethorpe's images of black men are racist objectifications see Hemphill (1992).
15. Mercer (1993), 354.
16. White (1991), x.
17. Ibid.
18. Stambolion (1991), 153.

19. See Fabian (1983) for a discussion of the ways in which imperialist anthropology fixes Third World peoples in a never changing present and always primitive history.
20. I want to emphasize that I am not here commenting on Grumley and Ferro themselves, to whose personal desires I do not have access, and in which I am not particularly interested. Rather, my analysis centers on the words of White and Stambolion, since these commentaries probably reveal more about the commentators than they do about the supposed subjects of the commentaries, and since my interest in this chapter revolves around the ways in which various kinds of representation of interracial desire collude with racist discourses and reduce the complex interplay of sexuality and race.
21. Nelson (1995), 11.
22. Ibid.
23. Ibid.
24. Ibid.
25. In the social sphere, the national US organization Black and White Men Together (recently renamed Men of All Colors Together in most of its chapters, despite the revealing reluctance of some members to include Asian men in the organization) typifies the misguided aphorism that intercourse signals alliance. For while lip-service is paid to the organization's supposedly reconciliatory political functions, it is understood (but hardly ever stated openly) by participants and observers that the organization in fact provides a forum for black men to find white sexual partners and white men to find black sexual partners. Gay racism is sometimes addressed, but the possible racism of the participants' desires or the possible racism built into the organization's structure is not up for discussion. Sunil Gupta (1989) draws a similar conclusion about analogous organizations in the United Kingdom:

    > One great gay mythology is that in this arena of desire we are all equal, and that there is a great crossing of barriers: class, race, etc. Well, that is clearly not the case. There is some provision for the fulfillment of fantasy, and there are institutionalized settings for white men to meet the other races. In these settings, racial stereotypes about the other races seem self-fulfilling for both parties. The Long Yang Club in London exists to bring together "Orientals and interested Westerners" in a social setting where racial assumptions can hardly be challenged. (166)

26. Nelson (1995), 11.
27. Stambolion (1991), 152.
28. Goldsby (1990), 12.
29. See Scott (1994) for an evaluation of the ways in which this slogan has been misinterpreted. For further discussion of the slogan as it was used by Marlon Riggs, see Riggs (1990, 1991).
30. Of course, similar arguments have been made in the case of black heterosexuals who seek or have white lovers or sexual partners. For one articulation of this argument, as well as a delineation of the gendering of race here, and the racist permutations of the white partner's desire in this kind of relationship, see Fanon (1967).
31. For an overview of the "black gay vs. gay black" debate, see Jordan (1990).
32. Hardy (1994), 79.
33. Scott (1994), 308.
34. For further discussion of the need to distinguish between different kinds of separatism, see Barnard (1998).
35. Hardy (1994), 201.

36. Ibid., 201–02.
37. Ibid., 202.
38. Ibid., 250.
39. Ibid., 251.
40. Ibid., 250.
41. See Manalansan (1994), 82, for further discussion of the ways in which nationalist critiques of interracial desire can in fact deny agency to people of color.
42. Hardy appears to attempt to correct this "oversight" in the recently published sequel to *B-Boy Blues*. In *2nd Time Around* (1996) Raheim recalls having sex with Angel (25–26), and Angel apparently has a lover by the novel's end (146). However, *2nd Time Around* recapitulates the sexism of its predecessor by failing to present any critique of Raheim's femphobia.
43. Scott (1994), 308.
44. Hardy (1994), 24.
45. For discussion of a similar dynamic of intra-racial racism in lesbian desire, see Goldsby (1990), 13. For further discussion of the impossibility of representing interracial desire outside of racism, see Fung (1993), 359.
46. Nelson (1995), 11.
47. Manalansan (1994), 82–84.
48. See Alexandre (1983) and the video *Sex Is . . .* (1993) for discussion of black gay masochism. For discussion of S/M in the context of race see Julien (1994). The ground-breaking anthology *Coming to Power* provides an important discussion of S/M in general, and in a lesbian feminist context, in particular. See SAMOIS (1987).
49. Califia (1991), 154.
50. Bersani (1995), 64.
51. See Scott (1994).
52. See Dowell (1990). This extraordinary but little known novel, does describe such a relationship, though it is a heterosexual one, and, tellingly, the white character, Ivy, gives up her political work after she begins to pursue her sexual desire for black men. The book's other central white character, the gay male narrator, also pursues black men, and while politically quite sophisticated, nevertheless is not an activist like Ivy is.
53. *Machismo*, v.3, n.9 (August/September 1995).
54. Mercer (1993), 357.
55. Goldsby (1990).
56. Scott (1994), 312.
57. White (1991), vii.
58. Scott (1994), 310.
59. Hardy (1994), 142. For a critique of the femphobia of Riggs' *Tongues Untied*, see Goldsby (1993), 114.
60. Lyle Ashton Harris (1991), 13.
61. Julien (1992), 19.
62. Julien (1994), 125. In 1990 in the United Kingdom, for engaging in consensual sado-masochistic sex, five gay men were convicted of assault and aiding and abetting assault. The verdict became known as the Spanner Case Ruling.
63. Mercer (1991), 357–58.
64. Scott (1994), 318.
65. Scott (1995), 92.

66. Ibid., 158–59.
67. Ibid., 213.

Chapter 4

1. Quoted by Cooper (1992), 31.
2. For a more detailed discussion of the queer 'zine phenomenon, see Barnard (1996). An extensive annotated queer 'zine bibliography appears as *Queer Zine Explosion*, published about twice a year.
3. Quoted in *Holy Titclamps Zine Explosion* 3 (1992).
4. See Brownworth (1993).
5. *Holy Titclamps* 9 (1991–92). Spew is the name of an annual 'zine "convention."
6. Salvador (1992), 8.
7. See Ellen Rooney (1989) for a discussion of the ways in which pluralist ideologies assume a universally persuadable readership.
8. Anzaldúa (1991), 249–50.
9. I will in this chapter use the pronominal "Anzaldúa" to blur the distinction between Anzaldúa and the narrator(s) of her book, as the text itself invites such blurring with its inclusion of apparently autobiographical anecdotes, even though the "I"'s in its fragmented and multiple component parts are clearly not consistent (in one of the poems in the book, for instance, the "I" is a racist white male rapist and murderer).
10. Yarbro-Bejarano (1991), 74.
11. Anzaldúa (1999), 94.
12. Ibid., 19.
13. Ibid., 20.
14. Wittig and Zeig (1979), 165.
15. See de Lauretis (1990) for an explication of Wittig's (re)conceptualization of the meaning of lesbian in Wittig's essay "One is Not Born a Woman":

    > Wittig's "we" is not the privileged women of de Beauvoir, "qualified to elucidate the situation of woman"; nor does her "lesbian society" refer to some collectivity of gay women, any more than "lesbian" refers to an individual woman with a particular "sexual preference." They are, rather, the theoretical terms of a form of feminist consciousness that can only exist historically, in the here and now, as the consciousness of a "something else." (145)

    It is difficult to get a full sense of Wittig's witty manipulation of pronouns in English translations of her work. For discussion of Wittig's pronoun usage, see Wittig, "Author's Note" (1986); and Wenzel (1981).
16. Anzaldúa (1999), 193.
17. Alarcón (1989), 81. Malinche is one version of the name of the Aztec woman who supposedly became Cortez's mistress, and served him as a translator and informer against her own people. The term *malinche* has thus come to be used in Mexico and in Chicana/o culture to denote any kind of collaborator, though some feminist writers, in particular, have recently attempted to rehabilitate Malinche's reputation by suggesting that her position might have been more complex than is usually assumed.

18. Anzaldúa (1999), 41, 24, 154.
19. Ibid., 81.
20. Anzaldúa, Lectures (1990).
21. Anzaldúa (1999), 102.
22. Ibid., 25. When quoting from *Borderlands/La Frontera*, I have followed the text's use of italics, which is sometimes problematic since it can be seen as re-enforcing the hegemony of English by italicizing non-English words and thus marking them as "foreign."
23. Alarcón (1990), 249.
24. Ibid., 252.
25. Anzaldúa (1999), 216.
26. Engelbrecht (1990) writes that the "internal plurality that *la mestiza* experiences is not unlike the male and lesbian Subjectivities which a lesbian living in the patriarchy may enact" (105). This is a comparison that could be perceived as avoiding discussion of racial oppression by substituting homophobia and sexism for racism.
27. Anzaldúa (1999), 102. See also the following assertion: "Being the supreme crossers of cultures, homosexuals have strong bonds with the queer white, Black, Asian, Native American, Latino, and with the queer in Italy, Australia and the rest of the planet" (106).
28. Ibid., 43. For further discussion of this paradoxical strategy of deconstructing identity from within a particular identification (in particular, identity formed around gender and sexual orientation) see Barnard (1993, 1994).
29. See Lugones (1992) for a further discussion of the problematic of pluralism in relation to Anzaldúa's text. Here Lugones distinguishes Anzaldúa's "dualism" from pluralism.
30. Ibid., 31.
31. Anzaldúa (1999), 43.
32. Ibid., 44.
33. Ibid., 84.
34. Ibid., 59. Anzaldúa blames Western culture for splitting the brain and reality into two functions, psychic and material.
35. Ibid., 32.
36. Ibid., 70.
37. Ibid., 80.
38. Ibid., 38.
39. Ibid., 27.
40. Ibid., 53, 55.
41. Ibid., 42.
42. Ibid., 25–26. (My emphasis.)
43. For instance, Anzaldúa (1999) writes of the Mexico/US border,

>   1,950 mile-long open wound
>   dividing a *pueblo*, a culture,
>   running down the length of my body,
>   staking fence rods in my flesh,
>   splits me splits me
>   *me raja me raja* (24)

44. Annamarie Jagose, for instance, criticizes Anzaldúa for contradicting herself in *Borderlands/La Frontera*. See Jagose (1994), 138, 152.

45. Anzaldúa (1999), 49.
46. Ibid., 69.
47. Ibid., 101-02.
48. Calderón (1991), 25.
49. Yarbro-Bejarano (1991, 1995).
50. See, for example, Trujillo (1991).
51. Dasenbrock (1987), 16.
52. Anzaldúa, "Bridge, Drawbridge" (1990), 225.
53. Angela Y. Davis (1989). For further discussion of "inclusion without influence," see Yarbro-Bejarano (1995) and Uttal (1990).
54. See Michel Foucault, "The End of the Monarchy of Sex" (1989) and *The History of Sexuality, Volume I: An Introduction* (1980).

Chapter 5

1. Schwartz (1992), 84.
2. For chronicles of the initial homophobic coverage of the Dahmer case in Milwaukee, see Schmidt (1994), Peck (1993). Peck (1993) points out that the term "homosexual overkill" had previously been used by the Milwaukee County medical examiner to describe the 1990 murder and bodily mulilation of James Madden by Joachim Dressler (55).
3. Every account of the Dahmer case that I have read and that mentions Dahmer's gayness, points out that for almost all of his adult life Dahmer was unable to accept his homosexuality, and made disparaging remarks against other gay men. For an unusually explicit account of the role that internalized homophobia might have played in Dahmer's killings see "Debate Rages in Milwaukee's Gay Community as Dahmer Sanity Trial Unfolds" (1992), especially 26. One exception to these accounts comes from Dahmer's attorney, who claimed at Dahmer's trial that his client had as an adolescent "discovered and accepted his homosexuality." See *The Trial of Jeffrey Dahmer* (1992). Dahmer did perhaps accept his sexuality near the end of his life. His probation officer noted in 1991, Dahmer 'has admitted to self he is gay. Told agent that's the way he is so 'fuck it.'" This exchange is recounted in Don Davis (1992), 129; Norris (1992), 219; Schwartz (1992), 84; and Dvorchak and Holewa (1991), 158.
4. My imputation that Dahmer's sexual orientation should have been publicly discussed would apply equally to a heterosexual serial killer. I certainly would not want to imply that a straight serial killer should be referred to as a "serial killer" while a gay serial killer is called a "gay serial killer," or that heterosexuality as an institution and as a state could not be a murderous shaping influence for a straight serial killer. Homophobia might play a part in the actions of both the gay and straight serial killers.
5. Schmidt (1994), 84, documents this argument.
6. "17 Killings in 13 Years Stunned U.S." (1994). The word "could" in Dahmer's statement might be read as symptomatic of a racism underlying Dahmer's claims to racial indifference if we understand Dahmer's own insecurities interfacing with a racist assumption of the inferiority of people of color. In other words, with his victims he had to "make do" with people of color.
7. Schwartz (1992), 53-54; Baumann (1991), 205, 265.
8. *The Trial of Jeffrey Dahmer* (1992).

9. Hirsch (1996) is one of the few Dahmer writers that does point to societal homophobia as a cause of Dahmer's killings. In his efforts to establish a larger social accountability for Dahmer, Hirsch also delineates the continuities between Dahmer and other social discourses. However, in his zeal to claim Dahmer's victimhood Hirsch does not account for what might be read as Dahmer's cynical deployment of the same gay rights discourse that informs Hirsch's article. Hirsch does not develop any theory of race in the Dahmer case though he does several times mention the races of the men Dahmer killed.
10. Don Davis (1992), 303.
11. Schwartz (1992), 69; Don Davis (1992), 99; Baumann (1991), 74; Norris (1992), 182. Here I am not using the language of Schwartz, Davis, Baumann, and Norris, none of whom quote Dahmer directly, and all of whom use the word "homosexual" rather than "gay," some also adding that Dahmer's homosexuality was a "sexual problem."
12. Don Davis (1992), 137.
13. Ibid., 109.
14. These suspicions were confirmed, for many, when the transcripts of one of the police officers' radio reports to the dispatcher after the encounter were made public. The officer, John Balcerzak, laughed, apparently derisively, about the incident. In another possibly derogatory reference to Dahmer and/or Sinthasomphone, he noted that his partner would get "deloused" at the station. See Schwartz (1992), 88–105. Chua (1993) has further pointed out how "Orientalphobia" was exemplified by the understanding of the Dahmer/Sinthasomphone relationship

> in the mind of Joseph T. Gabrish, the Milwaukee police officer who told the press, "There was just nothing that stood out, or we would have seen it," after he returned naked and bleeding fourteen-year-old Konerak Sinthasomphone to blond massmurderer Jeffrey Dahmer. (316)

15. Tellingly, none of the Dahmer books mentions the races of the police officers who were called to the scene—suggesting, therefore, that they were white.
16. Quoted by Schwartz (1992), 94–95. See also Don Davis (1992), 51; Jamakaya (1992), 24; and Dvorchak and Holewa (1991), 118. The caller, incidentally, also makes a nod in an antihomophobic direction by responding to the officer's comment, "I can't do anything about anybody's sexual preferences in life," with "Well, no, I'm not saying anything about that." This exchange is quoted in Dvorchak and Holewa (1991), 118.
17. Quoted in Dvorchak and Holewa (1991), 181–82.
18. Burke (1994).
19. Joel Norris's book *Jeffrey Dahmer* (the book stresses that its author is *Dr.* Joel Norris, presumably to convince readers of the expert nature of the testimony given) was published in 1992, just after the Dahmer trial. Although, after Dvorchak and Holewa's *Milwaukee Massacre*, this is the least homophobic of the Dahmer books—it does mention internalized homophobia as a contributing cause to Dahmer's self-loathing and outward evil—Norris makes several symptomatic conflations. His prologue begins with the verdict in the hands of the judge: "The pages in the judge's hand were the results of jury deliberations that followed weeks of complicated and conflicting testimony about homicide, violent aberrant sex, torture, and necrophilia" (7). Here, too, "violent aberrant sex" seems to be equivalent to gay sex.
20. Fuss (1993), 182, 188.

Notes | 131

21. Don Davis (1992), 4. Referring to the seven thousand Laotians who settled in Milwaukee, Dvorchak and Holewa (1991) note, "It offered the promise of a second chance. Better yet, it had no communist thugs butchering the population" (85).
22. Other kinds of conflations also give to gayness a necessarily pathological trajectory, as in Don Davis's (1992) diagnosis of Dahmer's 1986 arrest for lewd and lascivious behavior: "The eventual full expression of Dahmer's gay life-style was still in the future, but his exhibitionist tendency was about to land him in serious trouble for the first time" (82). By constructing Dahmer's murders as the "eventual full expression of Dahmer's gay lifestyle," Davis equates gayness with murderousness. Ed Baumann's and Joel Norris's Dahmer books are no more able to imagine a nonmurderous gay relationship. Baumann's chapter listing and describing the men Dahmer killed is titled, "The Men in His Life," and the back cover blurb of Norris's book promises "exclusive interviews with his friends and ex-lovers." Baumann's chapter title mockingly reduces gay relationships to serial murder, and Norris's book suggests that any kind of gay sexual encounter, no matter how brief, superficial, or coercive, represents the fullest potential gay relationship—the book contains no interviews with ex-lovers, but does document the words of some of Dahmer's escaped victims.
23. *The Trial of Jeffrey Dahmer* (1992).
24. See Foucault, *The History of Sexuality, Volume I* (1980).
25. "Judge Orders Brain Scan for Dahmer" (1991).
26. Schwartz (1992), 217-18. I have taken all quotations from Dahmer's speech from Schwartz's transcription of the speech. Dahmer's father, a fundamentalist Christian, made disparaging references to lesbians and gay men during Dahmer's childhood and remained unrepentantly homophobic even after Dahmer's trial. While he was growing up, Dahmer knew that his father would not approve of his gay sexual orientation. Dvorchak and Holewa (1991) quote Lionel Dahmer saying in retrospect of his son, "I've always felt he was somewhat of a social misfit . . . I tried my damnedest to instill interests, in trying to become interested in something in life, education, trying to get him to accept Christ" (76). In a 1994 television interview with Stone Phillips, Lionel Dahmer admitted that he would have "tried to change" his son if Jeffrey had told him that he was gay, and that he still believed that homosexuality was a sin. See "Dahmer and Dahmer" (1994). According to Jamakaya, "Jeffrey Dahmer's Grisly Homophobia: The Hate Crime that Wasn't" (1991), a lay brother of the Episcopal Church who talked with Jeffrey Dahmer at length, concluded that the son himself was "'extremely homophobic,' with an almost Christian fundamentalist view of homosexuality" (15). Dvorchak and Holewa (1991) suggest that Jeffrey Dahmer's biological mother appears to have been more tolerant: in a March 1991 telephone conversation with her son, Joyce Flint apparently told her son that she had no problem accepting his gayness (144). After his parents divorced, Dahmer lived with his grandmother. Although I have found no direct evidence of her homophobia, she attended a conservative church, to which her grandson sometimes accompanied her, and ejected him from her home when she discovered a partially naked man with him in the house—See "Dahmer and Dahmer" (1994); and Norris (1992), 153, 165, 249-50.
27. *The Trial of Jeffrey Dahmer* (1992).
28. From what I can gather, the men Dahmer murdered (and those who escaped him) embraced a variety of sexual identities. Some identified as gay, while some apparently did not; some were in the closet about their gayness or bisexuality, while others were not. It is impossible, of course, to fathom their reasons for having sex with Dahmer: for some, no doubt, money was the

prime motivator; for others, it might have been desire; for others, still, there might have been other reasons, or a combination of reasons. Although some of those who survived encounters with Dahmer have denied their queerness, it seems clear that almost all Dahmer's victims had at least moments of gay/bisexual/queer desire/identity/practice. My use of terms like "gayness" to describe these men, then, does not necessarily indicate my/their assumption of their/a gay identity, but includes, as well, moments of "gayness," such as fleeting homoerotic desires and practices.

29. Baumann (1991), 36.
30. Mathews et al. (1992); Norris (1992), 220; Baumann (1991), 173; Dvorchak and Holewa (1991), 100.
31. Dvorchak and Holewa (1991), 5.
32. Quoted by Schwartz (1992), 56. See also Baumann (1991), 160.
33. This incident occurred on *A Closer Look with Faith Daniels*, as presented in Boneyard Press's compilation video of footage surrounding the Dahmer comic controversy. See Fisher (1993).
34. Schwartz (1992), 87. See also Dvorchak and Holewa (1991), 107.
35. Schmidt (1994), 89. Ironically, Schmidt's article reproduces the very refusal to recognize Dahmer's gayness that enabled racists and homophobes to celebrate Dahmer, in that Schmidt fails to point to the logical flaw in the argument of those who congratulate Dahmer for killing queers: Dahmer himself is queer. It is difficult not to see a continuity between this kind of omission and the blinkeredness that refused to see Dahmer's own murder as a gaybashing. Ultimately, these types of omissions and blinkers contribute to a culture that condones and promotes such murders/gaybashings.
36. For further accounts of homophobic harassment and violence in Milwaukee following the publicity generated by Dahmer's arrest, see Schmidt (1994), 88-89; "Debate Rages" (1992), 25; Baumann (1991), 243; Dvorchak and Holewa (1991), 205-06; and Jamakaya (1991), 15. It's also quite possible, of course, that queerbashing in Milwaukee after Dahmer's arrest was carried out with mixed or uncertain motives. People who were angry at the course of events might have enacted this anger against Milwaukee queers merely because queers have already been set up by government, religious, educational, and social institutions as appropriate targets of persecution, or because the bashers didn't know where else to vent their anger.
37. Don Davis (1992), 271.
38. Blau and Griffin (1991), 12.
39. Bass (1995), 126.
40. Norris (1992), 108-09.
41. Lionel Dahmer(1995), 225-26; "Why Jeffrey Dahmer Killed So Many Black Men" (1994).
42. Prison homophobia directed at Dahmer is documented and discussed in the following texts: Kaplan et al. (1992), 50; Schwartz (1992), 35; Baumann (1991), 199. In an Afterword to a review of Lionel Dahmer's book the editor of the zine *Everard Review* notes that the locale of Jeffrey Dahmer's murder (a prison bathroom), as well as other characteristic features of the murder, suggest that it may have been a gaybashing. See Spiro (1995).
43. "Serial Killer Dahmer Slain in Prison" (1994), Terry (1994).
44. Schwartz (1992), 216.
45. In some cases, rallies and protests in Milwaukee did articulate anger at both racism and homophobia: the prejudices of a police department that had failed to vigorously investigate the reports of missing men at the time of the murders, and the societal racism and homophobia that Dahmer seemed to exemplify.
46. Quoted by Schwartz (1992), 182. See also Dvorchak and Holewa (1991), 184.

47. For documentation of the mail, monetary, and other gifts Dahmer received in prison, see the following: "For a Serial Killer, Money From Around the World" (1991); Lionel Dahmer (1995), 217–18; Holleran (1992)
48. Holleran (1992), 3.
49. Quoted by Brizzolara (1993), 25.
50. As my discussions of the word "queer" throughout this book suggest, this is not to say that lesbian and gay writers, filmmakers, 'zines, etc., identified with a queer sensibility have not also celebrated gaybashing in their suspicion of the possibility of a unified "gay community" or of the imperative for "positive" gay representation. See also Barnard, "Fuck Community, or Why I Support Gay-Bashing" (1996).
51. Quoted by Brizzolara (1993), 25.
52. The t-shirts are advertised in *The Further Adventures of Young Jeffy Dahmer*, the sequel comic to the infamous *Jeffery* [sic] *Dahmer* comic, both created by Hart Fisher.
53. Holleran (1992), 3.
54. Fisher, *Jeffery* [sic] *Dahmer: An Unauthorized Biography of a Serial Killer* (1992), 11.
55. Loud (1992).
56. Holleran (1992), 3.
57. "Dahmer," *Day One* (1993). For further discussion of Dahmer's "ordinariness," see, for instance, Masters (1991), Sproul (1991), Suplee (1991), and DeRamus (1991).
58. *The Trial of Jeffrey Dahmer* (1992).
59. See Schmidt (1994).
60. See Schwartz (1992).
61. Lionel Dahmer (1995).
62. Dale Peck (1993), 54.
63. Ibid., 114.
64. Ibid., 54.
65. Ibid., 113.
66. See Haney López, "White By Law" (1995) for one answer (in the negative) to this question.

Chapter 6

1. Masters (1991), 185.
2. See Harper, *Are We Not Men? Masculine Anxiety and the Problem of African-American Identity* (1996), 127–31, for analysis of some of the racially marked representations of O.J. Simpson following his arrest.
3. See Amanda Berry (1995) for a discussion of the lesbian subtext of the Simpson criminal trial. In the same article, Berry discusses Faye Resnick's account of her homoerotic evening with Nicole Brown Simpson, as well as tabloid versions of Resnick's revelations, and television representations of the trial lawyers, to conclude that the trial pitted black men against white lesbians, compelling television viewers "to participate in creating a hierarchy of oppressions" (22). Berry does not queer O.J.

Ostrom (1994) is one of the few public utterances linking O.J., however indirectly, to queerness, suggesting that he might suffer from a Chronic Fatigue Syndrome Dementia that affects many AIDS patients.

4. See Clark (1995).

5. "Mexico Celebrates Pride" (1995).
6. Wockner (1995).
7. See "Saddam's a Sex Pervert" (1991).
8. "Mad Bombers' Kinky Secret" (1995).
9. See Schulman (1994), 289–312, for a discussion of the ways in which the Lesbian Avengers (should) re-envisage political activism. See Daniel Harris (1991) for a critique of postmodern theory's role in queer activism.
10. Stein and Plummer (1994), 184.
11. Said (1993), 52.
12. Harper, White, and Cerullo, "Multi/Queer/Culture," 36.

Works Cited

Abelove, Henry. "Critically Queer: Interview with Henry Abelove." *Critical InQueeries* 1.1 (1995): 7-14.

———. "The Queering of Lesbian/Gay History." *Radical History Review* 62 (1995): 44-57.

Adam Gay Video 1995 Directory. Compiled by Dave Kinnick. *Adam Gay Video* 2.10 (March 1995). Los Angeles: Knight, 1994.

Adams, Kate. "Northamerican Silences: History, Identity, and Witness in the Poetry of Gloria Anzaldúa, Cherríe Moraga, and Leslie Marmon Silko." *Listening to Silences: New Essays in Feminist Criticism*. Ed. Elaine Hedges and Shelley Fisher Fishkin. New York: OUP, 1994. 130-45.

Alarcón, Norma. "Chicana Feminism: In the Tracks of 'The' Native Woman." *Cultural Studies* 4.3 (1990): 248-56.

———. "Traddutora, Traditora: A Paradigmatic Figure of Chicana Feminism." *Cultural Critique* 13 (Fall 1989): 57-87.

Alexandre, Wayne. "Interview: Black Homosexual Masochist." *Black Men/White Men: A Gay Anthology*. Ed. Michael J. Smith. San Francisco: Gay Sunshine, 1983. 77-83.

Almaguer, Tomás. "Chicano Men: A Cartography of Homosexual Identity and Behavior." *The Lesbian and Gay Studies Reader*. Ed. Henry Abelove, Michèle Aina Barale, and David M. Halperin. New York: Routledge, 1993. 255-73.

Almaguer, Tomás, et al. "Sleeping with the Enemy?" *OUT/LOOK* 15 (Winter 1992): 30-38.

Alonso, Ana Maria, and Maria Teresa Koreck. "Silences: 'Hispanics,' AIDS, and Sexual Practices." *differences* 1.1 (1989): 101-24.

Altman, Dennis. "On Global Queering." *Australian Humanities Review*. Online. July 1996. <http://www.lib.latrobe.edu.au/AHR/archive/Issue-July-1996/altman.html>.

———. "Rupture or Continuity?: The Internationalization of Gay Identities." *Social Text* 48 (Fall 1996): 77-94.

Angelides, Steven, and Craig Bird. "Feeling Queer: It's Not Who You Are, It's Where You're At." *Critical InQueeries* 1.1 (Sep. 1995): 1-5.

Anzaldúa, Gloria E. *Borderlands/La Frontera: The New Mestiza*. 1987. 2nd Ed. San Francisco: Aunt Lute, 1999.

———. "Bridge, Drawbridge, Sandbar or Island: Lesbians-of-Color Hacienda Alianzas." *Bridges of Power: Women's Multicultural Alliances*. Ed. Lisa Albrecht and Rose M. Brewer. Santa Cruz: New Society, 1990. 216-31.

———. Lectures for Ethnic Studies Program. University of California, San Diego: 21-22 May 1990.

———. "To(o) Queer the Writer—Loca, escritora y chicana." *InVersions: Writing by Dykes, Queers & Lesbians*. Ed. Betsy Warland. Vancouver: Press Gang, 1991. 249-63.

Anzaldúa, Gloria, and Cherríe Moraga, eds. *This Bridge Called My Back: Writings by Radical Women of Color*. 2nd Ed. New York: Kitchen Table, 1983.

Appiah, Kwame Anthony. *In My Father's House: Africa in the Philosophy of Culture*. New York: OUP, 1992.

———. "Race." *Critical Terms for Literary Study*. Ed. Frank Lentricchia and Thomas McLaughlin. 2nd Ed. Chicago: UCP, 1995. 274-87.

Barnard, Ian. "Another Take on the Oscars." *Gay & Lesbian Times* (San Diego) 23 April 1992: 18.

———. "Fuck Community, or Why I Support Gay-Bashing." *States of Rage: Emotional Eruption, Violence, and Social Change*. Ed. Renée R. Curry and Terry L. Allison. New York: NYUP, 1996. 74-88.

———. "Macho Sluts: Genre-Fuck, S/M Fantasy, and the Reconfiguration of Political Action." *Genders* 19 (1994): 265-91.

———. "Queer Fictions: Gay Men With/And/In/Near/Or Lesbian Feminisms?" *LIT: Literature, Interpretation, Theory* 4.4 (1993): 261-74.

———. "Queerzines and the Fragmentation of Art, Community, Identity, and Politics." *Socialist Review* 26.1-2 (1996): 69-95.

———. "Toward a Postmodern Understanding of Separatism." *Women's Studies: An Interdisciplinary Journal* 27.6 (1998): 613-39.

Barry, Peter. *Beginning Theory: An Introduction to Literary and Cultural Theory*. New York: St. Martin's, 1995.

Basic Instinct. Screenplay by Joe Eszterhas. Dir. Paul Verhoeven. Perf. Michael Douglas and Sharon Stone. Carolco, 1992.

Bass, Vernell. "A Beer and Some Chips with Jeffrey Dahmer." *Esquire* April 1995: 125-26.

Baumann, Ed. *Step Into My Parlor: The Chilling Story of Serial Killer Jeffrey Dahmer*. Chicago: Bonus, 1991.

Bawer, Bruce, Ed. *Beyond Queer: Challenging Gay Left Orthodoxy*. New York: Free, 1996.

———. *A Place at the Table: The Gay Individual in American Society*. New York: Poseidon, 1993.

Beam, Joseph, Ed. *In the Life: A Black Gay Anthology*. Boston: Alyson, 1986.

Beaver, Harold. "Homosexual Signs." *Critical Inquiry* 8.1 (1981): 99-119.

Berlant, Lauren, and Michael Warner. "What Does Queer Theory Teach Us About X?" *PMLA* 110.3 (1995): 343-49.

Berry, Amanda. "O.J. Versus the Lesbians." *Girlfriends* 2.3 (May/June 1995): 20-22.

Berry, Chris. "Sexual DisOrientations: Homosexual Rights, East Asian Films, and Postmodern Postnationalism." *In Pursuit of Contemporary East Asian Culture*. Ed. Xiaobing Tang and Stephen Snyder. Boulder, Colorado: HarperCollins, 1996. 157-82.

Berry, Chris, and Annamarie Jagose. "Australia Queer: Editors' Introduction." *Meanjin* 55.1 (1996): 5-11.

Bersani, Leo. *Homos*. Cambridge: Harvard UP, 1995.

Bérubé, Allan, and Jeffrey Escoffier. "Queer/Nation." *OUT/LOOK* 11 (Winter 1991): 12-14.

Bhabha, Homi. "The Commitment to Theory." *New Formations* 5 (Summer 1988): 5-23.

Bianco, David. "The Origins of the Word 'Queer.'" *Gay and Lesbian Times* (San Diego) 25 April 1996: 41.

Blau, Robert, and Jean Latz Griffin. "Why Preventing Repeat Murders is so Difficult." *Chicago Tribune* 28 July 1991: 11, 12.

Bloom, Lisa. "Constructing Whiteness: Popular Science and *National Geographic* in the Age of Multiculturalism." *Configurations* 2.1 (1994): 15-34.

Blount, Marcellus, and George P. Cunningham, Eds. *Representing Black Men*. New York: Routledge, 1996.

Boone, Joseph A. "Vacation Cruises; or, The Homoerotics of Orientalism." *PMLA* 110.1 (1995): 89-107.

Brizzolara, John. "'Eating People is the Ultimate Control': The Young Gentlemen of Dahmer's Diner Discuss Their Craft." *Reader* (San Diego) 14 Oct. 1993: 1+.

Browning, Frank. *The Culture of Desire: Paradox and Perversity in Gay Lives Today*. New York: Crown, 1993.

Brownworth, Victoria A. "The Porn Boom." *Lesbian News* 18.7 (1993): 42+.

Burke, Andrew. "Brutal Death of a Beast." *You* (South Africa) 22 Dec. 1994: 19.

Butler, Judith. "Against Proper Objects." *differences* 6.2-3 (1994): 1-26.

———. *Bodies That Matter: On The Discursive Limits of "Sex."* New York: Routledge, 1993.

Calderón, Héctor. "Texas Border Literature: Cultural Transformations and Historical Reflection in the Works of Américo Paredes, Rolando Hinojoso and Gloria Anzaldúa." *Dispositio* 16.41 (1991) 13-27.

Califia, Pat. *The Advocate Adviser*. Boston: Alyson, 1991.

Cameron, Edwin. "'Unapprehended Felons': Gays and Lesbians and the Law in South Africa." *Defiant Desire: Gay and Lesbian Lives in South Africa*. Eds. Mark Gevisser and Edwin Cameron. Johannesburg: Ravan, 1994. 89-98.

Carnaval in Rio. Video. Dir. Kristen Bjorn. Paladin, 1989.

Champagne, John. *The Ethics of Marginality: A New Approach to Gay Studies*. Minneapolis: UMP, 1995.

(Charles,) Helen. "'Queer Nigger': Theorizing 'White' Activism." *Activating Theory: Lesbian, Gay, Bisexual Politics*. Ed. Joseph Bristow and Angelia R. Wilson. London: Lawrence and Wishart, 1993. 97-106.

Chee, Alexander S. "A Queer Nationalism." *OUT/LOOK* 11 (Winter 1991): 15-17, 19.

Chin, Justin. "Doing it On the Oriental." *Lavender Godzilla* 4.2 (Fall 1991): 22-24.

Chua, Lawrence. "Desiring Conquest." *Queer Looks: Perspectives on Lesbian and Gay Film and Video*. Ed. Martha Gever, Pratibha Parmar, and John Greyson. New York: Routledge, 1993. 303-17.

Clark, Keith. "The Global Village of Gay/Lesbian Rights." *Gay & Lesbian Times* (San Diego) 15 June 1995: 38-39.

Coetzee, J. M. *White Writing: On the Culture of Letters in South Africa*. New Haven: Yale UP, 1988.

Constitutional Talk (Official Newsletter of the Constitutional Assembly). Working Draft Edition. Cape Town, 1995.

Cooper, Dennis. "Queercore." *The Village Voice* 30 June 1992: 31-33.

Corbin, Steven. *Fragments That Remain*. Boston: Alyson, 1993.

Cornwell, Anita. "Three for the Price of One: Notes from a Gay Black Feminist." *Lavender Culture*. Ed. Karla Jay and Allen Young. New York: Harcourt, 1979. 466-76.

Crying Game, The. Screenplay by Neil Jordan. Dir. Jordan. Perf. Jaye Davidson, Miranda Richardson, Stephen Rea, and Forest Whitaker. Miramax, 1992.

"Dahmer." *Day One.* Host Forrest Sawyer. ABC. KGTV, San Diego. 18 April 1993.

"Dahmer and Dahmer." NBC. KNSD, San Diego. 8 March, 1994.

Dahmer, Lionel. *A Father's Story.* 1994. New York: Avon, 1995.

Dasenbrock, Reed Way. "Intelligibility and Meaningfulness in Multicultural Literature in English." *PMLA* 102.1 (Jan. 1987): 10–19.

Davidson, Gerry, and Ron Nerio. "*Exit:* Gay Publishing in South Africa." *Defiant Desire: Gay and Lesbian Lives in South Africa.* Eds. Mark Gevisser and Edwin Cameron. Johannesburg: Ravan, 1994. 225–31.

Davis, Angela Y. Address for Panel on "Re-Thinking Alliance-Building." Parallels and Intersections Conference. Iowa City, 9 April 1989.

Davis, Don. *The Milwaukee Murders: Nightmare in Apartment 213: The True Story.* 1991. London: Virgin, 1992.

"Debate Rages in Milwaukee's Gay Community as Dahmer Sanity Trial Unfolds." *NYQ* 16 Feb. 1992: 25–26.

De Lauretis, Teresa. "Eccentric Subjects: Feminist Theory and Historical Consciousness." *Feminist Studies* 16.1 (Spring 1990): 115–50.

——. "Habit Changes." *differences* 6.2–3 (1994): 296–313.

——. "Queer Theory: Lesbian and Gay Sexualities: An Introduction." *differences* 3.2 (1991): iii–xviii.

——. "Sexual Indifference and Lesbian Representation." 1988. *The Lesbian and Gay Studies Reader.* Ed. Henry Abelove, Michèle Aina Barale, and David M. Halperin. New York: Routledge, 1993. 141–58.

DeRamus, Betty. "When the Bogeyman's Normal-Looking, He Takes Us Unawares." *Detroit News and Free Press* 28 July 1991: C-1.

Dev, Elango. "Cultural Diversity and the Politics of Assimilation." *New Indicator* 28 Nov. 1990–1 Jan. 1991: 1,7.

Dhairyam, Sagri. "Racing the Lesbian, Dodging White Critics." *The Lesbian Postmodern.* Ed. Laura Doan. New York: Columbia UP, 1994. 25–46.

Diedoardo, Christopher. "Strands of the Rainbow: Gay and Lesbian Interracial and Inter-Ethnic Couples." *Gay & Lesbian Times* (San Diego) 27 Jan. 1994: 34–35.

Dixon, Melvin. "Other Voices, Other Rooms: An Interview with Melvin Dixon." Interview by Clarence Bard Cole. *Christopher Street* 157: 24–27.

——. *Vanishing Rooms.* New York: Penguin, 1991.

Dollimore, Jonathan. "Homophobia and Sexual Difference." *Oxford Literary Review* 8.1–2 (1986): 5–12.

Dotton, Thomas. "Nigger in the Woodpile." *After You're Out: Personal Experiences of Gay Men and Lesbian Women.* Ed. Karla Jay and Allen Young. New York: Links, 1975. 218–26.

Doty, Alexander. *Making Things Perfectly Queer: Interpreting Mass Culture.* Minneapolis: UMP, 1993.

Dowell, Coleman. *White on Black on White.* 1983. London: Serpent's Tail, 1990.

Duggan, Lisa. "Making it Perfectly Queer." *Socialist Review* 22.1 (1992): 11–31.

Duplechan, Larry. *Blackbird.* New York: St. Martin's, 1986.

——. *Eight Days a Week.* Boston: Alyson, 1985.

Dvorchak, Robert J., and Lisa Holewa. *Milwaukee Massacre: Jeffrey Dahmer and the Milwaukee Murders.* New York: Bantam, 1991.

Dyer, Richard. "Idol Thoughts: Orgasm and Self-Reflexivity in Gay Pornography." *Critical Quarterly* 36.1 (1994): 49–62.

——. "White." *Screen* 29.4 (1988): 44–65.

Edelman, Lee. *Homographesis: Essays in Gay Literary and Cultural Theory.* New York: Routledge, 1994.
———. "Queer Theory: Unstating Desire." *GLQ* 2.4 (1995): 343-46.
Engelbrecht, Penelope J. "Lifting Belly is a Language: The Postmodern Lesbian Subject." *Feminist Studies* 16.1 (Spring 1990): 85-114.
Epstein, Steven. "Gay Politics, Ethnic Identity: The Limits of Social Constructionism." *Socialist Review* 7.3-4 (1987): 9-54.
———. "A Queer Encounter: Sociology and the Study of Sexuality." *Sociological Theory* 12.2 (1994): 188-202.
Fabian, Johannes. *Time and the Other: How Anthropology Makes Its Object.* New York: Columbia UP, 1983.
Fanon, Frantz. *Black Skin, White Masks.* 1952. Trans. Charles Lam Markmann. New York: Grove, 1967.
Farley, Pamella. "Lesbianism and the Social Function of Taboo." *The Future of Difference.* Ed. Hester Eisenstein and Alice Jardine. Boston: Hall, 1980. 267-73.
Fernández, Charles. "Undocumented Aliens in the Queer Nation." *OUT/LOOK* 12 (1991): 20-23
Fisher, Hart, ed. "50 Minutes of Boneyard News." Videotape. 1993.
Fisher, Hart. *The Further Adventures of Young Jeffy Dahmer.* Milwaukee: Boneyard, 1992.
———. *Jeffery* [sic] *Dahmer: An Unauthorized Biography of a Serial Killer.* 2nd Ed. Milwaukee: Boneyard, 1992.
"For a Serial Killer, Money From Around the World." *New York Times* 7 Mar. 1991: A10.
"Forum on the Political Implications of Using the Term 'Queer,' as in 'Queer Politics,' 'Queer Studies,' and 'Queer Pedagogy.'" *Radical Teacher* 45 (1994): 52-57.
Foucault, Michel. "The End of the Monarchy of Sex." Interviewed by Bernard-Henry Levy. 1977. *Foucault Live: Interviews 1966-84.* Ed. Sylvère Lotringer. Trans. John Johnson. New York: Semiotexte(e), 1989. 137-55.
———. "Friendship as a Way of Life.'" Interview. 1981. Trans. John Johnston. *Foucault Live: Interviews 1966-84.* Ed. Sylvère Lotringer. Trans. John Johnson. New York: Semiotext(e), 1989. 203-09.
———. *The History of Sexuality, Volume I: An Introduction.* 1976. Trans. Robert Hurley. 1978. New York: Vintage, 1980.
Frankenberg, Ruth. *White Women, Race Matters: The Social Construction of Whiteness.* Minneapolis: UMP, 1993.
Frye, Marilyn. "Lesbian Feminism and the Gay Rights Movement: Another View of Male Supremacy, Another Separatism." *The Politics of Reality: Essays in Feminist Theory.* Freedom, CA: Crossing, 1983. 128-51.
———. "On Being White: Thinking Toward a Feminist Understanding of Race and Race Supremacy." *The Politics of Reality: Essays in Feminist Theory.* Freedom, CA: Crossing, 1983. 110-27.
Fung, Richard. "Looking for My Penis: The Eroticized Asian in Gay Video Porn." *How Do I Look?: Queer Film and Video.* Ed. Bad Object-Choices. Seattle: Bay, 1991. 145-60.
———. "Shortcomings: Questions About Pornography as Pedagogy." *Queer Looks: Perspectives on Lesbian and Gay Film and Video.* Ed. Martha Gever, Pratibha Parmar, and John Greyson. New York: Routledge, 1993. 355-67.
Fuss, Diana. "Monsters of Perversion: Jeffrey Dahmer and *Silence of the Lambs*." *Media Spectacles.* Ed. Marjorie Garber, Jann Matlock, and Rebecca L. Walkowitz. New York: Routledge, 1993. 181-205.
Gaines, Jane. "White Privilege and Looking Relations: Race and Gender in Feminist Film Theory." *Screen* 29.4 (1988): 12-27.
Gates, Henry Louis, Jr. *Loose Canons: Notes on the Culture Wars.* New York: OUP, 1992.

———, Ed. *"Race," Writing, and Difference*. Chicago: UCP, 1986.
"Gay Abandon." *Weekly Mail* (South Africa) 15-21 Oct. 1993: 4.
Gevisser, Mark. "A Different Fight for Freedom: A History of South African Lesbian and Gay Organisation—the 1950s to the 1990s." *Defiant Desire: Gay and Lesbian Lives in South Africa*. Eds. Mark Gevisser and Edwin Cameron. Johannesburg: Ravan, 1994. 14-86.
Gevisser, Mark, and Edwin Cameron, Eds. *Defiant Desire: Gay and Lesbian Lives in South Africa*. Johannesburg: Ravan, 1994.
Goldsby, Jackie. "Queens of Language: *Paris is Burning*." *Queer Looks: Perspectives on Lesbian and Gay Film and Video*. Ed. Martha Gever, Pratibha Parmar, and John Greyson. New York: Routledge, 1993. 108-15.
———. "What it Means to be Colored Me." *OUT/LOOK* 9 (Summer 1990): 8-17.
Gomez, Jewelle. "Imagine a Lesbian . . . a Black Lesbian." *Trivia* 12 (Spring 1988): 45-60.
Gómez-Peña, Guillermo. "The Multicultural Paradigm: An Open Letter to the National Arts Community." *High Performance* (Fall 1989): 18-27.
"Government Ban Gay Publication." *Esteem* (South Africa) 1.2 (1992): 1, 10.
Gray, Stephen. "The Building-Site." *The Invisible Ghetto: Lesbian and Gay Writing From South Africa*. Ed. Matthew Krouse and Kim Berman. Johannesburg: COSAW, 1993. 65-75.
———. *Time of Our Darkness*. London: Muller, 1988.
Grewal, Inderpal. "Autobiographic Subjects and Diasporic Locations: *Meatless Days* and *Borderlands*." *Scattered Hegemonies: Postmodernity and Transnational Feminist Practices*. Ed. Inderpal Grewal and Caren Kaplan. Minneapolis: UMP, 1994. 231-54.
Gupta, Sunil. "Black, Brown, and White." *Coming on Strong: Gay Politics and Culture*. Ed. Simon Shepherd and Mick Wallis. London: Hyman, 1989. 163-79.
Gutíerrez, Ramón A. "Must We Deracinate Indians to Find Gay Roots?" *OUT/LOOK* 1.4 (Winter 1989): 61-67.
Halberstam, Judith. "Queer in Hollywood." *On Our Backs* July/Aug. 1992: 10, 11, 45.
Hall, Donald E. *Queer Theories*. New York: Palgrave-Macmillan, 2003.
Halperin, David M. *Saint Foucault: Towards a Gay Hagiography*. New York: OUP, 1995.
Hammonds, Evelynn. "Black (W)holes and the Geometry of Black Female Sexuality." *differences* 6.2-3 (1994): 126-45.
Hanawa, Yukiko. Guest Editor's Introduction. *positions* 2.1 ("Special Issue: Circuits of Desire") (Spring 1994): v-xi.
Haney López, Ian F. "The Social Construction of Race." *Critical Race Theory: The Cutting Edge*. Ed. Richard Delgado. Philadelphia: Temple UP, 1995. 191-203.
———. "White by Law." *Critical Race Theory: The Cutting Edge*. Ed. Richard Delgado. Philadelphia: Temple UP, 1995. 542-50.
Hardy, James Earl. *B-Boy Blues*. Boston: Alyson, 1994.
———. *2nd Time Around*. Los Angeles: Alyson, 1996.
Harper, Phillip Brian. *Are We Not Men? Masculine Anxiety and the Problem of African-American Identity*. New York: OUP, 1996.
Harper, Phillip Brian, E. Francis White, and Margaret Cerullo. "Multi/Queer/Culture." *Radical America* 24.4: 27-37.
Harris, Daniel. "AIDS and Theory." *Lingua Franca* June 1991: 1, 16-19.
Harris, Lyle Ashton. "Revenge of a Snow Queen." *OUT/LOOK* 13 (Summer 1991): 8-13.
Hawley, John C. "Afterword." *Postcolonial and Queer Theories: Intersections and Essays*. Ed. Hawley. Westport, CT: Greenwood, 2001. 197-208.

Hemphill, Essex, Ed. *Brother to Brother: New Writings by Black Gay Men*. Boston: Alyson, 1991.

Hemphill, Essex. "Does Your Mama Know About Me?" *Ceremonies: Prose and Poetry*. New York: Penguin, 1992. 37–49.

Hirsch, David A. H. "Dahmer's Effects: Gay Serial Killer Goes to Market." *Disciplinarity and Dissent in Cultural Studies*. Ed. Cary Nelson and Dilip Parameshwar Gaonkar. New York: Routledge, 1996. 441–72.

Holleran, Andrew. "Abandoned." *Christopher Street* 181 (1992): 3–6.

Holy Titclamps 9 (Winter 91–92).

Holy Titclamps Zine Explosion 3 (February 1992).

hooks, bell. "Feminist Theory: A Radical Agenda." *Talking Back: Thinking Feminist, Thinking Black*. Boston: South End, 1989. 35–41.

———. "Representations of Whiteness in the Black Imagination." *Black Looks: Race and Representation*. Boston: South End, 1992. 165–78.

Hovey, Jaime. "'Kissing a Negress in the Dark': Englishness as a Masquerade in Woolf's *Orlando*." *PMLA* 112.3 (May 1997): 393–404.

"How About Us?" *Exit* (South Africa) 66 (1994): 1.

Hwang, David Henry. *M. Butterfly*. New York: Penguin, 1989.

International Wavelength News 4.5 (October 1993).

International Wavelength News 4.7 (December 1993).

Jackson, Earl, Jr. *Strategies of Deviance: Studies in Gay Male Representation*. Bloomington: Indiana UP, 1995.

Jagose, Annamarie. *Queer Theory: An Introduction*. New York: NYUP, 1996.

———. "Slash and Suture: The Border's Figuration of Colonialism, Phallocentrism, and Homophobia in *Borderlands/La Frontera: The New Mestiza*." *Lesbian Utopics*. New York: Routledge, 1994. 137–57.

Jamakaya. "Blood on Its Hands: Homophobia and Racism in Milwaukee." *NYQ* 16 Feb. 1992: 22–25.

———. "Jeffrey Dahmer's Grisly Homophobia: The Hate Crime that Wasn't." *San Francisco Sentinel* 1 Aug. 1991: 1, 15.

Jolly, Rosemary. "Rehearsals of Liberation: Contemporary Postcolonial Discourse and the New South Africa." *PMLA* 110.1 (1995): 17–29.

Jordan, L. Lloyd. "Black Gay vs. Gay Black." *BLK* 2.6 (June 1990): 25–30.

"Judge Orders Brain Scan for Dahmer." *Washington Post* 10 Nov. 1991: A-3.

Julien, Isaac. "Confessions of a Snow Queen: Notes on the Making of *The Attendant*." *Critical Quarterly* 36.1 (Spring 1994): 120–29

———. "Young Soul Rebel: A Conversation with Isaac Julien." Interview by Don Belton. *OUT/LOOK* 16 (Spring 1992): 15–19.

Kaplan, David A., Karen Springen, Bob Cohn, Patricia King, and Peter Annin. "Silence of the Wolves." *Newsweek* 3 Feb. 1992: 50–51.

Katz, Jonathan Ned. *The Invention of Heterosexuality*. New York: Penguin, 1995.

Keating, AnnLouise. "Interrogating 'Whiteness,' (De)Constructing Race." *College English* 57 (1995): 901–18.

Kirk, Marshall, and Hunter Madsen *After the Ball: How America Will Conquer its Fear and Hatred of Gays in the 90's*. New York: Doubleday, 1989.

Kroll, Jack. "Cry the Beloved Country: South Africa's Powerful Black-Theater Movement." *Newsweek* 22 Sep. 1986: 85.

Landers, Nedhera. "The Black and White of Writing and Publishing." *Lambda Rising Book Report* 1.3: 1, 16.

Lane, Christopher. *The Ruling Passion: British Colonial Allegory and the Paradox of Homosexual Desire.* Durham: Duke UP, 1995.

Lee, Jayne Chong-Soon. "Navigating the Topology of Race." *Critical Race Theory: The Key Writings That Formed the Movement.* Ed. Kimberlé Crenshaw, Neil Gotanda, Gary Peller, and Kendall Thomas. New York: New, 1995. 441-49.

Lee, N'Tanya, Don Murphy, and Juliet Ucelli. "Whose Kids? Our Kids! Race, Sexuality and the Right in New York City's Curriculum Battles." *Radical America* 25.1 (1993): 9-21.

Levine, Judith. "The Heart of Whiteness: Dismantling the Master's House." *Village Voice Literary Supplement* 128 (September 1994): 11-16.

Leyva, Yolanda Chávez. "Breaking the Silence: Putting Latina Lesbian History at the Center." *The New Lesbian Studies: Into the Twenty-First Century.* Ed. Bonnie Zimmerman and Toni A. H. McNaron. New York: Feminist P at CUNY, 1996. 145-52.

Loh, Sandra Tsing. "The Taking of Dinah Shore." *Buzz* March 1994: 62-65, 105-06.

Lotringer, Sylvère, Ed. *Foucault Live: Interviews, 1966-84.* Trans. John Johnston. New York: Semiotext(e), 1989.

Loud, Lance. "No Hatchet Job." *The Advocate* 615 (3 Nov. 1992): 93.

Lugones, María. "On *Borderlands/La Frontera*: An Interpretive Essay." *Hypatia* 7.4 (1992): 31-37.

Ma, Ming-Yeun S. "Tofu Between Rocks." *Found Object* 1.1 (Fall 1992): 40-50.

Mackey, M. Corinne. "Life Behind the Bars." *GLN* (San Diego) 13 April 1990: 14-15.

———. "A Promise." *GLN* (San Diego) 2 Feb. 1990: 17, 19.

"Mad Bombers' Kinky Secret." *Globe* 30 May 1995: 6-7.

Manalansan, Martin F, IV. "(Dis)Orienting the Body: Locating Symbolic Resistance among Filipino Gay Men." *positions* 2.1 (Spring 1994): 73-90.

———. "(Re)Locating the Gay Filipino: Resistance, Postcolonialism, and Identity." *Journal of Homosexuality* 26.2-3 (1993): 53-72.

Masters, Brian. "Dahmer's Inferno." *Vanity Fair* Nov. 1991: 182+.

Mathews, Tom, Karen Springen, Patrick Rogers, and Gregory Cerio. "Secrets of a Serial Killer." *Newsweek* 3 Feb. 1992: 44-49.

Men of South Africa. Video. Trekker Productions-International Wavelength. 1991.

Men of South Africa II: Boereseuns/Boer Boys. Video. Voortrekker Productions-International Wavelength. 1992.

Mercer, Kobena. "Looking for Trouble." 1991. *The Lesbian and Gay Studies Reader.* Ed. Henry Abelove, Michèle Aina Barale, and David M. Halperin. New York: Routledge, 1993. 350-59.

"Mexico Celebrates Pride." *Update* (San Diego) 21 June 1995: 1.

Miller, Stephen H. "Who Stole the Gay Movement?" *Christopher Street* 218 (October 1994): 16-19.

minnesota review, the: A Journal of Committed Writing. Issue #47 ("The White Issue"): 1997.

Mohanty, Chandra Talpade. "Under Western Eyes: Feminist Scholarship and Colonial Discourse." *boundary 2* 12.3-13.1 (1984): 333-58.

Moraga, Cherríe. *Loving in the War Years. Lo que nunca pasó por sus labios.* Boston: South End, 1983.

Morrison, John. "Is Feminism Hurting Gay Men?" *Christopher Street* 14.2: 17-23.

Morrison, Toni. *Playing in the Dark: Whiteness and the Literary Imagination.* Cambridge: Harvard UP, 1992.

Morton, Donald. "Birth of the Cyberqueer." *PMLA* 110.3 (1995): 369-81.

———. "Changing the Terms: (Virtual) Desire and (Actual) Reality." *The Material Queer: A LesBiGay Cultural Studies Reader.* Ed. Donald Morton. Boulder, Colorado: HarperCollins, 1996. 1-33.

Mulvey, Laura. "Visual Pleasure and Narrative Cinema." *Screen* 16.3 (1975): 6-18.

Mumford, Kevin J. "Homosex Changes: Race, Cultural Geography, and the Emergence of the Gay.' *American Quarterly* 48.3 (Sep. 1996): 395-414.

Muñoz, José Esteban. *Disidentifications: Queers of Color and the Performance of Politics*. Minneapolis: UMP, 1999.

Nelson, Emmanuel S. "African-American Literature, Gay Male." *The Gay and Lesbian Literary Heritage: A Reader's Companion to the Writers and Their Works, From Antiquity to the Present*. Ed. Claude J. Summers. New York: Holt, 1995. 8-11.

Nguyen, Hoang T. "Across the Lines." *Lavender Reader* Winter 1993: 20-21.

———. "Challenging the Roles: The Heterogeneity of Asian American Males." *Momentum* 3.2 (1994): 16-17.

Norman, Connie. "Tribal Rites." *Update* (Southern California) 10 Feb. 1992: A-16.

Norris, Joel. *Jeffrey Dahmer*. New York: Pinnacle-Windsor, 1992.

Omi, Michael, and Howard Winant. *Racial Formation in the United States: From the 1960s to the 1990s*. New York: Routledge, 1994.

Omosupe, Ekua. "Black/Lesbian/Bulldagger." *differences* 3.2 (1991): 101-11.

Ostrom, Neeyah. "O.J. and CFS: The HHV-6 Dementia Defense." *New York Native* 19 Sep. 1994: 13.

Parker, Andrew. Contributor to "Forum on the Political Implications of Using the Term 'Queer,' as in 'Queer Politics,' 'Queer Studies,' and 'Queer Pedagogy.'" *Radical Teacher* 45 (1994): 55-56.

Parker, Canaan. *The Color of Trees*. Boston: Alyson, 1992.

Patton, Cindy. "Tremble, Hetero Swine!" *Fear of a Queer Planet: Queer Politics and Social Theory*. Ed. Michael Warner. Minneapolis: UMP, 1993. 143-77.

Peck, Dale. "Town Without Pity: Milwaukee After Dahmer." *Out* July 1993: 52+.

Penn, Donna. "Queer: Theorizing Politics and History." *Radical History Review* 62 (1995): 24-42.

Pratt, Mary Louise. *Imperial Eyes: Travel Writing and Transculturation*. New York: Routledge, 1992.

Pratt, Minnie Bruce. "Identity Skin Blood Heart." *Yours in Struggle: Three Feminist Perspectives on Anti-Semitism and Racism*. By Pratt, Elly Bulkin, and Barbara Smith. 1984. Ithaca: Firebrand, 1988. 9-63.

Preston, John. "Goodbye, Sally Gearhart. Gay Men and Feminists Have Reached a Fork in the Road." *Christopher Street* 59: 17-26.

"Queer is not a Substitute for Gay." *Rant and Rave* 1.1 (Autumn 1993): 15.

Raiskin, Judith. "Inverts and Hybrids: Lesbian Rewritings of Sexual and Racial Identities." *The Lesbian Postmodern*. Ed. Laura Doan. New York: Columbia UP, 1994. 156-72.

Rashid, Ian Iqbal. "Naming Names, or How Do You Say 'Queer' in 'South Asian'?" *Rungh: A South Asian Quarterly of Culture, Comment and Criticism* 3.3 (1995): 7.

Ratti, Rakesh. "A Question of Color." *A Lotus of Another Color: An Unfolding of the South Asian Gay and Lesbian Experience*. Ed. Ratti. Boston: Alyson, 1993. 98-102.

Reid-Pharr, Robert F. *Black Gay Man: Essays*. New York: NYUP, 2001.

Retief, Glen. "Keeping Sodom Out of the Laager: State Repression of Homosexuality in Apartheid South Africa." *Defiant Desire: Gay and Lesbian Lives in South Africa*. Ed. Mark Gevisser and Edwin Cameron. Johannesburg: Ravan, 1994. 99-111.

Rich, Adrienne. "Compulsory Heterosexuality and Lesbian Existence." *Signs* 5.4 (1980): 631-60.

Rich, B. Ruby. "Reflections on a Queer Screen." *GLQ* 1.1 (1993): 83-91.

———. "When Difference Is (More Than) Skin Deep." *Queer Looks: Perspectives on Lesbian and Gay Film and Video*. Ed. Martha Gever, Pratibha Parmar, and John Greyson. New York: Routledge, 1993. 318-39.

Riggs, Marlon. "Marlon Riggs Untied." Interview by Revon Kyle Banneker. *OUT/LOOK* 10 (Fall 1990): 15-18.

———. "*Tongues Untied:* An Interview with Marlon Riggs." Interview by Ron Simmons. *Brother to Brother: New Writings by Black Gay Men.* Ed. Essex Hemphill. Boston: Alyson, 1991. 189-99.

Rooney, Ellen. *Seductive Reasoning: Pluralism as the Problematic of Contemporary Literary Theory.* Ithaca: CUP, 1989.

Roscoe, Will, Ed. *Living the Spirit: A Gay American Indian Anthology.* New York: St. Martin's, 1988.

Ross, Andrew. *No Respect: Intellectuals and Popular Culture.* New York: Routledge, 1989.

"Saddam's a Sex Pervert." *National Examiner* 12 March 1991: 4-5.

"S. Africa Ban on *Advocate* Remains." *Frontiers* (Los Angeles) 28 August 1992: 22.

Said, Edward W. *Culture and Imperialism.* New York: Knopf, 1993.

———. *Orientalism.* 1978. New York: Vintage, 1979.

Saillant, John. "The Black Body Erotic and the Republican Body Politic, 1790-1820." *Journal of the History of Sexuality* 5.3 (1995): 403-28.

Salvador, Christian. "Queer Generations." *Infected Faggot Perspectives* 11 (Sep./Oct. 1992): 8-9.

SAMOIS, Ed. *Coming to Power: Writings and Graphics on Lesbian S/M.* 1981. Boston: Alyson, 1987.

Savage, Jon, and Isaac Julien. "Queering the Pitch: A Conversation." *Critical Quarterly* 36.1 (1994): 1-12.

Schmidt, Martha A. "Dahmer Discourse and Gay Identity: The Paradox of Queer Politics." *Critical Sociology* 20.3 (1994): 81-105.

Schulman, Sarah. *My American History: Lesbian and Gay Life During the Reagan/Bush Years.* New York: Routledge, 1994.

Schwartz, Anne E. *The Man Who Could Not Kill Enough: The Secret Murders of Milwaukee's Jeffrey Dahmer.* Secaucus, NJ: Birch Lane, 1992.

Scott, Darieck. "Jungle Fever?: Black Gay Identity Politics, White Dick, and the Utopian Bedroom." *GLQ* 1.3 (1994): 299-321.

———. *Traitor to the Race.* New York: Penguin, 1995.

Sedgwick, Eve Kosofsky. *Epistemology of the Closet.* Los Angeles: UCP, 1990.

———. "Gender Criticism." *Redrawing the Boundaries: The Transformation of English and American Literary Studies.* Ed. Stephen Greenblatt and Giles Gunn. New York: MLA, 1991. 271-302.

———. "QUEER SEX HABITS (Oh, no! I mean) SIX QUEER HABITS: Some Talking Points." *Queer-e: An Interdisciplinary Electronic Journal of Gay, Lesbian, Bisexual, Transgender, and Queer Writing* 1.1 <http://www.qrd.org/qrd/media/journals/queer-e-v1.n1/article.3>. 24 May 1995. 11 Feb. 2004.

Segrest, Mab. *A Bridge, Not a Wedge.* Plenary remarks at National Gay and Lesbian Task Force Creating Change Conference, 12 November 1993. Distributed by OUT Fund for Lesbian and Gay Liberation.

———. *Memoir of a Race Traitor.* Boston: South End, 1994.

Seidman, Steven. "Symposium: Queer Theory/Sociology: A Dialogue." *Sociological Theory* 12.2 (1994): 166-77.

"Serial Killer Dahmer Slain in Prison." *Facts on File* 54.2818 (1 Dec. 1994): 894.

"17 Killings in 13 Years Stunned U.S." *The San Diego Union-Tribune* 29 Nov. 1994, street final: A-1, 17.

Sex Is . . . Dir. Marc Huestis. 16 mm film. 80 minutes. USA. Distributor: Outsider Enterprises. 1993.

Smith, Paul Julian, and Emilie L. Bergmann. "Introduction." *¿Entiendes?: Queer Readings, Hispanic Writings.* Ed. Bergmann and Smith. Durham: Duke UP, 1995. 1-14.

Smyth, Cherry. "Crossing the Tracks." *On Our Backs* 10.2 (1995): 17-21.

———. *Lesbians Talk Queer Notions*. London: Scarlet, 1992.
Somerville, Siobhan. "Sicentific Racism and the Emergence of the Homosexual Body." *Journal of the History of Sexuality* 5.2 (1994): 243-66.
Spiro, Daniel. "His Heart Belongs to Daddy: A Father's Story by Lionel Dahmer." *Everard Review* Winter 1995: 49-51.
Sproul, Dick. "Dahmer: Distant, or Similar?" *USA Today* 1 Aug. 1991: A-8.
Stambolion, George. "Afterword: Michael's Room." *Life Drawing*. By Michael Grumley. New York: Grove, 1991. 143-56.
Stein, Arlene, and Ken Plummer. "'I Can't Even Think Straight': 'Queer' Theory and the Missing Sexual Revolution in Sociology." *Sociological Theory* 12.2 (1994): 178-87.
Stella, Bill. "Manifesto For Progressive Queers—A Pro-Active Agenda." 1994. E-Directory of Lesbigay Scholars. 25 November 1994.
Suplee, Curt. "Serial Killers: Frighteningly Close to Normal." *Washington Post* 5 Aug. 1991: A-3.
Terry, Don. "Violent Life, Violent Death." *New York Times* 4 Dec. 1994: E-2.
The Trial of Jeffrey Dahmer. Court TV/Video. Magnum Video Distributors. 1992. 120 minutes.
Trinh T. Minh-ha. "Interview with Trinh T. Minh-ha." Interview by Constance Penley and Andrew Ross. *Camera Obscura* 13-14 (1985): 87-103.
Trujillo, Carla, Ed. *Chicana Lesbians: The Girls Our Mothers Warned Us About*. Berkeley: Third Woman, 1991.
Uttal, Lynne. "Inclusion without Influence: The Continuing Tokenism of Women of Color." *Making Face, Makin Soul/Haciendo Caras: Creative and Critical Perspective by Women of Color*. Ed. Gloria Anzaldúa. San Francisco: Aunt Lute, 1990. 42-45.
Vaid, Urvashi. *Virtual Equality: The Mainstreaming of Gay and Lesbian Liberation*. New York: Anchor, 1995.
Warner, Michael. "From Queer to Eternity: An Army of Theorists Cannot Fail." *Village Voice Literary Supplement* 106 (June 1992) ("Perfectly Queer"): 18-19.
———. "Introduction: Fear of a Queer Planet." *Social Text* 29: 3-17.
———. "Media Gays: A New Stone Wall." *The Nation* 14 July 1997: 15-19.
Waugh, Thomas. "Men's Pornography: Gay Vs. Straight." *Out in Culture: Gay, Lesbian, and Queer Essays on Popular Culture*. Ed. Corey K. Creekmur and Alexander Doty. Durham: Duke UP, 1995. 307-27.
Wenzel, Helene Vivienne. "The Text as Body/Politics: An Appreciation of Monique Wittig's Writings in Context." *Feminist Studies* 7.2 (Summer 1981): 264-87.
Weston, Kath. "Theory, Theory, Who's Got the Theory? Or, Why I'm Tired of That Tired Debate." *GLQ* 2.4 (1995): 347-49.
White, Edmund. "Foreword." *Life Drawing*. By Michael Grumley. New York: Grove, 1991. vii-xii.
"Why Jeffrey Dahmer Killed So Many Black Men." *Jet* 19 Dec. 1994: 14-17.
Williams, Linda. *Hard Core: Power, Pleasure, and the "Frenzy of the Visible."* Los Angeles, UCP, 1989.
Wittig, Monique. "Author's Note." *The Lesbian Body*. 1973. Trans. David Le Vay. 1975. Boston: Beacon, 1986. 9-11.
———. *The Lesbian Body*. 1973. Trans. David Le Vay. 1975. Boston: Beacon, 1986.
Wittig, Monique, and Sande Zeig. *Lesbian Peoples: Material for a Dictionary*. New York: Avon, 1979.
Wockner, Rex. "British Gays to Colonize Island." *Gay & Lesbian Times* (San Diego) 7 Dec. 1995: 30.
Wolf, James B. "A Grand Tour: South Africa and American Tourists Between the Wars." *Journal of Popular Culture* 25.2 (Fall 1991): 99-116.

Yarbro-Bejarano, Yvonne. "Expanding the Categories of Race and Sexuality in Lesbian and Gay Studies." *Professions of Desire: Lesbian and Gay Studies in Literature.* Ed. George E. Haggerty and Bonnie Zimmerman. New York: MLA, 1995. 124–35.

———. "Reclaiming the Lesbian Body: Cherríe Moraga's *Loving in the War Years.*" *OUT/LOOK* 12 (Spring 1991): 74–79.

Zimmerman, Bonnie. "Placing Lesbians." *Concerns* 23.3 (Fall 1993): 10–16.

gender & culture

sexuality

William J. Spurlin
General Editor

This new series is a forum for the investigation and analysis of the contested terrain between culture, gender, and sexuality. Titles in the series can include, but are not limited to, (re)theorizations of gender in relation to, or its constitution through, sexuality, race, class, or culture, studies of sexuality and sexual identity that produce new understandings of gender, or new inquiries into culture, broadly defined, that raise compelling implications for the ways in which we think about gender and sexuality in the contemporary social world. Of particular interest are manuscripts that cirtique and/or broaden traditional constructions of gender and take into account sexuality, race, class, or the pressures of other constitutive categories, analyze nonwestern literary and cultural representations of gender and their relationship to sexuality, especially in postcolonial contexts, and theorize transgender from feminist, queer, postcolonial, or cultural studies frameworks.

For additional information about this series or for the submission of manuscripts, please contact:
      Peter Lang Publishing, Inc.
      275 Seventh Avenue, 28th floor
      New York, New York 10001

To order other books in this series, please contact our Customer Service Department:
      (800) 770-LANG (within the U.S.)
      (212) 647-7706 (outside the U.S.)
      (212) 647-7707 FAX

Or browse online by series:
      www.peterlangusa.com